Politics and Guilt

European Horizons

Series Editors

Richard Golsan, Texas A&M University

Christopher Flood, University of Surrey

Jeffrey T. Schnapp, Stanford University

Richard Wolin, Rice University

POLITICS AND GUILT
The Destructive Power of Silence

(**Politik und Schuld** Die zerstörerische Macht des Schweigens)

Gesine Schwan

Translated by Thomas Dunlap

UNIVERSITY OF NEBRASKA PRESS   •   LINCOLN AND LONDON

Publication of this book was
assisted by a grant
from Inter Nationes, Bonn.

Originally published as
*Politik und Schuld: Die
zerstörerische Macht
des Schweigens*
© Fischer Taschenbuch
Verlag GmbH,
Frankfurt am Main,
1997

Library of Congress
Cataloging-in-Publication
Data

Schwan, Gesine, 1943–
[Politik und Schuld. English]
Politics and guilt : the destructive
power of silence / Gesine
Schwan ; translated by Thomas
Dunlap.
p. cm — (European horizons
series)
Includes bibliographical
references and index.
ISBN 0-8032-4280-8 (cloth :
alk. paper)
1. Democracy—Germany.
2. Political culture—Germany.
3. Guilt—Psychological aspects.
4. National socialism—
Psychological aspects. I. Title.
II. European horizons.
JN3971.A91 S38 2001
301.5'4—dc21   00-045629

“N”

Contents

Introduction

It may seem strange to make guilt the topic of a discussion—let alone an analysis—on the level of political theory. At best, such an undertaking might seem naïve; at worst, obscene. For does not talk of guilt involve a careless transfer of experiences and needs from daily life to the harsh business of politics, which calls for dispassionate analysis? Does it not conceal what is really at stake in politics: interests, structures, functions, organizations, governments, and, above all, power? What place is there in all of this for the individualizing and subjective word *guilt*?

But the questions run even deeper than that. Is it possible to come up with an unambiguous definition of *guilt* in the first place? Doesn't the word mean something different to everyone who uses it? And if we really take this matter of guilt seriously, is it not true that we are dealing with something so personal that any public use of the term merely renders it shallow, often reducing it to something simply sentimental or utilitarian? Or is it possible, after all, to come up with an analysis of guilt that is sober and meaningful as political theory and gets by without vapid moralizing or the attempt to inspire self-reproach in others? Are there perhaps good reasons for embarking on such an analysis? A random selection of press reports during the past few years compels us to reflect on these questions:

Two-thirds of the children in Rwanda were involved in massacres, often as both victims and perpetrators at the same time. The incoherent report of a sixteen-year-old prisoner culminates in the declaration: "I am innocent!" (*Der Tagesspiegel*, 12 December 1994).

Japan's parties quarrel over a parliamentary motion concerning war guilt. Opponents of the motion argue that the question of Japanese guilt is not clear and that trust is best created by silence. However, concession should be made where "the constant denials are threatening to harm business in new markets" (*Frankfurter Allgemeine Zeitung*, 13 March 1995). The Chinese, Koreans, Filipinos, and Malaysians will not become reconciled with Japan as long as the Japanese refuse to take responsibility for their deeds and acknowledge their guilt (*Der Tagesspiegel*, 12 April 1995). A clever business ploy involving morality?

Ten thousand Ethiopians take to the streets to call for the punishment of the communist leaders. An international commission of jurists supports the demonstrators. Is there a comparable need to determine and punish guilt across cultures? ("A Nuremberg Trial in Addis Ababa," *Der Tagesspiegel*, 17 December 1994).

In his very first year in office, the South African minister of justice, Abdullah Mohamed Omar, sets up an official "Truth and Reconciliation Commission" (*Frankfurter Allgemeine Zeitung*, 10 June 1995). Does the new South African democracy need to take ethical stock of the past?

During the demonstrations in Belgrade against the Serbian government in the fall of 1996, Rolf Paasch, a correspondent for the *Tagesspiegel*, wrote: "It is evident that even one year after the Dayton Peace Accords it is still impossible to talk about guilt in Serbia." Addressing this dissonance between protests and genuine debate, the writer and translator Drinka Gojkovic explained: "It is so much easier to blame Milosevic than to grapple critically with the causes of the war." Did those who were marching against Milosevic feel they were adequately informed about what had happened earlier in Bosnia? "We can't claim that we didn't know anything," responds Ana, an art student. "But we didn't know whether it was the truth" (*Der Tagesspiegel*, 5 December 1996). Always the same "excuses"?

When the Argentine chief of staff Balza admitted his guilt and the navy and air force followed with more cautious admissions, Martin Gester interpreted these actions as part of a tactical election debate: "Today the murders, which occurred only fifteen years ago, are nearly forgotten" (*Frankfurter Allgemeine Zeitung*, 16 June 1995). In contrast, Walter Haubrich, in the same paper, reported on remorseful officers who had suffered for years from depression. President Menem is said to have told them to seek out a confessor, for this matter lay outside the sphere of competence of the government and the courts. The officers could not deal with the fact that they had thrown opponents of the regime from airplanes into the sea, alive. "A doctor who accompanied the flights supervised the administering of drugs to knock out the victims. This doctor, however, would look away when the prisoners were pushed out alive, because — as one contrite officer explained — of that Hippocratic oath." Numerous officers are in psychiatric treatment; "now some are hoping that a public admission of guilt might help them to continue living more easily" (*Frankfurter Allgemeine Zeitung*, 2 May 1995).

All these reports raise the question of whether the public admission of guilt is, after all, more than an obscene farce. For example, is it possible to detect among the Argentine officers, who were socialized through Catholic beliefs, the aftereffects of the way in which the Judeo-Christian tradition deals with guilt: that is, the three steps of *contritio cordis* (contrition, repentance), *confessio oris* (public admission), and *satisfactio operis* (restitution through works)? Could it be that this three-step approach is more than some dusty old dogma?

And what could a secularized world set up in its place? Or does it fail to put anything in its place, and is this possibly the central problem of democratic politics today?

We live, as Fritz Stern has observed, in a time of a general admission that injustices have been committed. And he adds: "It is difficult to admit one's own guilt; it is easier to lament one's own suffering." [1] Why does this asymmetry exist? Does guilt still play a role in our secularized world in which "anything goes" and in which cruelty is perpetrated with indifference? Does it play a role for the individual? For society at large?

Robert McNamara, former U.S. secretary of defense, attributes the cynicism and contempt "with which so many people view our political institutions and leaders" to the deceptions and disappointments of Vietnam and Watergate. He fears that cynicism is corroding American life because trust in politics is being lost. Does this also have something to do with the question of guilt in politics? Why is McNamara writing about the decision-making process that led to the Vietnam War and about the long and difficult process that ended it? Countless atrocities were committed during the Vietnam War. Who bears the guilt? Who bears the responsibility? Could a clarification of these questions help overcome the cynicism of the American people and restore their trust in the political system? Does trust require a prior admission of guilt, or can it be founded on silence? "I truly believe," McNamara writes, "that we made an error not of values and intentions but of judgment and capabilities." [2] Why is this distinction so important? Does trust in the political system depend on the subjective validity of and respect for the basic values on which it is founded? Is politically explosive guilt established through a disregard for these values, that is, by conduct that goes beyond mere error? Does the clarification of guilt—in the private and individual sphere as well as in the public realm—thus serve to provide reassurance about the values on which both individual and collective life is based? Are these values perhaps essential to that life because without them individual and public trust would disappear?

In any case, our brief selection of reports from the daily press confirms that the question of guilt in politics plays an important role in public discourse all over the world, especially in the task of establishing and maintaining democracies following the collapse of dictatorships.

By *democracies* I mean political systems that derive their legitimacy from the *sovereignty of the people*. Within the context of a *pluralistic society*, the institutions of democracy organize the process of political decision making in a setting that is based on the *separation of powers* and *the rule of law* and is largely *representative* in nature. The goal of these institutions is to secure the *personal autonomy and integrity of the citizens* as well as their political freedom, that is, their responsible participation in making decisions and formulating the political will of society. The counterpart to this institutional structure of democracy on a subjective and cultural level is the *capacity of the citizens to participate responsibly in politics*. This capacity incorporates a number of *political virtues*—a sense of justice, tolerance, solidarity—and corresponding psychological dispositions and attitudes, above all, trust in oneself and in strangers, a solid sense of competence, openness, as well as empathy and an ability to cooperate.

In this book, we will discuss the meaning of guilt chiefly in a historical context in which democracies have replaced *dictatorships*. These transitions have confronted people with problems of guilt that have been triggered, if not caused, by the political structures of the dictatorships themselves. For that reason, it is useful to identify briefly the salient characteristics of dictatorship that form the basis of the discussion. The central feature of dictatorship is the *concentration of state power with no legally guaranteed control of politics and with a process of formulating the political will that is neither pluralistically organized nor founded on popular sovereignty*. The most important consequence both for communal political life and for daily life is the potential or real *abuse of power, arbitrary actions*, and the *arbitrary treatment of people*: a disregard for people's dignity, basic rights, and—in aggregate—for their physical and psychological integrity. The counterpart to this system on a subjective and cultural level is the willingness of people to submit to the demands of uncontrolled state power and to accommodate themselves to it. In other words, while ignoring their conscience, people are also willing to forego the exercise of political responsibility, personal autonomy, and political freedom, especially in situations where state power ignores, oppresses, or extinguishes the dignity and integrity of human beings.

It is above all this latter consequence of dictatorship—participating in the violation or destruction of the physical and psychological integrity of fellow citizens or the passive acceptance of such violations—that is experienced as a feeling of guilt following a change in government from dictatorship to democracy. This book poses the following question: what does it mean for democracies when such guilt is not clarified and processed but is left standing and covered with silence? I do not maintain that by definition one lives without guilt in a democracy and that one necessarily incurs personal guilt in a dictatorship. Rather, it is my intent to elucidate the effects of guilt on the personal lives of people, on their attitudes, and on the lives they share in a context of freedom. What I am after, therefore, is the effects of guilt on political democracy and the possibilities that may exist to counter and overcome its destructive consequences.

History is replete with political crimes. What makes the twentieth century unique, however, is that politics seized entire nations or laid claim to doing so. Defining themselves as the "rule of the people," the dictatorships of our century not only invoked the people as legitimation but also involved them in their criminal acts in a way very different from the regicides in Shakespeare's plays: as participants, as affirming and thus legitimizing voices, as spectators. By the twentieth century, it was no longer possible to escape the grasp of politics by simply withdrawing into private life.

Or was it? Just how close is the relationship between reprehensible acts of politics and individuals? Is it possible to ascribe the—generally undisputed—crimes of past and present dictatorships to individual perpetrators, or should the latter be seen merely as "implementing organs" or indifferent spectators who bear no personal responsibility and thus no guilt? What is implied by the frequently used images of a people "seduced" by a handful of individuals and of crimes that are interpreted as the consequence of a large, anonymous context of guilt? Clearly, what is implied is an image of human beings that is utterly contrary to the idea of a responsible citizenry in a democracy. For if we accept this vision it would mean that human beings are not free, but generally act either unintentionally (having been seduced), under coercion (fearing for their lives or their careers or their standing among their comrades), or blindly (failing to understand what is going on). Can one create a democratic state with people who are described in these terms? Hardly.

And what if one simply distinguishes between two historical conditions? In a dictatorship we lack freedom and responsibility; we are without guilt and incapable of incurring it. In a democracy, by contrast, we are free and responsible and therefore capable of incurring guilt. But how, in this scenario, do we one day magically pass from one condition to the other?

At the same time, there can be little doubt that the dictatorships of the twentieth century significantly constrained the scope of freedom of action and threatened people with death. Under these regimes, one often had to be a hero to remain a decent person. In contrast, the claim that democracy makes on us is merely that our conduct be not entirely cowardly or conformist. Does this not establish a distinction in the question of guilt and responsibility?

Empirically, in each individual case, it certainly does establish a distinction, but not in principle and in theory. For either we are free as human beings, and thus responsible and capable of incurring guilt (in which case dictatorships merely put us to a harsher test than democracies), or we are not. Only by accepting the proposition that we are not free can one dismiss out of hand the question about our responsibility and guilt under dictatorial conditions. The crucial distinction is *not* whether we (for example, as the "post-Nazi generation") are willing to take into account the historical constraints on a person's ability to act when assessing a concrete situation. It goes without saying that we must do so. No, the real difference is whether we take this individual assessment seriously, along with the reflections on our standards of judgment and motives this necessarily entails, or whether, by using the slogan about "different times," we redefine people a priori as mere instruments incapable or incurring guilt and hence free of responsibility. That is what we would be doing if we assigned guilt only to political systems. In that case, we could not possibly imagine how the transition that turns individuals from subjects into democratic citizens takes place, while simultaneously ignoring the many clues that indicate that people in dictatorships are capable of incurring and in fact experience guilt. At the same time, such a stance would abandon people to their guilt: for guilt continues to fester if one refuses to acknowledge it and treats it with silence.

But the general premise that people are either capable of incurring guilt or not, regardless of the political conditions under which they live, does not say anything specific about a particular guilt, about the criteria on which it is based, about personal motives, and about political consequences. We would be making it too easy on ourselves if we failed to grapple seriously with the repeated assertions by defendants that they bore no guilt. Such questions cannot be answered from the lofty heights of fundamental philosophical-anthropological decisions. We must descend to the "depths" of documented experience and examine whether —subjective—guiltlessness is possible even in a situation where individuals participated in criminal acts.

Of course, this only throws up further questions: What is the necessary condition before we can speak of guilt? Is it a *subjective feeling* or *consciousness* of guilt? Is it an *objective factual situation*? Are there rules that are timeless and valid in all cultures? If a person does not feel guilt, am I permitted to talk him or her into feeling guilt or to simply impose it? Would I not be violating that person's autonomy and embarking upon a course of psychological or political manipulation? Must we not leave it up to each individual to determine his or her guilt and responsibility and how to deal with it? Most societies, following a change of political regimes, choose the path of keeping silent to themselves and others about guilt. Is this perhaps the right path to take because it is the most successful way of lifting a heavy burden and opening the future to something new?

If one could assume that the path of silence is the right one, I would not have written this book. I am *not* interested in heaping false or additional feelings of guilt on people in situations where the burden is already sufficiently heavy. I am *not* interested in demonstrating moral superiority where humility is called for. I *am* interested in uncovering interconnections and contexts, and in the process discovering opportunities for genuine relief and liberation from guilt. For I am convinced that silence about guilt only appears to help (even if it sometimes seems unavoidable), that its cost is high because it has destructive consequences under the surface—for people (the perpetrators, victims, and the next generation) and for the political life of democracy. In all of this, the question revolves primarily—but not exclusively!—around moral guilt.

Moral guilt is not inherited—"It is the soul that sins, and no other, that shall die; a son shall not share a father's guilt, nor a father his son's," says the prophet Ezekiel (Ezek. 18:20)—*but the psychological and*

*moral consequences of treating it with silence harm even the subsequent
generation and the basic consensus of a democracy.* This is my thesis.

Chapter 1 begins by showing that guilt is a central category of the basic
human experience, one that reflects a person's self-understanding about
freedom, responsibility, and dignity as well as his or her relationship to
society, politics, and the world. Chapter 2 lays out the many historical
manifestations of this abstract structural premise in an effort to discover
elements of an understanding of guilt that are constant and endure in
spite of historical change. Chapter 3 is an attempt to draw insights from
this treasury of concrete historical situations and experiences into the
ways in which people deal with guilt, the consequences of different approaches, and whether—in the experience of tradition and psychology—there is such a thing as a successful or unsuccessful handling of
guilt. Chapter 4 will attempt to define "silenced guilt" in the case of National Socialism. Chapter 5 looks in greater detail at the consequences
that arise from silenced guilt for the perpetrators and the next generation. Chapter 6 will seek to show how treating guilt with silence damages
democracy and can destroy it. Finally, chapter 7 is devoted to identifying more precisely the conditions that make it possible to break the vicious cycle of silenced guilt, destruction, and renewed guilt.

I have chosen National Socialism as the test case for my examination of
the destructive power of silenced guilt. The reason for this choice was my
desire to be as precise as possible in my empirical and theoretical analysis. One shortcoming of my approach, which I regret, is the fact that only
the former West Germany forms the empirical basis for examining the
consequences of the Nazi aftermath. In other words, the former GDR (after 1989, eastern Germany) has been, for all practical purposes, excluded
from this study. I did not do this out of some "west German" arrogance
or thoughtlessness, but rather because the source material and inter-
pretive literature on West Germany is far more extensive as far as the
scope of this book is concerned. Moreover, I did not have enough time
to study the situation in eastern Germany in sufficient depth to hazard
an opinion. After all, it would have been necessary for my interpretation
to have incorporated the special situation of the political system of the
GDR in subtle and very specific ways. I did not want to make rash statements. That said, there is a good deal of evidence to suggest that the
personal handling of guilt and the family dynamics in East Germany were,
in this respect, not substantially different from West Germany. Lutz

Niethammer's archaeology of "his people's experience" has uncovered traces in the GDR that are much like those we can find in West Germany.[3] However, to assess with greater precision the significance that the respective political systems had for the subjective, private handling of guilt it would be necessary, and interesting, to have more detailed studies.

1

Guilt—A Basic Human Condition

MYTHOLOGY, GREEK ANTIQUITY, AND THE BIBLE: EXPERIENCING AND UNDERSTANDING GUILT

The world is an inheritance that we enter upon on the day of our birth. At some point, which cannot be pinned down precisely, we come to understand that this inheritance always leaves us a choice: we can reject it by rejecting life. But from the very moment that we know about the possibility of voluntary death and yet go on living, we take on the debts of the world as our own. Living also means simply accepting all the rot and shame, acknowledging that it is worth accepting the inheritance in spite of the debts, or that life is worthy of our participation in spite of the suffering and shamefulness. In truth, we are incapable of reckoning the assets and liabilities of the estate, of tallying the sum of good and evil in the inheritance, and—contrary to the hopes of the ancient theodicies—we will never be able to do so.[1]

The Polish philosopher Leszek Kolakowski concludes from this description of our basic experience of the world that "our primary relationship to the world . . . is that of a responsibility voluntarily assumed," the responsibility, namely, of reducing the debts of the world. From the beginning of our existence in the world, Kolakowski asserts, we distinguish between good and evil and feel called upon to redeem the debts that accumulate in the account of evil. But are we in fact dealing with an incontestable, universal basic human experience?

Surely we must admit that we are not. Since the end of the eighteenth century, at the latest, from the time of the Marquis de Sade, people have imagined in ever more radical terms a world that places itself in conscious opposition to every accepted social order (which is regarded as "boring") and declares its allegiance to evil. To be sure, even these visions have generally retained the distinction between good and evil, even if they explicitly—often aesthetically—affirmed evil. "In the act of senseless destruction, the spirit of perversion revels in the awareness that it is committing a mortal sin"—as Norbert Bolz interprets Edgar Allan Poe's "The Black Cat."[2] In these visions there is an unwillingness to continue following the seemingly self-evident commandment to do good, an unwillingness to feel guilty about evil, yet the distinction between good and evil as such is not abandoned. This is peculiar. Are we unable to do without this distinction? Do we need it, even if we decide to pervert it?

Good versus Evil

Ethnologists, scholars of religion, and philosophers have searched for the origins of this distinction. The creation stories of ancient myths, which both describe creation and establish social norms, express concrete experiences of daily life, experiences whose "material" significance is no longer readily apparent to us. But the basic moral distinctions between good and evil on which they are based carry over into the present. This is particularly true for the cultural sphere that was shaped by the monotheistic religions and for the culture of ancient Egypt.

The Iranian prophet and priest Zarathustra, one of the first in this cultural sphere to give poetic expression to the fundamental distinction between good and evil, was evidently driven by an elemental revulsion against violence. In his poems—the practical implications of which were regarded by his contemporaries as so revolutionary that he was forced to flee his homeland—he was chiefly concerned with banning violence and protecting animals and farming against the constant recurrence of murderous frenzy. He generalized the social destructiveness of violence and the individualized murder into the notion of the lie, which is opposed to the truth. As Colpe has described it: "The decision for truth is a choice for *good thought* or good sense, which can be exercised by the Wise Lord as well as by human beings. Whatever is done by the Lord, for truth, through good thoughts, is *salvation-bringing spirit*. This is done in opposition to the killing of cattle, which is a lie, works through *evil thought*, and is, on the whole, *evil-bringing* or *evil spirit*. The latter can, all on its own, set into motion the *murderous frenzy* that menaces cattle and people. In that way, as well, the lie and evil thought or evil mind manifest themselves."[3]

Truth, falsehood, murderous frenzy—these three concepts encapsulate archaic and primordial distinctions of what sustains or destroys the human community. They point to early experiences, but ones we can still reconstruct centuries later in other historical contexts. These concepts were joined by others that offered points of orientation, in part through juxtaposition (clean/unclean; light/dark; warmth/coldness; spiritual/material), in part by bundling together discrete, concrete situations that were regarded as negative and experienced as suffering. For example, cold, dryness, heaviness, darkness, stench, death, and disease go together. In this way, in the geographic region between Iran, northern Syria, and Greece, individual bad experiences coalesced during the course of history into a *single* "evil." "It would appear," Hermann Trimborn wrote, "that in the border area between Iran, where the collectivization of evil had been conceptualized, and northern Syria, where the general character of evil—thanks to the characteristic Semitic way of making it real—could become present in the shape of a person, Greek thinking about substance contributed to the final reification. The latter, in turn, was the prerequisite for making evil universal and cosmic." [4]

Evidently, human beings since time immemorial have had the need to distinguish between good and evil in order to secure their coexistence. This is supported by the observation that the distinction itself and many of its concrete specifications recur, centuries later, in other parts of the world as well. According to Mexican pictographic codices and reports by missionaries, the Aztecs knew not only the distinction between good and evil (one can even recognize a consciousness of sin), but similar associations with evil. Filth, excrement, adultery, fornication, and drunkenness formed a core part of these associations. The same is true for the Incas of ancient Peru: murder, abortion, witchcraft, adultery, incest, and rape were crimes that drew particularly draconian punishments. [5]

But the universality of the distinction between good and evil—a distinction evidently called forth by the mere fact of human cohabitation (although we should not reduce it to its social function)—does not answer the question of whether human beings are always able to distinguish between good and evil in their actions. In other words, it does not answer whether in any given case guilt or the capacity for guilt can be imputed to an individual.

Deed or Motive? The Greek Experience

In human perception, misdeeds on the one hand and individual guilt or a corresponding awareness of guilt on the other have clearly not always overlapped. For example, the Greeks at the time of Homer certainly did have a sense of good and evil and also of responsibility in the sense of accountability for the consequences of one's actions. But this did not presuppose either that human beings (rather than the gods) were in fact the cause of whatever went wrong or that one had to impute evil intent and thus an awareness of guilt if one wanted to hold individuals accountable. People had to answer for their actions, not for their reasons or motives. Here an evil or bad deed is not yet linked to an individual consciousness of guilt. Contact with death or sexual activities, for example, were defiling, but the causality was still envisaged in entirely material terms as pollution without any connection to the individual's inner life or intentions.[6]

It was only during the course of the sixth century B.C.E. that the central offense of the Greeks—hubris, that is, reaching beyond the boundaries set for human beings—came to rest not only on an objective deed but also on a false, subjective frame of mind. But even then, human beings did not decide autonomously whether to inflict harm and take guilt upon themselves. Instead, it was something that overcame them by the inscrutable decree of the gods, and nobody went through life without guilt.[7]

Early Greek law was also not concerned with the intent of the accused, only with the act itself. Responsibility had to be accepted even when the gods were the cause of the offense. The modern question about how the imputation of guilt, responsibility, and freedom are interconnected did not occur to the Greeks at that time. All deviations from normality were ascribed to supernatural powers, and the Erinyes—goddesses of retribution—were morally indifferent in the beginning. Accordingly, in early Homeric times the socially sanctioned response to bad acts was not guilt but shame, and elements of this shame-culture were preserved in the archaic and classical periods. Interestingly enough, this shame-culture eventually did give rise to an increasing sense of guilt, in which the Erinyes became helpers in vengeance and Zeus was transformed from an unpredictable, arbitrary ruler into the "embodiment of cosmic justice." At the same time, however, the fear of pollution and the need for ritual purification (catharsis) remained intact. In the words of E. R. Dodds, "Strictly speaking, the archaic sense of guilt becomes a sense of sin only as a result of what Kardiner calls the 'internalizing' of conscience—a phenomenon which appears late and uncertainly in the Hellenic world, and does not become common until long after secular law had begun to recognize the importance of motive. The transference of the notion of purity from the magical to the moral sphere was a similarly late development: not until the closing years of the fifth century do we encounter explicit statements that clean hands are not enough—the heart must be clean also."[8]

From "Externality" to "Internality": The Bible

In his classic work on the problem of guilt, *Symbolism of Evil,* Paul Ricoeur sheds light on an analogous development from "externality" to "internality," from pollution to sin to the feeling of guilt. He begins his examination with the Babylonian world, but his main focus is the Judeo-Christian tradition and, to a lesser extent, the Greek world. In the *first phase* of an external understanding of evil, in which it is conceptualized in the symbol of the stain or pollution, the desire to avoid evil arises from the fear of contaminating contact. Interestingly enough, theft, lying, and murder are not yet regarded as bad in this mental framework. Instead, the primary concern is the avoidance of pollution through sexuality. Theft, lying, and murder become evil only when the evil in a religion's system of reference touches on divine holiness, and in so doing disregards social "cohesion" and violates "self-esteem." What arises here, in a historically contingent form, is the connection between evil and harm, not only to the ties between human beings but also to individual self-esteem. This connection will take on systematic interest, and we shall return to it later.[9]

The phase in which a person felt shame for a stain or pollution, and in which purity was still understood in an entirely external way, was followed by an ambiguous oscillation between the physical and the ethical. Over time, this ambiguity slowly resolved itself in favor of ethical or spiritual purity. Parallel to this there also occurred a separation of suffering and sin: suffering had to become an inexplicable affliction in order for the evil of external, objective pollution to become the evil of internal, subjective guilt. Disease was now no longer to be regarded simply as the result of an offense. (This is one interpretation of the Job story.) Sin—defined as a transgression before and a break with God—was the next stage after pollution. It eventually gave rise to guilt: "Guilt represents an internalization and a personalization of the consciousness of sin."[10]

With this a momentous step had been taken, one that has reverberated down to the present day. Sin, after all, could still be experienced as something real, something distinct from human consciousness. For example, we read in Leviticus 5:17: "If and when any person sins unwittingly and does what is forbidden by any commandment of the Lord, thereby incurring guilt, he must accept responsibility. He shall bring to the priest as a guilt-offering a ram without blemish from the flock, valued by you." This real objective existence of sin also entailed the possibility of transferring it onto a scapegoat and sending it off into the desert, thereby cleansing oneself of sin (Lev. 5:16ff).

Guilt, however, shifts the transgression into subjective consciousness. Only on this new level does the *consciousness* of sin become the criterion and measure of fault; in contrast, sin was "objective," which means it could be committed without the sinner being aware of it. From a modern perspective, the fact that a transgression was imputed to an individual as personal guilt only if a corresponding subjective consciousness existed represents progress of some kind (in penal law, which we shall discuss further on, this criterion plays a central role). Now it was no longer possible to let a single person atone for the collective, no matter what his or her motive or how conscious he was of the deed. At the same time, however, the awareness that people were mutually dependent and interconnected in their transgressions faded into the notion of original sin (often no longer understood) because every individual was accountable only for his or her individual act. Above all, the human being now became the subjective arbiter of good and evil: "[I]t is 'conscience' that now becomes the *measure* of evil in a completely solitary experience. . . . [M]an is guilty as he feels himself guilty; guilt in the pure state has become a modality of man the *measure*."[11]

The consciousness of humanity united in the common sin before God is lost. As a result, the function of the distinction between good and evil, the foundation of a universal ethic, is lost sight of: to secure human coexistence without violence. Taken to the extreme, this new posture would mean that I am only guilty if I feel guilty—regardless of whether others are hurt by me, suffer at my hands, and protest against it.

This much, then, is clear: while the distinction between good and evil is rooted in many individual experiences of social life and appears to be an early phenomenon in all human communities, the attitudes toward that distinction—actual and commanded—have developed and changed through the course of history. This development shows a discernible trend: from the identification and evaluation of transgressions by means of a symbolism of the external and collective to a symbolism of the internal and individual-subjective; from magical and externally contagious pollution and its attendant shame to objective sin, which affects all members of the community but becomes known to God as the power that addresses and commands the individual person, and, finally, to an internal, purely subjective and individual feeling or consciousness of guilt.

The transitions, however, are not as clean as they may sound. Ricoeur, in referring to the language of the symbol, which he understands as "analogical meanings that are spontaneously formed and immediately significant," emphasizes that in the transition from one meaning to another the previous meanings are not lost without a trace. Instead, they are "sublated" in an almost Hegelian sense. The "external" symbolic meanings of pollution, filth, and contagion reverberate down to this day when we talk about guilt. Incidentally, these meanings are found not only in our current individual perceptions and in our language but also in the contemporary religions and ethical cultures of the world, with various degrees of emphasis and existing side by side. It would seem that shame tends to be the predominant reaction to offenses in African societies, but alongside shame we also find numerous indications of individual feelings of guilt. Whether Japan is today still a "shame-culture" through and through, to use the famous characterization of Ruth Benedict in her book *The Chrysanthemum and the Sword,* is very doubtful. In that country too there are many indications that suggest an intertwining of a predominant shame-culture with clear signs of individual consciousness of guilt.[12]

It therefore seems quite possible, and psychologically plausible, that the various stages in this development from externality to internality continue to be present to this day—beyond the vague feeling of many people. For example, it now becomes clear why the guiding notion of "pure blood" and a general fixation on unadulterated purity and cleanliness could be subjectively perceived as entirely "moral ideas." Conversely, seen in the light of this development, a great (collective) need for cleanliness or purity might indicate a feeling of guilt. Finally, one could use this insight to explain the practice of making a person or a group into a scapegoat as an older stage of moral development, a regression, while simultaneously gaining insight into the reason why human beings can feel that such a practice is morally right.[13]

All of this means at the same time that this evolutionary process, unquestionably conditioned by history, does not simply result in a lasting moral "essence," an essence that holds true and from which there is no going back—even though that is precisely the hope of all those who, while accepting the notion that morality and conceptions of guilt are historically conditioned, wish to cling to the belief that they are absolutely binding.

Ricoeur too seems to nourish that hope when he justifies the focus of his analysis on Jewish and Greek sources by declaring that these cultures "constitute the first stratum of our philosophical memory." He goes on: "More precisely, the *encounter* of the Jewish source with the Greek origin is the fundamental intersection that founds our culture; . . . the abstractly contingent fact of that encounter is the very fact of our occidental existence. Since our existence begins with it, this encounter has become necessary, in the sense that it is the presupposition of our undeniable reality." [14]

But what if the more subtle inspirations of these sources have been so deeply buried or are so thoroughly repressed that they no longer leave any admonitory traces in the modern consciousness of guilt? What if people, manipulated by the circumstances of their time or by demagoguery, remain stuck in these earlier moral experiences (for example, that of external "purity") or fall back into them, with the result that the historical development toward a subjective conscience and the universal morality of reciprocity—a central, substantive quality of this moral development—is blocked? No dogmatic answers are possible. But at the same time, Ricoeur's perspective on the complex symbolism of evil can stimulate us to take another, closer look at recent—"reduced"—manifestations of the experience of guilt, examining them for the original elements of a later development. Perhaps we may come to a better understanding of how and why people can think of themselves as moral subjects even on such a "regressive" level. It might then be possible to work from this self-conception as the starting point in an effort to overcome this moral regression. To that extent, the "reservoir" of historical experiences of evil offers us the chance, as we seek to define *guilt* today, to escape the unpalatable alternatives of philosophical or theological dogmatism, on the one hand, and an utter relativizing historicization, on the other.

In any event, for now we must observe that Kolakowski's claim that an "indebtedness" toward the world is a basic human experience does not hold true across time. Instead, this experience rests on foundations that are historically conditioned, fragile, and—at present—in need of specific affirmation. Conversely, this perspective renders plausible the notion that the understanding of guilt documents the prevailing way in which humans conceive of themselves, which is why it is important that there be a continual process in which people reaffirm the understanding of guilt and come to an agreement about it. Without such a reaffirmation and agreement, any discussion about imputable guilt, and hence responsibility, would not rest on firm ground. Democratic politics, however, depends on imputable guilt and responsibility.

Since the consciousness of guilt and the experience of responsibility are therefore not simply eternal anthropological truths but the creations of history, they are not universal but relative. We can no longer simply decree either one. But we can ask what will follow if we challenge the capacity for guilt and responsibility in principle or simply relativize them, that is, do not affirm them. Once we answer this question, we can examine with greater clear-sightedness whether we truly want these consequences.

Let us then pose the question from the perspective of the present: what happens if we challenge in principle the capacity of human beings for guilt or challenge guilt as a category for imputing responsibility for actions? The debate within legal theory over the question whether penal law [*Schuldstrafrecht*] ought to be replaced by prerogative law [*Maßnahmerecht*] can help us gain new insights: for penal law is a socially and politically binding agreement on the norms we must follow and on the extent of freedom and responsibility that are granted to us philosophically and demanded from us politically. The theoretical justification of penal law therefore reflects not only how we see ourselves privately, but also how we ought to see ourselves subjected to public sanction. It brings to light our basic understanding of ourselves and the changes that understanding undergoes. Above all, in the practical enforcement of justice, penal law cannot evade the question of whether we are fit to bear guilt—that is, whether we can be held responsible and are fit for democracy.

PENAL LAW: A POLITICAL CONSENSUS
ABOUT GUILT AND RESPONSIBILITY

Guilt-Based Law (*Schuldrecht*)
or Prerogative Law (*Maßnahmerecht*)

In a 1952 decision, the Great Criminal Panel [Große Strafsenat] of the German Federal High Court declared the principle of guilt to be the foundation of German criminal law. In the opinion that followed, the panel went on to offer a paradigmatic definition of the systematic connection between the conception of guilt and culpability and the view of humanity inherent in it:

Punishment presumes guilt. Guilt means accountability. The verdict of guilty accuses the culprit of failing to act properly, of choosing what was wrong even though he could have acted rightfully and could have chosen to adhere to the law. The inner reason for the charge of guilt is grounded in the fact that a person is capable of exercising self-determination that is free, responsible, and ethical. For that reason he is capable of deciding in favor of what is right and against what is wrong, of adjusting his conduct in accordance with the norms of legal obligation and avoiding what is legally prohibited, as soon as he has attained moral maturity and for as long as the disposition of free and ethical self-determination is not . . . temporarily paralyzed or permanently destroyed. The precondition for a person's decision—rendered on the basis of free, responsible, and ethical self-determination—for right and against wrong is the knowledge of right and wrong. The person who knows that what he is freely deciding to do is wrong behaves in a culpable manner if he does it nonetheless.[15]

Arthur Kaufmann is one of the most committed legal and philosophical defenders of the principle of guilt in criminal law. In a number of publications he has laid out the implications summarized in a nutshell in this opinion and has debated those who would replace a penal law based on guilt with prerogative law. Guilt-based penal law essentially starts from philosophical presuppositions about human nature than can not be scientifically proved but can only be elucidated or rendered plausible. They include, chiefly, a conception of a human being as someone who is able and called upon to live in freedom (defined as self-determination) and whose dignity derives from this condition. This freedom includes responsibility and the capacity to incur guilt.[16]

    The guilt that Kaufmann makes the basis of the verdict in criminal law is guilt of the will and the act. It presupposes the free will to knowingly do what is wrong, and in this respect it differs from rational guilt (meaning the inability to understand), emotional guilt (human beings are not responsible for their emotions since the latter do not obey the commands of reason), and character guilt (which deals with the evolution of the person, the "lead-up" to the crime; although such a "lead-up" is philosophically plausible—as Aristotle has shown—and surely also within the realm of a person's responsibility, it concerns his or her personal sphere, from which the legal system should in principle keep its distance out of respect for a person's privacy and because it is impossible to attain precise knowledge about this sphere). Guilt is thus culpable conduct, a voluntary offense against what the person knows to be right, though not necessarily in the sense of a formal knowledge of the law. This in turn presupposes that every person, by "exerting his conscience," can have insight into a "minimal ethical standard" that is binding upon everyone. And it is with this minimal standard that the judge, by virtue of her life experience and resultant conception of the "average person," can render a decision about the guilt of an accused person in a "substitute judgment of conscience." However, the judge can only do this if she engages the individual and establishes a personal communication with him or her. Judgments of this nature can never be rendered with absolute certainty. They are made by analogy and remain problematic since the "average person" is an intellectual "construct." [17]

The function of punishment, which follows a verdict of "guilty" rendered on culpable conduct, is neither revenge nor retribution but atonement. According to Kaufmann, "Regardless of whether actual practice reflects this or not: by its nature, punishment is the deserved response to culpable conduct and as such simultaneously a way for the guilty person to atone. It is only in guilt that punishment finds its intrinsic measure and justification." Punishment allows the punished person to free himself of his guilt. For Kaufmann, personhood, guilt, and punishment form a tightly linked whole, as he sums up:

It is remarkable that in cases where people, as a matter of principle, punished or even killed others who were guiltless, the validity of the principle of guilt itself was never questioned. Instead, these people were deprived of their full human dignity: degraded to objects (slaves!), witches, or inferior and burdensome life forms (Jews, the mentally ill!), they could become the objects of arbitrary treatment. This reveals that in any setting in which human beings are respected as persons, people are compelled at the same time to respect the principle of guilt. . . . Penal law based on guilt takes the perpetrator seriously; it accepts his conduct as an act of mind and spirit. It sees the perpetrator not only as an object. [18]

In Kaufmann's view, the alternative to guilt-based penal law has been formulated by proponents of law as "défense social," that is, as prerogative law. Advocates of this position do not necessarily regard themselves as explicit opponents of a personalized view of humankind. However, they are not willing to accept the philosophical premises of Kaufmann's position, especially the general assumption of human freedom, as the premise of penal law. Since freedom of conscience cannot be proved, special attention would have to be paid to the conditions that could possibly restrict or nullify it. New knowledge about the spheres and parameters of freedom needs to be scrupulously examined. Guilt-based penal law must be rejected in principle not only because of its numerous internal contradictions (which Kaufmann admits are necessary difficulties, which is why any judgment remains problematical). The primary reason for opposing it is that it loses sight of society's role in the offense, that is, it keeps us from understanding a deed as a potentially ineluctable result of "social contexts." This social dimension, so the argument goes, is concealed in the interest of stabilizing the system, so as to "avoid the need for society to create concrete freedoms": "If criminal conduct intrudes into the social order as a free deed, this leaves only the negation of this negation, that is, the repression of evil." In this scenario, evil is detached from its social context, and this makes it easy "to draw a line of separation between society and the criminal offender, . . . to see a perfect order where in reality the reproduction of evil is *systemic.* The doctrine of penal law promotes the tendency to conceal all of this by invoking guilt, culpability, and the freedom of self-determination as fundamental theoretical concepts." [19]

The basic assumption that evil is reproduced by society or the system is thus opposed to the assumption that individual freedom and self-determination exist. To be sure, critics of the guilt principle are aware that, under specific circumstances, it certainly allows for the possibility that a person may be unable to incur guilt and, if necessary, it responds to a deed not with punishment but "disciplinary intervention" (for example, confinement to a psychiatric facility). But there are two things that disturb the critics of the guilt principle: one, the fundamental belief in individual freedom (rather than the social reproduction of evil), which places upon the perpetrator an unreasonable burden of responsibility; two, the inconsistency of differentiating punishment and disciplinary intervention while ignoring the fact that both measures de facto involve a deprivation of freedom, that is, a substantial restriction of the basic rights of the accused. Anyone who truly proceeds only from the charge of guilt should have no right to lay hands on a perpetrator who is incapable of incurring guilt. The alternative to guilt-based penal law is penal law "without a charge of guilt," a law that makes a different legal principle the basis of punishment. "Without a charge of guilt" does not mean doing away with the notion of guilt. Rather, the concept should be understood in a strictly objective sense, not from the perspective of the perpetrator's range of possible conduct but solely from the perspective "of the objective violation of a duty, the perspective of the needs and demands of others."[20]

There is in this argument an interesting parallel to Kaufmann's premise. For Kaufmann also proceeds from an "objective" minimum ethical standard and is explicit in grounding his definition of guilt not in the perpetrator's subjective consciousness of guilt but in the offense against an objective order of values. Guilt, according to Kaufmann, does not arise only with a subjective evaluation of a deed (by the perpetrator or the judge). The reverse is in fact the case: conduct can only be judged culpable because it is objectively unethical. Guilt is not a psychological but a normative thing, regarded as a given in natural law: "Because a perpetrator *has* guilt, he deserves to be accused, only where there *is* guilt can a (justified) verdict of guilty be rendered."[21]

Thus, both guilt-based law and prerogative law start, respectively, from objective guilt and an objective offense, and it appears that neither approach can do without them. Both positions contain premises that are certainly open to challenge: one has ideas grounded in natural law, ideas whose inherent difficulties need to be subjected to a searching examination; the other erects the "needs and demands of others" as the measure of objective duty. In the latter case, the individual person is essentially exposed to the interests of society and its manipulation since the barrier of the proof of individual guilt no longer exists.

Moreover, in a system of penal law that seeks to do without the principle of guilt and culpability, punishment no longer has the function of atoning and redeeming individual guilt (which, strictly speaking, does not exist in the first place if society is the cause of the offense). Instead, its purpose is only that of "prevention in the interest of society," so-called general prevention. In answer to Kaufmann's critique that the principle on which this "défense sociale" is based opens the door to manipulation and degrades the individual to the status of object, proponents of this approach have sought to establish a legal maxim that incorporates a notion of justice and excludes, or at least limits, arbitrariness. This is the maxim of "proportionality," though the point is precisely that it may not take the perpetrator's guilt as the yardstick. Instead, the goal is to establish a "practical concordance between the exercise of the perpetrator's basic rights, on the one hand, and the protection of other legal values and rights, on the other." Moreover, the right methods should be used to achieve the desired ends, especially in regard to the perpetrator's therapy. Since the degree of punishment can therefore no longer be aligned with individual guilt, the basis on which it is determined is essentially an

assessment of how likely it is to have a therapeutic effect on the condemned perpetrator. The measures taken must be adapted to the perpetrator's unique characteristics: "Therapeutic experts must be entrusted
with deciding the question whether a perpetrator, in the process of serving a punishment, will be responsive to the notion of his own responsibility, or whether such an appeal will be futile or may even interfere with
the healing process."[22]

The desire to protect a potential perpetrator from the general
assumption and imputation of freedom of will and personal responsibility thus results in him being profoundly disenfranchised by psychiatry.
Doctors decide whether a perpetrator is responsive to "his" (why his?)
responsibility. Contrary to its original intent, this approach does not
strengthen an individual perpetrator's basic rights as a subject against an
(unjustified) accusation of guilt but deprives him of self-determination,
and thus of his standing as a subject. For it is the doctors who determine
the capacity to bear guilt and responsibility (meaning that they can, if
necessary, deny this capacity even against the perpetrator's will). What
this means is that the historical decoupling of suffering and disease from
sin in favor of the principle of individual guilt (as described by Ricoeur)
has been, for practical purposes, reversed—that is, guilt is equated with
illness. The person who is supposed to be found guilty is actually sick.
(And is the person who is sick once again guilty?) Individual responsibility is no longer the right and obligation of every person, but follows from
an attribution made by medical expertise. Evidently, the range of possible arguments concerning the connection between guilt and human
self-understanding is not only contingent upon history but limited by
logic.

The result of this theoretical debate is conflicting: On the one hand,
it is true that the definition of principles by the Federal High Court, the
implications of guilt-based penal law, and even penal law that rejects guilt
as the measure of and reason for punishment, all reveal that there is a systematically compelling link between the definition of guilt and human self-
understanding. The denial that human beings are, in principle, capable of
bearing guilt ineluctably leads to the denial of their freedom and responsibility. If one rejects the imputation of freedom one ends up by making
people the objects of decisions rendered by doctors and psychiatrists.

On the other hand, the stance of guilt-based penal law, with its basic assumption that human beings are persons and with its presuppositions in natural law, includes premises one can—but does not have to—
agree with. In particular, these premises are replete with considerable

difficulties with respect to a precise determination of natural law under current conditions.

Can We Leave Open
the Question of Determining Guilt?

Would it be a possible way out of this dilemma to not deny in general that people are capable of incurring guilt but to simply leave the question open since we are unable to come up with a binding and "objective" determination of either responsibility or the "minimal ethical standard"? This approach finds support in the fact that the separation of morality and legality, that is, the refusal to demand that citizens adhere to the law for *moral* motives as laid down by the state, should be seen as an advance in tolerance. For in this scenario the citizen does not have to make a state-sanctioned morality his own. He merely has to show outward obedience to the law, and beyond that he is free to hold to his own convictions.[23]

And yet this solution does not help, unless one wants to dispense with penal law in general (something only anarchists have so far demanded). For it is still necessary to justify punishment (and its severity) as a penalty imposed on an offense. And if punishment cannot invoke the personal guilt of the condemned person, the only thing left is the goals of so-called general and specific prevention. There are essentially two approaches to justifying punishment, a dual scheme that goes back to the time of Protagoras. There are the so-called absolute justifications that refer to the *past* of a deed; these justifications are articulated *because* a perpetrator has done something to incur guilt (punitur *quia* peccatum est). And there are the so-called relative justifications, in which the punishment is aimed *preventively* at the *future* and is subordinated to the goal *that* the deed will not happen (again) (punitur *ne* peccetur). Logically, this scheme does not appear to leave open a third alternative.

In their pure forms—the absolute, which calls for punishment as retribution and atonement, and the relative, in which punishment is intended to serve as prevention through deterrence and public affirmation of the law, as well as through the perpetrator's rehabilitation—these justifications are no longer advocated today. In particular, following the revival of punishment merely as general or specific prevention, as Ellscheid and Hassemer advocated prototypically in the 1970s, the limitations and dangers of this understanding of punishment have once again become apparent.

Today, we feel far more uncertain about the positive possibilities of rehabilitation and even more so about the ability of the disciplines of psychology and psychiatry to offer advice and guidance in determining punishment. This uncertainty arises because the latter disciplines can say little in the way of prognosis, and especially because it is in principle just as difficult to differentiate clearly between healthy and sick, normal and deviant, as it is to draw a line between guilty or responsible and not guilty. Definitions of health, normality, and responsibility are equally grounded in philosophical and normative choices that are simply beyond proof.[24]

Still, we cannot leave the question about guilt and responsibility open because in any verdict in criminal proceedings we de facto make a statement about guilt and responsibility that must be justified.

Moreover, leaving the question unresolved also has potentially destructive consequences for a liberal democracy based on the rule of law. By its very self-conception, such a political system depends on the vitality and support of democratic citizens, meaning citizens who are willing to take responsibility and are therefore capable of incurring guilt. If penal law, as a public and binding consensus about the parameters and content of guilt and responsibility, ceases to make pronouncements it cuts the ground from the normative, foundational consensus of the citizens. Instead of undergirding and affirming this consensus, the silence of penal law exposes it to arbitrary interpretations. Nobody would choose to live in a society without a prohibition against murder and without responsibility on the part of the citizens. That is why we simply cannot evade the task of establishing the content of the normative, foundational consensus and of defining a justified minimal ethical standard. The political consequences of these decisions make it impossible to avoid them. At the same time, we are fully aware that we no longer possess a definitive and unshakable basis for making these decisions.

Klaus Günther has sought to get out of this dilemma with the help of the so-called ethics of discourse. This approach, which relies on the work of Jürgen Habermas, seeks to derive the normative, minimum consensus—on which social and judicial imputations of guilt could base themselves—from the subtle exercise of reciprocity. In the tradition of Immanuel Kant, this method involves the essentially rational process of putting oneself in the place of another in order to devise fair rules of communal life. The question of whether this formal approach can truly produce a consensus about content triggers a complicated discussion that I will not pursue in detail here. Günther himself has also raised the problem that a rational understanding of what is right, in the absence of a sanctioning authority or convincing philosophical grounding, is not sufficient by itself to motivate people to actually do what is right, that is, to exercise responsibility. This is all the more true if one conceives of responsibility in purely functional and descriptive terms as something ascribed and allocated by society. In this case, there is no longer an elementary foundation that societies are prevented from disregarding when allocating responsibility. Moreover, the individual conscience as the final, internal instance of responsibility would, in theory, be stripped of its authority.[25]

In practice, contemporary penal theory solves this dilemma through a variety of "unification theories" that combine the two justifications for punishment (compensation for past injustice through atonement and the future-oriented purpose of general and specific prevention) even though they are logically contradictory. To prevent this inconsistency from fracturing the theoretical justification of penal law and leading in practice to the disintegration of the awareness of the law, the different unification theories all center around a "core" supplemented with elements drawn from the other side. In this way, the theories preserve a minimum degree of internal coherence and persuasiveness.

The German Federal High Court has so far clung to the "core" of the theory of guilt, a stance that accords with the need for responsible citizens. But this once again raises the question of how to justify responsibility and what the content of the criteria of guilt is, given that the theoretical uncertainties are fundamentally unresolvable. Adolf Arndt has responded to this difficulty with the hope and persistent demand that we continually create a new social consensus about the basic determinations of good and evil in natural law within the context of a concrete historical situation, and that we create along with it another consensus about the parameters of guilt and responsibility. Such an approach would demand even more urgently that we imagine not only the systemic implications of a particular conception of guilt. In this case, it would also be necessary and compelling to initiate and maintain an ongoing—and therefore more lasting—discourse about the *content* of guilt, about the "minimal ethical standard" that Kaufmann (joining Jellinek) accepts as a matter of course. In taking this stance we may share Arndt's "trust that every person can be won over to the law," that it is possible to establish a basic ethical and moral consensus.[26]

One of the primary goals of this book is to contribute to such a basic moral consensus. Perhaps by shedding light on the destructive consequences of silenced guilt, which leaves us in the dark about the reach of moral responsibility, we can help attain a normative agreement about the basic values that guide us and about the ethos we must follow if we wish to live together in a free and democratic system. Insight into the suffering and destruction caused by treating guilt with silence may offer us a new foundation for formulating the content of a democratic ethos and putting it into practice in the form of a shared, normative basic consensus. Such a foundation, while not objectively binding, binds us together voluntarily and is not arbitrary.

The next step toward this goal is to examine in greater detail the notion of guilt—both its formal structure and its many concrete historical manifestations.

2

Shared Elements in the Historical Notions of Guilt

THE FORMAL STRUCTURE OF GUILT

We have seen that the distinction between good and evil has accompanied human social existence since earliest times. Evidently, human communities need this distinction as a guide to live and survive. At the same time, we have had to recognize that attitudes toward this distinction, and the specifics that people have attributed to it, have undergone historical changes: from an early view of evil as an external, objective, and material contagion or stain to the community-centered notion of objective sin as an offense against the love of God (Israelite), or the idea of transgression as an objective responsibility (independent of subjective intent or design) centered on the polis (Greek), and finally to the notion of a subjective awareness of sin as determined by the individual conscience.[1]

Pushed to its extreme, this last, subjective stage, in which the individual consciousness of sin beyond any objective system of values is turned into the criterion of guilt, raises the following question: does the radical extension of this stage lead to arbitrary definitions, thereby undercutting the original function of the distinction between good and evil, namely, to promote social coherence? Are we, with our "solitary conscience," compelled to conclude that the determination of guilt and the definition of what it means can only be private matters now and as such are detached from any socially grounded distinction between good and evil? Or is it possible to find philosophical, theological, and maybe even sociological or psychological considerations that point to intersubjectively recognizable boundaries to such a radical subjectivization and relativization of the determination of guilt? I believe that one can demonstrate the existence of such boundaries, for example in the close interconnection between individual or personal identity on the one hand and social integration on the other.

The concept of identity has many proponents and opponents. Proponents see it as a foil on which the conditions of individual and social existence can be imprinted especially well. Opponents dislike the arbitrary nature of the specific elements associated with the concept. I introduce it here because it is a place where insights from theology, philosophy, sociology, and psychology concerning guilt intersect and can be highlighted. We shall begin with the more vivid observations of theology and religious philosophy.

In his comparative study of the "wages of guilt" in Germany and Japan, the Dutch journalist Ian Buruma reports of being told about a Japanese diplomat who felt "that Germany's preoccupation with its past sins, and its willingness to apologize to its former victims, had surely led to a loss of German identity." The Japanese Right, meanwhile, is afraid that the war guilt imposed upon them by the Americans has damaged Japanese identity. In Germany, the new Right is articulating similar views, arguing that the sense of guilt instilled in the Germans by the Allies and later the so-called generation of '68, is having a destructive effect on a healthy German national identity.[2] Does the acceptance of guilt in fact destroy personal or social identity? Does this danger exist at the very least in situations where individuals are burdened with unjustified accusations of guilt? What is the connection between guilt and identity? I will look for answers by going back to the biblical understanding of sin and guilt.

Biblical Answers:
Sin and Guilt as a Rupture of Relationship

The Bible has no uniform words for sin and guilt but expresses these concepts through a host of concrete images: missing the mark, a crooked path, an error and aimless wandering, obstinacy or turning from God, estrangement, dereliction, God-forsakenness. All told, sin is experienced not as the transgression of an abstract rule but as the violation of a personal and communal relationship, both with God and, inseparably linked to that, with one's fellow human beings. The transgression arises from a person's obstinacy, from the evil inclination of the "hardened heart" against which the prophet Jeremiah rails. From a Catholic perspective, Karl Rahner has defined guilt as "a person's total and definitive decision against God" and thereby against the very ground of her existence. That is why guilt is self-destructive, is "suicide, without the subject being able to escape into nothingness through it." Analogously, the Jewish philosopher Pinchas Lapide has called sin "the turning away from God . . . , a straying onto loveless paths that are in the service of selfishness."[3]

In the notion of sin, the biblical message thus from the outset weaves together the relationship between God and humankind and the relationship among human beings. Imperiling or destroying one of these relationships does the same to the other. In theological terms, the Bible underscores that the successful pursuit of the relationship to God, to one's fellow human beings, and to oneself—or the destruction of this relationship—is of a piece. The reason why subjective moral guilt and sin against God overlap in the Christian perspective is because guilt toward one's fellow human beings and toward one's own conscience is always a "rejection of divine love" and vice versa. This theological idea is complemented etymologically by the derivation of sin from segregation, separation, the abrogation of community. As selfishness, as a turning from God and a disordered turning toward mortal creatures, sin destroys human relationships. The violation of love and the termination of trust in God and the human community are inseparably connected. Incidentally, in African nature religions as well, sin is often described as an offense against the harmony of the human community. If a person separates himself from God, his other relationships are also disturbed. In Shintoism too, a person incurs guilt by hurting the feelings of others or by upsetting the harmony of social coexistence.[4]

In the Judeo-Christian experience of *sin*, and in its theological interpretation, a close link thus exists between the people's relationship to God, to their community, and to themselves because sin has destructive effects on all three relationships simultaneously. It is therefore only natural to examine how this interlinked triad expresses itself in a context where sin is radically subjectivized in the consciousness of *guilt* as a subjective conscience and how it may manifest itself in a nonreligious or secularized garb.

Guilt as the Abandonment of Personal Identity

The possibility of fallibility—that is, of guilt—arises from the fact that there is no exact correspondence between a person and her self. In other words, we are not simply identical with our selves: thanks to our capacity for reflection, we enter—willingly or not—into a relationship to ourselves that we sometimes call freedom. In our conscience we simultaneously experience this situation as the task of reestablishing the congruence of self disturbed by transgressions against the norms. In my conscience I am charged with the task of personal identity, which contains a natural and a moral element. The natural element of identity (e.g.,

my fingerprint) is given to me; the moral element I must summon up myself. As a whole then, my personal identity is my own achievement. Arising from conscience, personal identity means the "preservation of the
congruence of the person with himself," that is, the congruence between
a person's norms and his conduct. Personal identity, however, is not
merely a formal state of noncontradiction. It arises materially "from the
blueprint of a successful life, a blueprint experienced as meaningful." It is
qualitative identity, the congruence of my actions and my ideas of what
is good.[5]

Incidentally, conscience is experienced as a fundamental moral arbiter not only in the Judeo-Christian and later the Greek tradition (for instance, as the daimon of Socrates), but also in the tradition of African
ethics, which is often misinterpreted as collectivist. Evidence of this are
the practice of name-giving found among many tribes, which underscores the worth of each individual, and the practice of traditional public courts. Long before the Christianization of Africa, these courts in-
quired into the motive and intent behind a deed; for example, these
courts considered not only an actual murder punishable, but the intent
itself.[6]

A long tradition, stretching from Aristotle and Thomas Aquinas all
the way to Kant, sees the human being as fundamentally endowed with
the will to do what is good. Although the temptation and possibility
of doing evil is ever present, to want evil for the sake of evil is utterly
"inhuman" and "diabolical." It is in this sense that Kant draws a distinction between "depravity" [Bösartigkeit] and "wickedness" [Bosheit] in
human nature: "We are not, then, to call the depravity of human nature
wickedness, taking the word in its strict sense as a subjective principle of
the maxims or a disposition to adopt evil as evil into our maxims as an incentive, for that is satanic; we should rather term it the perversity of the
heart, which then because of what follows from it is also called an evil
heart."[7]

Thomas Aquinas, on the basis of the same assumption (that human
beings in principle want the good, or at least do not want evil for the sake
of evil), differentiated between disposition and the act of conscience. By
disposition, a human being knows in general that one ought to do good.
This is not an individual judgment, but a principle that is plain and convincing because it is part of God's law and because we are endowed with
natural reason. The individual act of conscience appears afterward "as a
judgment of my judgment, as the self-examination of practical reason." If
I follow my act of conscience, I create my personal identity. In the words

of Honnefelder: "The judgment of conscience is the preservation of the distinctive unity of the individual person in the face of changing parameters of conduct, or the reestablishment of that unity after guilt has been incurred." [8]

Guilt thus means, conversely, that a person foregoes the act of reestablishing this distinctive personality. If one follows the traditional view that human beings generally do not want evil for the sake of evil, guilt exists in "contradiction to what a person fundamentally and essentially desires. Instead of a successful self-realization, it means the loss of self-identity through a clash with what a person truly wants and wants to be, and it thus leads to disruption of the self." [9]

In all of this, however, identity cannot simply be undifferentiated sameness, otherwise once a person has incurred guilt he could not reestablish identity. Personal identity exists when and as long as there are serious efforts to avoid contradiction of the self or, if a contradiction has occurred, to resolve it by recognizing and correcting it.

For a human being, the experience of evil is painful. It impels the individual to reestablish her identity. And it is that act that creates dignity, and dignity consists of taking responsibility for oneself and one's acts and admitting that one can incur guilt and has done so. Todorov defines dignity as "the capacity to satisfy, through one's actions, criteria that one has internalized. Dignity in this sense is synonymous with self-respect." [10]

Hannah Arendt has described the need for such dignity through self-congruence as essential for life. It is unbearable for a person to be in a state of contradiction with his own self. Todorov draws a similar conclusion from his experiences in the concentration camps: "The kind of coherence between internal standards and external behavior that leads to self-respect is no less common among the guards than among their prisoners and gave rise in both to the same feeling of dignity. Höß was a confirmed Nazi who acted on his convictions. So was Mengele, who apparently did not suffer from the split personality characteristic of so many others." [11]

We thus have evidence that all humans have the feeling, evidently rooted in conscience, that dignity and self-respect stand opposed to guilt, defined as an accepted contradiction of the self. And we can even invoke the likes of Höß and Mengele as examples that human beings do not, by their very nature, seek evil for the sake of evil but to maintain self-respect construct their unique "guiltlessness" as a congruence of self or identity. Yet it also becomes abundantly clear that a purely formal definition of guilt—as the willingness to let the contradiction of self be what it is—is insufficient. The congruence of ideal and conduct becomes a convincing example of personal identity that transcends guilt only if the ideal is also identified in terms of *content* and is convincing in its own right. That is the reason why we must later return to the question of content.

If guilt means foregoing the reestablishment of personal identity and accepting the contradiction of the self, and if personal identity cannot simply be sameness without tension or differentiation but demands the continual creation of a complex personal unity, it would make sense to expect another defining characteristic of guilt and misconduct on the other pole of this equation, that is, in the search for a false unity. For guilt can also manifest itself in a dishonest identity in the form of a false unity. In a paradoxical way, a person can also fail to attain the necessary identity by eliminating the contradiction—the committed transgression—from his personal identity instead of integrating it. One way of doing that would be, in the words of Odo Marquard, to "de-evilize" evil, for example, by trying to abolish in general the distinction between good and evil or by recasting one's worldview in thoroughly "scientific" terms. According to Marquard, this kind of "de-evilizing" creates in people a compulsion to make enemies of others and to denigrate them, which would attest once again to the link between intrapersonal and interpersonal relationships that we know from the Bible and which in any case would provide an indication that we don't mean an identity free of tension when we talk about the overcoming of guilt.[12]

In psychological terms, another way of creating a false unity of personal identity is through separation or fragmentation. The American psychologist Ervin Staub, in a comprehensive study entitled *The Roots of Evil*, has pointed out the mechanisms of "compartmentalization" and the "splitting" of the self: schizophrenics cease to have any feelings of guilt. These mechanisms make it possible to do evil and to do it apparently without a bad conscience. From a sociological perspective, Zygmunt Baumann, continuing the work of Max Weber, has examined in detail the contribution of modern bureaucratization to separation, that is, to the process that leads people to block out interconnections, thereby keeping them from shouldering responsibility and guilt. And Todorov, in his compelling study *Facing the Extreme: Moral Life in the Concentration Camps*, points to the repeated observation that concentration camp guards, and even camp commandants, fragmented their conduct into a ghastly job, on the one hand, and their "praiseworthy" private life, on the other, which may even have been intended to compensate for the horrors of their work.

Todorov is fully cognizant of the fact that it is impossible for us to fully integrate all problems and all possible consequences of our actions into our own perception of guilt and personal identity, that a certain rejection or fragmentation is quite necessary for us to live: A "certain degree of fragmentation is . . . indispensable for the sheer psychological survival of the individual. . . . How can one discern the boundary beyond which this fragmentation becomes culpable, indeed, criminal?" His answer is a pragmatic one. The boundary, he declares, lies at the point where I no longer think about interconnections and banish the extent of the evil (such as torture and murder) completely from my mental horizon.[13] This boundary is not precise, a point to which I shall return when defining "silenced guilt."

Still, this aspect of a failed personal identity reveals that guilt — paradoxically enough — is present essentially when I reject it, that is, when I am unwilling to incorporate it into my personal identity, when I try to avoid or cover up the contradiction within me by not registering it or looking away. Consequently, liberation from guilt would not mean a rejection of guilt but in fact its acceptance, such that I would at the least stand up and take responsibility for it. "I have the hunch that innocence has gradually passed to the side of those who are willing to take on the guilt," says the consul in Siegfried Lenz's play *The Time of the Guiltless* [*Zeit der Schuldlosen*]. He will take the guilt upon himself and will shoot himself so that the others, who are being blackmailed along with him, will be set free.[14]

Without Conscience There Is No Free Society

The need to "preserve" the difficult and contradictory parts within personal identity is also discussed by sociologists and psychologists who ponder the conditions that must exist for individual identities to be able to connect through social interaction and integration. My concluding reflections on the connection between identity and guilt will thus explain why this precondition for free social coexistence may offer a clue to how we can define the meaning and content of the notion of guilt.

For decades, modern society has witnessed a process of differentiation and individualization that has confronted people with many and often quite contradictory expectations about the roles they should play. Against this background, there has been an ongoing sociological, sociopsychological, and psychoanalytical discussion about how individuals can react to these contradictory demands without relinquishing their internal coherence and without splitting themselves up completely. Once again, the concepts of fragmentation and identity have played a central role in this debate.

The contradictory nature of the expectations to which I find myself exposed in my various roles as a woman, mother, professional, member of a party or church, and so on could easily suggest that I should simply adapt to each set of expectations, in the process fragmenting myself not only temporally but also with respect to my views, specific reactions, and so forth. However, experiences have shown that this kind of fragmentation (i.e., dispensing with the formation of a coherent personal identity despite contrary expectations) is profoundly unsettling to my interactions with other people. This disturbance arises essentially because the condition of unresolved contradiction causes my words and actions to lack credibility and dependability. People do not like to deal with a person who is unable to regulate his conduct in accordance with his own logic—who is, psychoanalytically speaking, unable to form a self-identity—because they don't know what they are dealing with and what is coming next. Lothar Krappmann, in his classic overview of the relevant literature, summed it up this way: "It is not possible to interact with people who lack self-identity." Much as in our earlier discussion of identity in connection with the definition of guilt and conscience, a genuine self-identity resists (a) the splintering into contradictory expectations (acceptance of contradictoriness) and (b) the attempt, when faced with the uncertainty caused by contradictory expectations, to attain a deceptive security by identifying completely with one role or person or ideology while refusing to let in other expectations in the first place or splitting them off. In addition, fragmentation—that is, the attempt to erect dividing walls between the various spheres of one's life—is opposed to free social intercourse, especially if it develops a tendency toward reciprocal, hermetical isolation.[15]

Social interaction with others is most likely to be successful if a person can muster the energy to continually create a plausible and justifiable balance, constantly keeping in mind past and present parameters of conduct and norms. Such a balance leaves a person open to old and new demands, while at the same time allowing for the kind of predictability and trustworthiness that others need, and without which social life is not possible in the long run.

We must recognize that it is entirely possible for our self-under-

standing and behavior to vary in different phases of our lives. What matters is that we establish a connection between these phases that others
can understand. Again Krappmann:

*The most difficult problem that individuals face is maintaining a bal-
ance between these self-interpretations and making this balance understandable to the people with whom they are interacting. Part of the
difficulty is that the individual must face up to unsettling events. Being
unable to explain how something could have happened is an uncomfortable state of affairs since the inability to reconstruct decision-making
processes raises doubts that one's acts are carefully considered in the
first place. An ambivalent life trajectory, meanwhile, could make the
people with whom a person interacts suspicious. They must be per-
suaded that their counterpart, even if he or she is unable to offer a consistent explanation for a course of events, acknowledges them with a
sense of responsibility, and in so doing makes it easier to know where
they stand.*

Of course, people must also be expected to put up with a certain degree
of ambivalence and uncertainty in the process. Incidentally, the more
complex the reflected psychic structure and biography of a person is and
the more it is able to knit together different experiences and self-interpretations, the greater is its ability to judge others in a differentiated
manner, to feel what it is like to be in their shoes, to resist prejudices and
thus contribute to the liberal integration of society. In sociopsychological terms as well, people who can rely on a strong sense of self make an
important emotional contribution to a free and democratic social coexistence. To trust in one's own identity means that an "individual is less
fearful and defensive, and instead more spontaneous, friendlier, and
more respectful." [16]

   This demonstrated connection between individual identity and social interaction reveals the central importance that attaches to a coherent identity as a result of its reliability. This reliability is, in the final analysis, grounded in its existential link to truth and truthfulness, which allow
the self to face even "unsettling events." Modern sociology and socio-
psychology thus offer a plausible explanation why the principled distinction—already outlined by Zarathustra—between truth and lie, between "good spirit" and "evil spirit" and later conscience as the shaper of
identity, takes on such importance for the social coexistence of human
beings. For it is these two elements—an ethical distinction between

good and evil and conscience—that form the basis of the indispensable minimum degree of reciprocal predictability and trust without which human beings could not interact or cooperate. And this is all the more true in a society in which conduct is shaped by personal freedom and not by prescriptions and unquestioned traditions.[17]

All this applies especially to those elements of a person's biography that are difficult to incorporate into individual identity, that is, to wrong or culpable conduct. It follows from this that the clarification of one's own guilt, a process that resists the temptation to engage in fragmentation or silencing, makes a contribution to free social intercourse and thus to the integration of society that should be greatly appreciated. Conversely, treating guilt with silence, leaving it unclear or failing to acknowledge it, opposes this kind of free social intercourse: it has a destructive effect both on a person's identity—leading, in the extreme case, to the schizophrenic split of the self—and on the liberal cohesion of society.

To answer the question we raised at the outset: the acceptance of guilt—provided it is authentic and not falsely imposed—thus does not in any way compromise identity, either on an individual or a national level. On the contrary, it is one of its essential prerequisites if the national identity we strive for or conceive of—that is, the national unity that undergirds our social coexistence—is to be a liberal one. Karl Jaspers, in a groundbreaking and still influential study on the categorical distinctions of guilt, splendidly illuminated how important the acceptance of guilt is to social coexistence in liberty and to the connection between the formal and substantive conception of guilt.

SUBSTANTIVE SIMILARITIES

Karl Jaspers's Categories of Guilt

Only a year after the end of World War II, Karl Jaspers delivered an illuminating series of lectures—unsurpassed to the present day—in which he addressed the question of guilt with which the Germans were frequently confronted after 1945 and which they in turn responded to or pushed away in different ways. Revealingly enough, he began his reflections with a statement that pointed to the connection between the internal unity of Germany and the way it dealt with its historical guilt: "We have to get our spiritual bearings in Germany, with one another. We have no common ground yet. We are seeking to get together. . . . Finding the common in the contradictory is more important than hastily seizing on mutually exclusive points of view and breaking off the conversation as hopeless." As Jaspers saw it in 1946, what was common to the Germans was "noncommunity."[18] To what extent then does the way in which the Germans dealt with guilt affect their potential common ground?

At the outset, Jaspers made his well-known, and to this day exceedingly helpful, distinction between criminal, political, moral, and metaphysical guilt. These various forms of guilt are connected and arise from a single substratum, but it is easier to talk about them individually.

Criminal guilt stems from crimes that can be proved objectively and violate established laws. *Political* guilt is responsibility for acts of state. It arises from a shared citizenship and for Jaspers even more generally from the mere fact that people are subject to the power of the state and live under the order it establishes. *Moral* guilt expresses itself in the individual's responsibility for everything she does, including the political and military spheres. It thus encompasses these spheres, which is why political and military orders cannot suspend it. The simple statement "orders are orders" is never a valid excuse or justification. *Metaphysical* guilt lays the foundation for all guilt. In its absence it would be theoretically impossible to establish the other, specific forms of guilt. Jaspers describes it as follows: "There exists a solidarity among men as human beings that makes each co-responsible for every wrong and every injustice in the world, especially for crimes committed in his presence or with his knowledge. If I fail to do whatever I can to prevent them, I too am guilty. If I was present at the murder of others without risking my life to prevent it, I feel guilty in a way not adequately conceivable either legally, politically, or morally. That I live after such a event has happened weighs upon me as indelible guilt." A lofty standard—akin to the earlier statement by Leszek Kolakowski and surely questionable to many. But if we don't assume the existence of a fundamental duty of solidarity among human beings, all others conceptions of guilt—not only those of Jaspers—are up in the air.

In all of this, it is important to remind oneself of the various tribunals before which the specific kinds of guilt are professed and that can bring a charge of guilt: the *court* charges *criminal* guilt; the *victorious side* demands the *political* responsibility of the *defeated side*; a person's *conscience* or loving fellow human beings can raise the charge of *moral* guilt (not the court, not the state, or simply any fellow citizen); *God* alone is the arbiter of *metaphysical* guilt.[19]

The two kinds of guilt that have a special relationship to the inner unity of a community are moral guilt and metaphysical guilt. Every person alone must profess them before his conscience or his god. Insisting on their public profession through legal means is not only impossible (because inappropriate to this kind of guilt), it also leads to the opposite of understanding and acceptance, namely, hardening, defensiveness, and defiance. And yet it is essential, especially for the public political community, that people also grapple honestly with their guilt. The more likely response is all kinds of superficial excuses, which promote aggressiveness and defiance, arise from self-deception, and favor deception toward oneself and others. "Whoever has not yet found himself guilty in spontaneous self-analysis will tend to accuse his accusers." In such a situation people are sensitive to questions. They try to reckon their own guilt against that of others, even though it is only "the anxiety that as human beings we share with all others for mankind" that provides a legitimate reason for determining the guilt of others. This gives rise to self-pity. In its fixation on the self, self-pity is just as wrong as instinctive and lusty confessions of guilt, which demonstrate a person's seeming moral superiority and aggressively seek to force others into making a confession of their own.

True community cannot be created in this way. Community is also undermined if we deceive ourselves about our concrete share of guilt, by letting it sink into the vast ocean of universal original sin or claiming that in the past we were defenseless and impotent. If this happens, we continue living impotently—and not "out of our self." This renders impossible the transition to a free community with which we associate ourselves with a sense of responsibility and belonging: "The first sign of the awakening of a people's political liberty is the understanding of its culpability and responsibility." As long as I deceive myself and others about my guilt and responsibility, I will not attain a shared sense of political responsibility. The engagement with guilt, which creates genuine community, lies in truthful self-examination, in "purification" and reparation. Purification does not happen externally through magic. It is an "inner process that is never ended but in which we continually become ourselves. Purification is a matter of our freedom. Everyone comes again and again to the fork in the road, to the choice between the clean and the murky." Purification makes us humble; we don't withdraw defiantly, do not accuse others, and, conversely, are not sensitive to false accusations because they no longer really touch us. We become "aware of being humanly finite and incapable of perfection. Then we are capable of nonaggressive silence [a critical distinction!]—it is from the simplicity of silence that the clarity of the communicable will emerge." In our own bond to the truth, we are no longer in need of guile. "Purification is the premise of our political liberty too; for only consciousness of guilt leads to the consciousness of solidarity and co-responsibility without which there can be no liberty." And while the "awareness of guilt is no guarantee of new happiness," we become free "so as to be ready for whatever may come."[20]

It is only a clear view of moral guilt within the realm of metaphysics that enables us to overcome the deception of self and others, to achieve a sustainable community based on political responsibility and truth, and to acquire a realistic perception of political possibilities. It is a perception that does not lead us astray and whose aim is not to see one's opponent only as an enemy or a fool but preserves a fundamental common bond with him despite political opposition. (If we compare this scenario as outlined by Karl Jaspers in 1946 with what actually happened in the following years in both West and East Germany, we cannot be surprised by the fundamental lack of a shared community that became apparent in the controversies—between the "Left" and the "Conservatives," as well as later, after 1989, between western and eastern Germany—over where responsibility should be placed. Germans on both sides of the Iron Curtain lacked the willingness to recognize the part that Nazi guilt had played in the division of their country.) The acceptance of guilt is not opposed to individual identity (Jaspers would say "selfhood") and social integration; it is in fact an indispensable precondition of both. And the attempt to talk people into an unjustified sense of guilt can have a destructive effect—because it arouses understandable and also justified aggression—only where no genuine examination of guilt has taken place: "Once we have been shaken by the inner tremors, however, the external attack will merely brush the surface. It may still be offensive and painful, but it does not penetrate to the interior of the soul."[21]

Our discussion now shifts to a search for other constant, substantive elements in the way in which guilt has been defined or experienced in the religious and philosophical tradition since antiquity. In doing so, we may be able to uncover a foil against which we can explain what precisely we mean when we talk about "silenced" guilt. This hope is based on the presumption that centuries-old notions of culpable behavior take root in human beings and continue. Even intensive "reeducation" or ideologization cannot simply eradicate these notions, which remain vital as (semi)conscious standards.

Guilt in Egyptian, Biblical, and Greek Traditions

In the remainder of the book, our efforts to arrive at a more precise substantive definition will focus primarily on moral and metaphysical guilt as
understood by Jaspers. We must bear in mind that guilt as a subjective
perception or as a subjective criterion of moral misconduct comes to
characterize human attitudes toward evil only in their late stage of development.[22] This change shifts the emphasis in the substantive definition of guilt increasingly away from the objective deed and toward the
subject's volitional decision. As we have already seen in our discussion of
Ricoeur's phenomenology of guilt, this shift has the tricky potential consequence that individual feelings of guilt could be declared the decisive
and final criterion of guilt. Accordingly, a person who has no feelings of
guilt or denies having them would therefore be guiltless. To gain a better
grasp of these questions, it seems appropriate to begin by distinguishing more precisely between three concepts that have often been used
synonymously in our discussion up to now: feelings of guilt, consciousness of guilt, and guilt.

In our context, the term *feelings of guilt* is used in the sense of an
emotion. This emotion—measured by "objective" standards or by those
the subject accepts for herself—can indicate guilt but does not necessarily do so. Feelings of guilt designate a questioning impulse, but this impulse is not yet an indicator of guilt. *Consciousness of guilt* describes
the reflective knowledge of one's misconduct, and *guilt* describes the de-
viation from the accepted standard that is manifested in an act of misconduct.[23]

In world religions that proclaim a personal notion of God, guilt describes chiefly an abandonment of faith, from which all else flows. As
far as worldly relations—that is, relations between people—are concerned, the emphasis is on two central offenses: lying and violating another person's physical and psychic integrity. You shall not murder, you
shall not commit adultery, you shall not steal, you shall not bear false witness against your fellow man: these four injunctions from the Ten Commandments encapsulate the essential transgressions of the norms of social conduct, norms that have survived for centuries as the core of public
morals, that is, of objectively valid morality. These injunctions are either
broken down into individual acts or condensed into abstract rules: of justice, of reciprocity, the "golden rule," or of solidarity.

We should mention another kind of guilt that is found in Greek tradition and comes close to the notion of pride, egotism, or a false sense

of autonomy: hubris.[24] It is, first of all, a transgression not against one's fellow human beings but against the gods or fate. But because hubris is a grossly inflated sense of self-importance and the absence of a sense of reality and proportion, the consequences for those exposed to it are potentially disastrous. Especially in view of the extraordinary crimes of the twentieth century—often based on theories of utopia one could certainly call hubristic—it is useful to note the Greek experience that a person who acts with hubris not only fails but incurs guilt.

Respect and Care:
The Core of Traditional Morality

It is not clear whether the injunction of reciprocity means that only the willful harming of another person and the willful violation of the norm constitute misconduct or whether mere indifference should also be seen as culpable. The second "major" commandment of the Decalogue—"You shall love your neighbor as yourself"—indicates that the point is not merely to avoid harm. The obligation extends further. Like the Good Samaritan, one should care for one's fellow human beings. Failure to act is therefore guilt.

Incidentally, the roots of this Judeo-Christian tradition are already found in the Persian and Egyptian cultures. Here too the protection of the weak (primarily widows and orphans) was an important element of morality. For instance, an inscription on the tomb of Darius the Great declares: "Right I have loved, and Wrong I have not loved. My will was that no injustice should be done to any widow or orphan, and that injustice should be done to widows or orphans was not my will. I strictly punished the liar, (but) him who labored I well rewarded." And in the famous hymn to the Egyptian sun god Shamash, we read: "He who does not take a bribe, who espouses the cause of the weak, is well pleasing to Shamash."[25] Positive solicitude for another person, care for those who need it, is an element of central importance. For it means that the orbit of guilt comes to encompass even behavior that arises not from the intent to inflict willful harm but from thoughtlessness, unkindness, from the averting of one's eyes out of convenience or cowardice. We generally conclude from the finiteness of human beings that they are not, or need not be, heroes, at least in their natural state. But when it comes to defining the core content of traditional morality, it does not follow from this that people need not have any concern for their neighbors, that they can watch their suffering with indifference or simply look away. Just how dangerous to one's own life it may be to look is the next question that needs to be answered in order to render a moral judgment. However, a moral transgression against this tradition, that is, guilt, is present even if this second question is never asked at all and averting one's eyes is regarded as a morally legitimate act. Relatedly but carrying the thought further, we must inquire of this tradition whether only deliberate betrayal should be considered guilt or also the careless deception of deceiving oneself.

With the growing importance of the individual conscience and the simultaneous transition from case law (seemingly objectively definable morality) to subjective-individual morality, self-examination took on increasing weight and with it the difficult question of deception and self-deception.[26] Eventually, in the philosophy of Jaspers it took center stage. Kant, in a subtle differentiation, had already expressed the logic and psychology that leads to a change in the moral determination of guilt away from the explicit intent toward veiled self-deception:

This innate guilt (reatus), which is so denominated because it may be observed in man as early as the first manifestations of the exercise of freedom, but which, none the less, must have originated in freedom and hence can be imputed—this guilt may be judged in its first two stages (those of frailty and impurity) to be unintentional guilt (culpa), but in the third to be deliberate guilt (dolus). It displays the character [of this guilt] in a certain insidiousness of the human heart (dolus malus), which deceives itself in regard to its own good and evil convictions. . . . This dishonesty by which we "kid" ourselves and which thwarts the developing of genuine moral convictions, broadens itself into falsehood and deception of others. If this is not to be termed wickedness, it at least deserves the name of worthlessness, and is an element in the radical evil of human nature. Inasmuch as such evil puts out of commission the moral capacity to judge what a man is to be taken for, and renders wholly uncertain both internal and external attribution of responsibility, it constitutes the foul taint in our race. So long as we do not eradicate it, it prevents the seed of goodness from developing as it otherwise would.[27]

If it is only the explicitly evil intent that is punishable, it makes sense for the conscience to seek out avoidance strategies of self-deception. Eventually, these strategies make it difficult even for the individual to clearly determine his own guilt. At the same time, it becomes quite evident that it is problematic to link moral guilt only to its subjective perception (in one's feelings or consciousness). For this heightens the temptation to engage in self-deception and makes it nearly impossible for the responsible subject as well as his social environment (whether neutral or the victim of the subject's acts) to come to an understanding about guilt as a correlate of a crime or act of misconduct. It is essential for a subjective self-examination, as well as for the social—and public—discourse about guilt, that we incorporate the objective facts about a transgression into the process of determining subjective guilt. Otherwise we fall into a hopeless relativization of good, evil, and guilt, which cannot do justice either to the social integration function of the distinction between good and evil or to the personal search for identity through the development of conscience.

Based on our discussion thus far, we can describe guilt in summary as a contradiction of the self. I incur guilt if I act against my norms. And there are solid grounds for believing that my own norms are linked to tradition or, at the least, are not left untouched by it; in any case, the evidence suggests that a thorough reflection on my norms cannot simply circumvent tradition. To that extent, the contradiction of self in all likelihood includes the contradiction of the core of norms that have been handed down over centuries and are in that sense "objective" (You shall not kill, You shall love your neighbor as yourself, and so on). We will address this problem in greater detail and empirically in the chapters on "silenced guilt."

A person need not always be aware of the contradiction of self, especially at the time she commits an act. However, on the basis of traditional moral reflection, the failure—or even refusal—to try to come to some kind of understanding about it constitutes another level of guilt. Transgressing a norm is a guilt "of the first degree"; failure to reflect upon this transgression is a "second," more serious guilt. As Jaspers put it, it is important that we "question even our best faith; for we are responsible for our delusions—for every delusion to which we succumb."[28]

Whether all human beings can arrive at such a reflection on guilt, or whether we can become incapable of guilt because of our familial or political imprinting, must remain an open question for now. I shall try to answer it later by looking at the case of National Socialism. Two borderline scenarios are conceivable: as we have already noted, certain experiences in psychiatry suggest that schizophrenic persons no longer activate a consciousness of guilt. This finding would square logically and psychologically with our definition of guilt. For a contradiction of self presupposes a prior and potential personal unity, something that can be lost in a schizophrenic person, at least in an acute stage. If it were possible to get used to the permanent separation of one's moral self, one could come close to the nature of a schizophrenic person.

The second scenario would exist if people could, from the outset, relinquish their responsibility willingly and generally in favor of obedience toward an organization or a person. Some observers, among them Hannah Arendt, have seen Adolf Eichmann as such a case: Arendt assumed that Eichmann had given up his conscience (almost) entirely in favor of obedience.

3

Tradition and Modern Psychology

Experiences in Dealing with Guilt

GUILT AS BURDEN

The great religions that proclaim a personal god share a central notion with the philosophies in their traditions and with modern psychological and psychoanalytic insights. It is the notion that guilt is experienced as a heavy burden and that a person's relationship to himself finds an especially incisive expression in the experience of guilt: guilt touches the very "core of the self." The "misuse of freedom" that guilt indicates is "felt as an inner loss of self-esteem." This loss is "such a disquieting basic fact of human existence that a person cannot simply endure it." Society too punishes the guilty person and stigmatizes him as inferior, which puts him into an isolated and lonely position. This is how the psychologist Janice Lidsay-Hartz has described it: "Not only are our motivations and our identity in question, but when guilty, we also feel lost, isolated, and out of place. We feel a tension between ourselves and others; we look around and avoid eye contact. We are alone with our guilt and unsure of our relation to others. We are not at home in the present since we are stuck in going over and over our role in some past event. There is no peace." Guilt is a burden that affects us in an existential way. It makes us feel worthless, isolated, and torn.[1] It comes as no surprise that nobody wants to be guilty, that our goal is to get rid of guilt and to do so in the easiest and least painful way possible.

False "Relief"

For example, we could pretend that we didn't commit a certain act, that we had nothing to do with an evil deed that took place, or that we were not responsible for an obvious crime. We encounter such a case in chapter 4 of Genesis (4:4–9), immediately following the expulsion from paradise and therefore at the very beginning of secular history:

The man lay with his wife Eve, and she conceived and gave birth to Cain. She said, "With the help of the Lord I have brought a man into being."

Afterward she had another child, his brother Abel. Abel was a shepherd and Cain a tiller of the soil. The day came when Cain brought some of the produce of the soil as a gift to the Lord; and Abel brought some of the firstborn of his flock, the fat portions of them. The Lord received Abel and his gift with favor; but Cain and his gift he did not receive. Cain was very angry and his face fell. The Lord said to Cain, "Why are you so angry and cast down? If you do well, you are accepted; if not, sin is a demon crouching at the door. It shall be eager for you, and you will be mastered by it." Cain said to his brother Abel, "Let us go into the open country." While they were there, Cain attacked his brother Abel and murdered him. Then the Lord said to Cain, "Where is your brother Abel?" Cain answered, "I do not know. Am I my brother's keeper?"

This is the archetype of a false and denying way of dealing with guilt. Cain does not own up to being a perpetrator and rejects his responsibility toward God.

Another type of denial is escape into cynicism and self-contempt, which eventually ends in the destruction of our selves. Alternatively, we could choose a somewhat more benign route and expunge our misconduct from memory by splitting it off. We might also refer to the universal guilt of the world or point the finger at others by accusing them or making them into scapegoats. We could simply withdraw into defiant silence, refusing to let any upsetting reminders—past and present—of our deed come close to us. Then again, we could indulge lustily and pointlessly in vague self-recriminations, either because we are no longer dealing with our deed or because we have lost the hope for genuine relief. We could also combine all these forms of behavior with no regard for internal contradictions.

However, the lessons that religions, theologians, philosophers, and psychologists have learned warn us against dealing with guilt in this way. It only leads us more deeply into misfortune, isolates us from God and humanity, fractures us internally, and destroys our trust and self-confidence. It "ends in mistrust, suspicion, and eventually self-contempt and humiliation." The prophet Ezekiel gave warnings of dire consequences to those of his "colleagues" who would allow people to not separate themselves from their idols and sins but rather "keep their eyes fixed on them": "Both shall be punished; the prophet and the man who consults him alike are guilty" (Ezek. 14:3, 10). Later, Paul would repeatedly emphasize the "subjective weight and the objective maleficence of sin that has not been forgiven." [2]

Genuine Relief from Guilt

The great religions counsel a different approach: they demand—as do African nature religions, incidentally—a genuine purification. Buddhism, Hinduism, and Shintoism, with their nonpersonal conceptions of God, demand less a personal accounting and changing of ways than a (partly ritualistic) purification, but also remorse or illumination. In any case, they call for a restoration of an original harmony or connection between people. The Aztecs, Incas, and the inhabitants of ancient Peru were also familiar with the demand for a change of heart in the form of repentance (among the Aztecs, however, as an outward act), active remorse, or confession.[3]

By contrast, the religions of the personal god—Judaism, Christianity, and Islam—have always regarded personal confession, remorse, and the changing of ways and restitution that goes along with it, as stations along the path of liberation from guilt, though with faith as the necessary and sure guide to that path. From a theological and psychological perspective, this—subjectively serious—faith is the precondition for the eventual attainment of forgiveness, reconciliation, and redemption.[4] It is psychologically easier for a person to take the risk and confront her guilt with faith in God because she can always hope for God's love and mercy in the knowledge that God supports us even when we have done wrong.

At the end of our inquiry, we shall return to ask: Do these two elements—supportive love and forgiveness—have a "functional equivalent" in a secular world marked by a loss of faith? Does their absence reduce the chances for an honest engagement with guilt so severely that pushing it away and keeping silent are not only the most logical responses but in fact become, psychologically, the only remaining survival strategy?

In searching for answers it is useful to take a closer look at the conditions, implications, consequences, and prospects of the individual steps in an appropriate handling of guilt, especially in the Judeo-Christian tradition.

THE PROSPECTS FOR LIBERATION

Admission (or, in ritual terms, *confession*) is the original way of speaking about guilt in the Judeo-Christian tradition. (Among the Aztecs and the Greeks it was not known or highly regarded; in fact it was looked down upon as humiliating.) One does not report guilt but acknowledges it, at

the same time accepting one's own freedom (one could have acted differently), the commandments that one has violated, and the clarity of the
motives or erroneous decisions that led to the wrong behavior. Of special importance in this process are the implicit affirmation of one's own
standards and the "purifying" effect that clarity has on us, in contrast to
what Jaspers called "murkiness."

Complementary to this first step of admission as laid down in theology and philosophy, empirical and analytical psychologists have repeatedly pointed to the finding that people who feel guilty (even if they may
not in fact be guilty) have an urge to talk about it and that this talking
alone can have a liberating effect. However, the effect occurs only if one
truly acknowledges one's guilt and accepts it as wrong behavior for which
one bears full responsibility. Once again, we see that only the acceptance
of guilt allows liberation from it.[5]

As the next step or next dimension in the internal handling of guilt,
this liberation includes *remorse* and a *changing of one's ways.* Psychologically speaking, the liberating element is found precisely in regret and
an honest self-reformation. Theologically speaking, it is found in mercy,
forgiveness, and absolution from God. In worldly terms (to the extent
that it is possible), it is found in the restoration of community with the
victim, provided the victim is willing and able. Genuine remorse and sin-
cere forgiveness can transform the perpetrator and the victim because
the attitude that both feel toward guilt changes. Both can experience
guilt as a burden weighing on them, and true liberation from this burden
creates between them the common bond of relief. Tradition's experience
in dealing with guilt also includes the encouraging discovery that remorse and the changing of one's ways not only frees a person from something negative but also offers an additional "benefit": the fact that one
has mustered the strength of mind to acknowledge guilt strengthens
one's self-confidence (and, conversely, alleviates fear). The acknowledgment of guilt can heighten self-respect by leading a person back to his
own self in a kind of roundabout way.

In religious experience and theological interpretation, this finding
has its counterpart in the belief that repented and atoned guilt is worth
more than righteousness that was never in doubt: "I tell you, there will be
greater joy in heaven over one sinner who repents than over ninety-nine
righteous people who do not need to repent" (Luke 15:7). That is also
why in Jewish understanding a changing of ways is not a sad thing. As the
"noblest impulse of man" it pleases the heart. Its special worth lies in the
fact that the "person who is changing his ways has conquered himself;

after a long struggle with himself, he has renounced a deep feeling and found a new path. The righteous person did not have to undergo such an unsettling ordeal and thus did not have to prove himself." However, the strict condition is honesty of intent. If the "real purpose" that creeps into the intent is to look good to oneself and others, this vain desire for recognition destroys all the value that could lie in a change of heart.[6]

Another element in a "proper" handling of guilt is *atonement*, which, even if it takes the form of punishment, should be seen within the context of reconciliation, not retribution. The element of sacrifice it contains is often regarded as psychologically useful for the perpetrator because he can see it as a kind of archaic restitution. In the Christian understanding, however, the true sacrifice of the guilty person lies in the fact "that he understands his failure and, through an inner change of heart and remorse, sets out on a new path." He sacrifices, as it were, his pride and vanity, and this gain in humility simultaneously strengthens his bond of understanding for the situation of his fellow human beings. Yet the primeval desire to make an atoning sacrifice in the wake of a wrong action can also have illusory consequences: namely, if one's own suffering following a culpable act is regarded—even without prior acknowledgment, without remorse and a change of heart—as an "exculpatory" compensation, which then leads one to believe that there is no further need to deal with the actual problem of guilt itself. Thus, many Germans presumably experienced the collapse and expulsions after 1945 unconsciously as "archaic punishment" that freed them from having to face the question of their guilt. Similarly, Ian Buruma reports that leftists and liberals in Japan saw Hiroshima as a kind of "divine punishment." Now that the Japanese themselves had gone through hell and purgatory, they, in turn, had earned the right to sit in judgment of the Americans.[7]

The final step in the handling of guilt as called for by tradition is *restitution*. Once again, psychologists too report that guilt feelings trigger the desire for restitution and that the impossibility of making amends for harm done extends or strengthens feelings of guilt. In the latter case, a guilty person will then seek self-punishment as a different sort of "relief." This phenomenon can be observed in a perverted fashion when "upstanding" citizens suddenly steal to satisfy a subconscious desire to be punished.[8]

Within the realm of faith in a personal god, what awaits the guilty person at the end of this sequence of steps is the firm hope for forgiveness, relief, liberation, and *redemption* from guilt. But where do we stand if this realm of faith disappears or is no longer discernible? The frequent answer is that without God and faith there is no end to guilt and that in hoping for liberation people are unable to deal with their guilt. Accordingly, Ricoeur sees no chance for an end to evil in the Greek paradigm of evil as tragedy: "What can the end of evil be like in the tragic vision? It seems to me that the tragic vision, when it remains true to its 'type,' excludes any other deliverance than 'sympathy,' than tragic 'pity'—that is to say, an impotent emotion of participation in the misfortunes of the hero."[9] This hopelessness gives us pause for thought if we recall that many Germans after 1945 also interpreted their past—often only half-consciously—within the paradigm of tragedy: misfortune simply befell them. Is it possible for them to find a "liberating" end to guilt? And is there not a good chance that compassion as "participation in the misfortunes of the hero" can turn into self-pity?

At least in theory there is still the secular possibility of forgiveness from the victims, though that is often not possible for practical reasons; moreover, many victims, understandably enough, cannot bring themselves to forgive on psychological and ethical grounds. Also, the increase in self-confidence and a feeling of self-esteem that can come from overcoming oneself in acknowledging guilt is, in principle, independent of religious faith.

Lastly, there is the benefit mentioned by Jaspers, that of regaining inner integrity through an honest examination of guilt. By engaging in such an examination one could create a better chance to trust oneself and others, thereby contributing to the creation of a viable political community based on freedom. To be sure, this doesn't mean that suffering simply ends—though it could be mitigated.

Let us return to our opening question: Given that the content of guilt and responsibility has been relativized and that our way of dealing with them is beset with uncertainties, are these two concepts still useful categories for analyzing human interactions and politics? A first clue comes from an analysis of the controversy in criminal law over whether guilt-based law should be replaced by prerogative law, which rejects the assumption that human beings are free and capable of incurring guilt (see the section "Guilt-Based Law [*Schuldrecht*] or Prerogative Law [*Maßnahmerecht*]" in chapter 1). Such an analysis reveals two insights: first, that humanity's fundamental self-conception finds expression in the category "guilt," which is why it remains central to the analysis of politics as an anthropological category; second, that the seemingly solicitous attempt to spare human beings from having their actions imputed as guilt eventually turns them into objects of outside forces that determine guilt and systematically and definitively block their access to self-determination. At the same time, however, it becomes clear that the substantive definition of guilt is no longer self-evident but needs to be continually reestablished in an ongoing process of social discourse and consensus.

As a contribution to such a social discourse, it makes sense to gather together experiences from religious, theological, and philosophical traditions, along with insights from sociology and psychology, in an attempt to carve out elements that could form the basis of a consensus in defining guilt. Part of this is the realization that guilt, from the very beginning of history, was experienced not primarily as a violation of abstract norms, but as a threat to or destruction of the relationships between people, between God and humanity, and between individuals and their selves.

Against this backdrop we can discern a remarkable coincidence between the structural definition of guilt as an abandonment of conscience (i.e., of personal identity) on the one hand, and on the other the sociological and psychological insight that free social interaction and integration can only succeed if people are able to establish an identity as a way of balancing varying self-interpretations. Evidently, there is a close connection between an understanding and acceptance of guilt and social integration—a connection not only handed down in theology and philosophy but plausibly articulated in sociology and psychology. Karl Jaspers, drawing on his own philosophical position and the experience of National Socialism, gave specific expression to this connection by arguing that the success of a politics of freedom in a new democracy, and especially of the basic consensus of German society that it required, depended on that society's honest engagement with guilt. However, there are understandable motives for shying away from such honesty: a world without God no longer holds out the plain hope of forgiveness and reconciliation. Yet the costs of a dishonest, "silenced" handling of guilt are high, and revealing those costs—especially by taking the transition from a dictatorship to a democracy as an example—can make clear how much we have to gain from a successful engagement with guilt.

4

Silenced Guilt

The Case of National Socialism

The "costs" of silenced guilt burden the individual citizen as well as society and political life. This chapter will examine primarily the negative effects of silenced guilt on the political culture of democracy. Empirically, my reflections are based for the most part on the experiences of the Federal Republic of Germany with the transition from the Nazi era to the democracy after 1945. But the insights I hope to gain are meant to be applicable to other transitions from dictatorships to democracy, and more generally to the normative and psychological burdens that silenced guilt imports into the political culture of a democracy.

In 1983, Hermann Lübbe delivered a widely discussed speech in the Berlin Reichstag. He vehemently rejected the notion that the culpable participation in National Socialism had been repressed and that this had impeded the transformation of the Germans from supporters and followers of National Socialism into democratic citizens of the Federal Republic. He countered this repression thesis by pointing to the complete public discrediting of Nazi ideology and to the impossibility of pushing aside the blatant and obvious crimes of the National Socialists. Instead, the "transformation of the German population, which had in some way or other escaped the downfall of the Reich, into the citizenry of the new Republic" took place under the protective umbrella of the radical public renunciation of National Socialism in an atmosphere of a "certain silence" and with a "communicative silence treatment" given to the brown-shirted elements in people's life stories. This silence "was the sociopsychologically and politically necessary medium of transformation"—necessary, because the majority of Germans had been supporters or followers of National Socialism and because the new state could be established in opposition to Nazi ideology but not in opposition to the majority of the German people. Integrating the Germans into the new democracy had been possible only in the setting created by the silent treatment, and it had been successful. To be sure, Lübbe noted, we know little about the "inner feelings" of the Germans, "but the inner feelings of individual subjects tell us little about what holds sway politically and morally." The latter emerges instead from the moral and political principles "that a person cannot contradict publicly without isolating himself morally and politically." [1]

Without saying so explicitly, Lübbe was explaining that authoritative public standards and the population's conformity to them were the vehicle of moral and political change and not an inner reversal, a change of the "inner feelings" on the personal initiative and responsibility of the citizens. Was conformity to public political guidelines truly a path to the democratic responsibility of the citizens? Or did this merely create a new version of conformism and mendacity? That was precisely Hannah Arendt's diagnosis. Much like Lübbe, she noted in 1962 the German people's far-reaching agreement with National Socialism, especially a moral agreement whose foundation was not only the loss of all traditional morality and religion but also a systematic mendacity. Yet unlike Lübbe, she perceived—at least in the early 1960s—an unbroken line of continuity in the mendacity and self-deception of the Germans: "But the practice of self-deception had become so common, almost a moral prerequisite for survival, that even now, eighteen years after the collapse of the Nazi regime, when most of the specific content of the lies has been forgotten, it is sometimes difficult not to believe that mendacity has become an integral part of the German national character." Even if typical elements of Nazi ideology (especially openly anti-Semitic ones) had retreated (and here Arendt may well have agreed with Lübbe), the political and moral habits and the psychic disposition of the German had remained the same after 1945. One would be hard-pressed to accept the pervasive mendacity or self-deception of the Germans that Arendt alleged as the marks of a democratic citizenry. To be sure, Hannah Arendt's diagnosis proceeded from the assumption that "what is commonly understood by conscience had been all but lost" in Germany prior to 1945. For many Germans, their conscience no longer told them "You shall *not* kill." On the contrary, the temptation was "*not* to murder, *not* to rob." [2]

Daniel Goldhagen alleges a similar reversal of values and a hermetically clean conscience in the Germans as they engaged in the joyful murder of the Jews. He considers it fundamentally wrong to assume that the Germans were "normal" and to ask how the mass murders of the Nazis could have happened without or against their will. Instead of proceeding from the erroneous assumption that common sense is universal and thus also applied to the Germans, Goldhagen argues, we must proceed from the assumption that they were not coerced but carried out the murder of the Jews willingly, knowingly, and in "good conscience." Responsibility for this "clean conscience," according to Goldhagen, lay with the historically evolved "demonizing" of the Jews and the "eliminationist antisemitism" that characterized nearly all Germans and only the Germans.

But in contrast to Hannah Arendt, Goldhagen maintains that the Germans after 1945 underwent a radical transformation into good democrats. Of course, he does not examine how this transformation from conscious and sadistic lust for murder to a democratic citizenry is supposed to have occurred; he does not even hint at an answer. Against the backdrop of his thesis that the "eliminationist antisemitism" that guided the Germans in their brutal murders of the Jews, with its conscious and intentionally murderous designs, dates from the nineteenth century at the latest, it is hard to come up with a plausible explanation for such a radical change in so short a time after 1945—and even less so since Goldhagen claims that the nineteenth century saw a continuity of the subterranean anti-Semitism even where it did not rise to the surface.[3]

We thus have three different positions. Hermann Lübbe argues that the Germans changed from supporters and followers of the Nazi dictatorship into democratic citizens of the Federal Republic and that they did so under the supportive conditions of treating their own past with silence and under the influence of the public and political establishment of norms and values. Hannah Arendt noted a near total loss of morality on the part of the Germans prior to 1945 and their continuing mendacity and self-deception after 1945—thus, no change. Daniel Goldhagen alleges a radical transformation of the Germans, whose quasi self-contained murderous mentality, devoid of a bad conscience, was changed into a solidly democratic spirit after 1945, though he does not spell out the reasons for and course of this transformation or offer a plausible explanation for it.

In contrast to Hannah Arendt and Daniel Goldhagen, I will seek to show that the Germans prior to 1945 had not completely lost their conscience, that all moral traditions had not simply ruptured, and that the Germans did not succumb to a *hermetic* self-deception. By the same token, they were not generally enthusiastic murderers of the Jews with a de facto clean conscience because they were supposedly convinced that the destruction of the Jews was justified. To be sure, the Germans were not coerced into committing murder; they could have refused, and so far we know of no single instance in which someone who did refuse was punished by death for his refusal. Daniel Goldhagen deserves credit for noting this fact, as Christopher Browning did before him in his own 1994 study. But the failure to refuse participation had many motives, and there is much to argue against the attempt to explain it exclusively with reference to the conviction of the Germans and the moral justification of the murders. Instead, it is precisely the fact—to be empirically demonstrated—that the conscience of the Germans was not hermetically sealed against challenges from traditional morality (which forbids murder) that makes the Germans capable of bearing guilt. Moreover, only this fact creates—logically and psychologically—the possibility of asking them about their guilt and of speaking about "silenced" guilt after 1945. Many Germans sensed their part in the crimes, but they kept silent about their guilt to themselves, to their immediate environment (especially their families), and in public discourse. They shied away from clarifying the matter to themselves either by acknowledging it to themselves or to the outside world.

Contrary to Hermann Lübbe, I want to show that this "communicative silent treatment" of one's own share of guilt has imposed significant human and political "costs." It did not promote a genuine transformation of the Germans into citizens of the Federal Republic but in fact impeded, and in part undermined, that process. To be sure, unlike Hannah Arendt, I do not deny that the German people underwent a partial change. However, that change concerned primarily the rather "superficial" individual attitudes toward institutions and processes of the republic. I am thus in partial agreement with Lübbe. But unlike Lübbe I want to reveal the destructive—and negative—effect of "silence," which extends not only to the generation of the "perpetrators" but also to their children and grandchildren. This effect concerns the conception that people have of themselves as citizens acting in a responsible manner. It concerns the public—and not merely rhetorical—agreement about the common values and the parameters of political responsibility, that is, the soundness of the basic democratic consensus or, as Lübbe would say, "common sense." It also concerns the psychic dispositions of people, which make it difficult for them to practice the kinds of attitudes and virtues that are generally considered necessary for the success of a democratic community. More specifically, the silencing of guilt has wrought its destructive effect on the willingness and ability to feel empathy on a personal and political level, to develop trust in oneself and others, and to take on responsibility.

TRADITIONAL MORALITY AND
MURDEROUS NAZI "MORALITY"

No reasonable person today would deny that millions of crimes were committed during the period of National Socialism. But the question to whom these crimes should be concretely attributed is, for many, an open one. Is it true that "what one generally calls conscience" (Arendt) was lost prior to 1945, so that on an individual level nobody really is to blame?

As early as the late 1960s, Herbert Jäger, in an extensive and subtle analysis of available court records, memoiristic recollections, and a variety of other sources, probed into the question of whether those who had been involved in Nazi crimes had been conscious of injustice. In his work (dedicated, incidentally, to Hannah Arendt), he came to the conclusion that it is not correct to speak about a pervasive loss of conscience. At the same time, however, it is impossible in many cases to detect a clear "consciousness of injustice." Many times, the moral or legal assessment of the situations was determined purely by emotion; the various elements of understanding in the people involved did not always "condense" into a clear awareness.[4] My interest here is precisely in this space between a clear consciousness of injustice or guilt, on the one hand, and a self-contained lack of conscience, on the other: the space in which — either at the time of an action or afterward — guilt was felt without the person getting it clear in his own mind, let alone acting on this feeling and guiding his action or nonaction by it or using it later to reflect on what he had done.

The central problem for the question of the connection between guilt and democratic political culture are not sadists or schizophrenics. Such people exist in every society, but they were not the typical Nazi perpetrators or the typical perpetrators in the Vietnam War, for instance, and they constitute a fairly small segment of the population.[5] It is the many others who pose the problem: those who still have a (rudimentary) conscience, who are still aware of remnants of traditional morality and yet participate in murder, lies, and betrayal. They are in the vague state of recognizing an act as an injustice but do not give a clear account of their own share in it; they are, then, in a state of "silenced guilt." I argue that they make up the large majority of the population, based on my contention — contrary to Hannah Arendt's dictum — that traditional morality was not expunged in the consciousness or feeling of the Germans.

There is much to support the notion that traditional morality persisted also under National Socialism and that it clashed with the murderous Nazi norms—Jäger has called this conflicted parallelism "dualism." Many statements even from high-ranking representatives of the system indicate as much. For Heinrich Himmler, the clash between traditional morality and Nazi morality was a primary concern when it came to motivating his SS men. In a speech to SS group leaders delivered in Posen in October of 1943, he laid out in detail how difficult it was to actually carry out the destruction of the Jews:

I am now talking about the destruction of the Jews, the extermination of the Jewish people. It is one of those things that are easily said.— "The Jewish people is being exterminated," says every party comrade, sure thing, it's in our program, elimination of the Jews, we'll do it! And then they all show up, those eighty million good Germans, and each one has a decent Jew. No question, the others are pigs, but this one is a first-rate Jew. Of those who talk like that, not one has watched, not one has endured. Most of you will know what it means when one hundred corpses are heaped up, when five hundred are heaped up, when one thousand are heaped up. Having endured this, and in the process—with the exception of human frailties—having remained decent, this has made us tough.[6]

Himmler was also concerned that the extermination actions against the Jews would cause a general lapse into undisciplined behavior, sadism, or immorality. Unauthorized shootings of Jews that were carried out not for purely political but "self-seeking or sadistic or sexual motives" were to be prosecuted under the law, "if necessary even on the charge of murder or manslaughter." The almost eerie existence side by side of traditional and murderous Nazi morality finds expression again in the Posen speech:

One principle must have absolute force for an SS man: we must be honest, decent, loyal, and comradely to members of our own blood and to nobody else. I simply don't care how the Russians are faring, how the Czechs are faring. We will get the good blood of our kind that is present in these peoples by stealing their children, if necessary, and raising them amongst ourselves. Whether the other peoples live in prosperity or bite the dust from hunger interests me only to the extent that we need them as slaves for our culture; I don't care about anything else. Whether or not ten thousand Russian women collapse from exhaustion during the construction of an antitank ditch interests me only to the extent that the ditch will be finished for Germany. We will never be rough or heartless if it is not necessary, that is clear. We Germans, who are the only people in the world who have a decent attitude toward animals, will naturally also take a decent attitude toward these human animals. But it is a crime against our own blood to worry about them and to bring to them ideals, with the result that our sons and grandchildren will have an even more difficult time with them.[7]

The persistence of traditional morality against the backdrop of a radical inequality of races and people and the absolute predominance of the "Germanic race" is also strikingly apparent when Himmler, in the same speech, describes in detail the "virtues of the SS man." Obedience, for example, is clearly important, but not blind obedience: "If a person believes that an order is based on a superior's false understanding or on a false foundation, it goes without saying that he—which means, every one of you—has the duty and responsibility to address this situation and to present his reasons in a manly and truthful manner if he is convinced that they run counter to the order."

Courage, in Himmler's eyes, included acting out of one's own "loyalty," not out of fear of the "commissar" (as was the case among the Russians), and an important aspect of courage was the "courage of one's own convictions" (one should voice one's criticism openly). Himmler demanded "truthfulness" (also when it came to passing on unpleasant war news, for example), keeping one's word, taking on responsibility, justice, and honesty.

Of course, this raises the question of whether the "Nordic race" itself lived up to the picture he painted of it. Since Himmler himself worked with the assumption that "presently in the war, in many areas, ninety-five of a hundred reports are lies or only partly true or partly correct," there is very good reason to doubt his entire ideological construct.[8] Still, people can continue to act while blinding themselves to the facts, but only at the expense of values or virtues they preach or formally accept. Blinding oneself then means accepting self-contradiction, which is precisely an important indicator of guilt.

Two interesting observations reveal that the population was aware of the contradiction between ideology and reality. After the National Socialists had drummed it into German society that the Russians and Bolsheviks were generally inferior subhumans, many Germans were surprised to see the honorableness, competence, and even faith of many Russians whom they encountered as "foreign workers" in their daily lives.

In its "Reports from the Reich," the security service of the SS was forced to acknowledge that the use of Soviet prisoners of war and east European workers in the Reich was overturning many clichés about them. The Russians were neither as starved nor as godless as the authorities had tried to convince the Germans. In relationships between the sexes, these foreigners—especially Russian women—were much more restrained than people had assumed they would be (and were possibly used to within the Reich). The technical and practical intelligence of many Russian prisoners of war astonished the Germans, who expressed their admiration candidly:

Numerous messages express the unanimous view that the workers from the former Soviet territories demonstrate a special understanding of all technical installations. For instance, time and again the German folk comrade would witness that an eastern worker, with the most primitive means, was able to repair all sorts of damage to motors and so on (Stettin). A number of reports are in line with this example from Frankfurt/ Oder: "A Soviet Russian prisoner of war on an agricultural estate was able, in a short time, to restore to working order a motor that had stumped the German experts. Moreover, he pointed out faults in the tractor gear that the German operators had not yet noticed."[9]

The despised Eastern workers also gave an impressive demonstration of the spirit of comradeship that Himmler demanded from his SS people, and that he believed they alone were capable of: "From Berlin comes a report of the following case, which German workers offer as an example that a *spirit of comradeship* exists also among the Eastern workers. In a speech to Eastern workers, the camp leader of the German Asbestos-Cement AG announced that they would have to work even harder. Whereupon one of the workers called out: 'In that case we will have to get more to eat.' When the camp commander demanded that the caller identify himself, no one responded at first, but then about eighty men and fifty women stood up."[10] The persistence of traditional moral elements alongside Nazi ideology was also confirmed by Hans Frank, chief of the Generalgouvernement of Poland. In passing on Hitler's order to kill the Polish intelligentsia, he underscored the following in a speech in 1940: "Gentlemen, we are not murderers. For the police officer or SS man who finds that *in his official capacity* and in the course of duty this measure requires him to carry out an execution, that is a fearful thing."[11]

Hans Frank's son Niklas recounted something even more macabre:

his father, having met the love of his youth again, presented his unloved wife with his wish to be divorced. He justified this by saying that he was involved in a "criminal regime," and in order to save his wife and son "he had to make the greatest sacrifice a loving husband would ever have to ask of his beloved wife: divorce." [12]

In his memoirs, Rudolf Höß, the commander of Auschwitz, captured not only the horror of the gassings but also the distinction between good and evil when he declared—perversely—that those under his command, especially the block eldest, were the embodiment of evil. The commandant of Treblinka, Franz Stangl, explicitly admitted to his interviewer Gitta Sereny that the sight of the gas ovens in Poland made him instantly aware that crimes awaited him in his new job. In addition, Jäger's broad and subtle study has documented many cases where individuals refused to obey orders. The *Wartheland Diary* of Alexander Hohenstein (a pseudonym) offers us a chance to read with frightening clarity the breathtaking existence side by side of traditional morality, clear-sightedness, and murderous participation. [13]

As we have already noted, the SS norms themselves attest to the partial continuation of traditional moral norms: honesty, loyalty, honor, truthfulness—even if they revalue them from a racist perspective. Beyond these verbal pronouncements, there are many indications that traditional morality persisted: the manifold and conscious efforts to keep the crimes secret; the euphemistic language rules; the "defensive" garb in which murderous orders were wrapped. For example, the so-called commissar order (which called for the immediate execution of captured Soviet troop commissars, in violation of international law) was justified as a "preventive" measure:

In the struggle against Bolshevism, we must not assume that the enemy's conduct will be based on principles of humanity or of international law. In particular, hate-inspired, cruel, and inhuman treatment of prisoners can be expected on the part of all grades of political commissars, *who are the real leaders of resistance. . . . Political commissars have initiated barbaric, Asiatic methods of warfare. Consequently, they will be dealt with immediately and with maximum severity. As a matter of principle they will be shot at once whether captured* during operations or otherwise showing resistance. [14]

The German officers were fully aware that this order was calling for the commission of an injustice. Even the "Ten Commandments of How the

German Soldier Conducts War," which appeared in many soldiers' handbooks in World War II (to what extent they were included as an insert if they were not printed is difficult to determine, according to the Institute of Research in Military History in Freiburg), bears witness to the continuity of traditional standards. They include the following: "1. The German soldier fights chivalrously for the victory of the nation. Acts of cruelty and senseless destruction are unworthy of him. . . . 3. No enemy who surrenders may be killed, not even the partisan or spy. They will receive their just punishment from the courts. . . . 10. Violations against the above-mentioned commandments in official matters are punishable."[15]

Christopher Browning has reconstructed the murders committed by the Police Battalion 101 in Poland. His study shows not only the shocking process by which the actions became increasingly brutal and routinized but also the initial departure of some policemen, who therefore had not lost a sense of moral standards. To be sure, and this is an observation of central importance, Browning also reveals how *few* men opposed the murders or avoided participating in them. Joachim Fest, in turn, has noted the almost incomprehensible equanimity with which the German people had accepted acts of injustice and violence following the Nazis' assumption of power. Jäger, drawing on trial records, estimates that of those perpetrators sentenced between 1958 and 1963, about 20 percent should be regarded as violent perpetrators, 20 percent as initiating perpetrators, and 60 percent as perpetrators following orders. This means that 60 percent of those sentenced tried to make clear to the court the contradiction between orders and their moral conviction, which implies that they saw this contradiction at least in hindsight.[16] Still, in Germany the number of people who resisted the violations of traditional morality was evidently far smaller than in Italy, Denmark, or Bulgaria. Why?

WHY DID SO MANY GERMANS PARTICIPATE?

Mentalities, Thoughtlessness, Fear, and Banal Cowardice

The racist Nazi ideology, which we encountered in the Himmler speech, surely promoted the readiness to participate: it radically negated the core of traditional morality, namely, respect for a person's physical and psychological integrity. In so doing, it was able to draw upon an older stock of anti-Semitic and racist attitudes. Of critical importance as well was the willingness with which the Germans accepted as moral guides the

National Socialist notion of "toughness"—the rejection of any compassion or empathy—and its attendant ideal of masculinity. Finally, instrumental virtues—such as the willingness to sacrifice, a sense of duty, personal loyalty, and the readiness to work hard—were set up as absolutes. These virtues certainly have a place in tradition, but they derive their moral dignity only from their relationship to the values they serve. The murderous potential of this absolutization became real through its seeming ability to provide moral justification for the suspension of personal conscience—what Buchheim calls "consciousness of wrongdoing . . . in partial suspense." Even more, it allowed Himmler, but also Heydrich and other protagonists of the Third Reich, to transfigure the abandonment of personal conscience and the suppression of feelings of compassion into acts reflecting an exemplary readiness to make sacrifices and to transform the despised compassion for the victims into self-pity on the part of the perpetrators, which even "strengthened" their morality. Typical of this is Himmler's famous answer to his masseur Kersten when the latter asked how he was able to come to terms with his evil deeds:

You oughtn't to look at things from such a limited and egotistical point of view; you have to consider the Germanic world as a whole—which also has its karma. A man has to sacrifice himself even though it is often very hard for him; he oughtn't to think of himself. Of course, it's pleasanter to concern yourself with flower beds rather than political dustheaps and refuse dumps, but flowers themselves won't thrive unless these things are seen to. I try to reach a compromise in my own life; I try to help people and do good, relieve the oppressed, and remove injustices wherever I can. Do you think my heart's in all the things that have to be done simply from reasons of state?[17]

This response, with its references to a readiness to help, justice, and reasons of state, documents at the same time the conscious and intentional continuation of traditional values. These values were invoked not only for tactical reasons: as Himmler's conduct toward his SS subordinates attests, they clearly remained partially valid and were undoubtedly of functional importance in holding together Nazi society itself.

Instrumental virtues turned into absolutes and toughness against one's own emotions—especially compassion—were important ideological bridges. They made it possible to combine in practice the ethical values of traditional morality and of National Socialism, two systems that were in theory mutually exclusive. The elimination of feelings, in particular, is one issue we shall return to later.

In addition to pseudomoral justifications, there were mental dispositions that also fulfilled this bridging function. To begin with, many Germans are evidently susceptible to ideology, that is, they are ready to perceive and judge multifarious reality by means of systematic or seemingly systematic theories. This disposition includes the habit of shutting out feelings and spontaneous intuition quickly and efficiently, thus eliminating factors that interfere with an ideological interpretation of reality. Many observers have asked in astonishment how the Germans of all people, a highly cultured "nation of poets and thinkers," were able to commit the monstrous crimes of the Nazi era. Perhaps it was precisely the thinker's (but not the poet's!) penchant for theories, philosophy, and systems—so deeply rooted in German culture—that provided a favorable setting for the Nazi process of thoroughly ideologizing society because the corrective element of compassionate spontaneity had long since been deadened or at least severely weakened. It is no coincidence that Rousseau argued that reason and reflection create and strengthen egotism because they destroy compassion, a sentiment through which a person puts himself spontaneously in someone else's place. Philosophy "isolates" a person; it is because of philosophy that a person will say to himself at the sight of another person's suffering: "Perish if you will, I am safe."[18]

It is also striking how frequently observers have highlighted the fact that essential behavioral patterns on the part of the perpetrators involved a readiness to blindly obey or submit, a strong need to fit in, and the childlike, almost immature desire to do everything one has been told "well" and "correctly." Eichmann showed himself quite compliant and polite, indeed solicitous, toward the Israeli authorities and the Canadian clergyman Hull, who tried to elicit an admission of guilt during the trial in Jerusalem and save his soul. And according to Broszat, Rudolf Höß, the commander of Auschwitz, took pains "to be helpful to his interrogators in a way that was almost strange." When the British writer Gitta Sereny first met the commander of Treblinka, Franz Stangl, he struck her as quiet and courteous. Browning is not the only one who has noted that German policemen and soldiers were more afraid of not participating and appearing weak than of the murders.[19] The willingness to fit in, the fear of standing alone, the need to be accepted by the existing authorities and to win their trust—all this reveals a low self-esteem. But a sense of self-esteem is the precondition of moral independence and nonconformism. I shall return to this point later.

Another striking disposition that tied traditional morality together with the murderous morality was a high degree of willingness to accept images of the enemy and adopt metaphors of cleanliness as models. We are familiar with the extent to which anti-Semitism and racism in general employed hygienic concepts and images—and how important purity (of blood and race) and cleanliness were to them. Höß recorded in his memoirs that he had felt a nearly "irresistible" attraction to water as a child: "I was perpetually washing and bathing. I used to wash all manner of things in the bath or in the stream that flowed through our garden, and many were the toys or clothes that I ruined in this way. This passion for water remains with me to this day."[20]

One need not be a staunch believer in psychoanalytical theories to realize that this urge toward washing and cleanliness reveals feelings of guilt and a desire for punishment. On a subconscious level it resonates with archaic myths of evil (as a stain or pollution); Paul Ricoeur, in his study on the *Phenomenology of Evil*, has reflected upon the persistence of these myths in the modern psyche. It is therefore not inappropriate to assume that the susceptibility to ideologies of cleanliness or purity is or was promoted by preexisting feelings of guilt and a desire for punishment.

Beyond that, it almost goes without saying that qualities such as thoughtlessness, ambition, and careerism contributed their share to the fact that the clash between traditional morality and murderous morality produced in so few Germans conflicts of conscience that influenced their behavior. There is no need to elaborate upon these qualities. Their amorality is obvious since no individual could seriously believe that ambition or careerism could justify unjust or immoral acts, while thoughtlessness as such runs counter to the exercise of conscience and can therefore in principle lay no claim to moral legitimacy.

The motive of fear in a totalitarian system is another factor I will not probe further. Undoubtedly, it was widespread and kept people from resisting. But in itself it already presupposes an awareness that the things one is involved in or is witnessing, without intervening, are unjust or morally wrong. It fails to explain why so many Germans participated without coercion or looked the other way and still maintained afterward that they bore no guilt. It also fails to explain why as late as the 1950s more than 50 percent of the Germans considered National Socialism a good thing in theory. For a person, if she wants to behave in accordance with her own values, is not likely to consider a regime of which she is truly afraid a "good thing."

Finally, the assertion that one was afraid conflicts with the far more frequent statement that one didn't know anything about the regime's atrocities and injustices. Incidentally, many Germans may not have known about the worst of the atrocities (though many did know! More on this later). But the illegality and brutality of the regime was evident even in the "Altreich," where no extermination camps existed and no mass executions took place.[21] Here too traditional morality did not induce the majority of Germans to rise up or at least offer passive resistance. Unlike careerism, fear, thoughtlessness, or "ignorance," the mentalities and psychological dispositions discussed above are important in determining "silenced" guilt insofar as they are not necessarily to be seen as immoral a priori. For that reason, their contribution to criminal forms of behavior is not readily apparent, and they are in fact suitable for providing "justifications" to oneself and for obscuring one's own share of guilt. Empirical observations and theoretical interpretations of the situations in which the crimes were committed may offer additional insights into the factors that—in spite of the continuity of traditional values and the recognition that they clashed with murderous Nazi morality—led a person to participate in crimes, incur guilt, and deceive himself about that guilt.

The Setting of the Crimes

Were the perpetrators in the circumstances of the crimes thoroughly evil or psychologically abnormal? Had they lost their conscience completely or were they like all other people? American psychologists and psychoanalysts have asked these questions not only with regard to National Socialism and the Holocaust. Evidently, most perpetrators (including high-ranking SS men) in, for example, the concentration camps or in the euthanasia programs were by no means evil in a self-contained way. Instead, they were quite capable of showing human feelings, or they tried to make up for the horror of their murderous daily life by turning to their family life, for instance. At times this could take on eerie forms: as late as 1993 (!), the German-Estonian functionary Otto von Kursell reported without embarrassment about the "renovations" in the former institution of Schwez after the mentally retarded Poles there had been killed and the place turned into a German old-age home. Soon he was able to note with satisfaction "that this dirty, run-down, gigantic insane asylum had become a pretty, cultured settlement for our old people, a place where the residents felt comfortable."[22]

Asked if and how he had gotten used to the killing that went on in the camp of Treblinka under his command, Franz Stangl responded:

"To tell the truth . . . one did become used to it."

"*In days? Weeks? Months?*"

"Months. It took months before I could look one of them in the eye. I repressed it all by trying to create a special place: gardens, new barracks, new kitchens, new everything; barbers, tailors, shoemakers, carpenters. There were hundreds of ways to take one's mind off it; I used them all."[23] In the entrance room to one of the gas chambers in Auschwitz, a mother was pleading with Höß, the camp commander, to take pity on her children: "Everyone was looking at me. I nodded to the junior noncommissioned officer on duty and he picked up the screaming, struggling children in his arms and carried them into the gas chamber, accompanied by their mother who was weeping in the most heart-rending fashion. My pity was so great that I longed to vanish from the scene: yet I might not show the slightest trace of emotion. I had to watch everything." It is revealing that Höß, in talking about the urge "to vanish from the scene," reveals his feeling of shame and thus also his sense of the crime in which he was participating. For the desire to become invisible speaks of shame, not pity. Elsewhere, Höß reports: "This mass extermination, with all its attendant circumstances, did not, as I know, fail to affect those who took part in it. With very few exceptions, nearly all of those detailed to do this monstrous 'work,' this 'service,' and who, like myself, have given sufficient thought to the matter, have been deeply marked by these events. Many of the men involved approached me as I went on my rounds through the extermination buildings and poured out their anxieties and impressions to me, in the hope that I could allay them." And Höß had this to say about the leaders of the party and the SS who visited Auschwitz: "They were all deeply impressed by what they saw. Some who had previously spoken most loudly about the necessity for this extermination fell silent once they had actually seen the 'final solution of the Jewish problem.'"[24]

Even if we can read in these recollections Höß's intention of presenting himself and the SS men as humane beings, there is much to indicate that they are accurate on this issue. They are not presented here with an apologetic intent on my part. Quite the contrary: they are meant to show that the perpetrators were morally open, that in principle they had the capacity of conscience and therefore also of responsibility.

In his compelling analysis of the realities of the camps under National Socialism and Stalinism, Todorov concluded that the perpetrators were "neither monsters nor beasts—ordinary people . . . Guards who committed atrocities never stopped distinguishing between good and evil. Their moral faculty had not withered away."[25] However, Todorov's interpretation is that the state had provided the guards with a new morality. Yet there is reason to doubt how complete or sealed off this new morality was, as individual reports reveal. The SS man who was given the task of burning the bodies in Treblinka always volunteered for the night shift:

"When I was on duty at night I used to go and just sit behind one of the barracks and snooze. I didn't *want* to do see anything. Yes, I think several people felt like I did. But that was the most positive thing one could do—you know, play possum."[26]

We have an image "of man in harmony with himself, coherent, monolithic," Primo Levi observed of his horrific camp experiences, but "that is not how man is." "Compassion and brutality can coexist in the same individual and in the same moment, despite all logic; and for all that, compassion itself eludes logic." On the other hand, therein lies that person's moral potential, his chance—at least against a petrifying ideologization. Incidentally, Primo Levi was not the only one who had to think of Dante's *Inferno* in Auschwitz. This is how Franz Stangl remembered the day he arrived in Treblinka: "Treblinka that day was the most awful thing I saw during all of the Third Reich. . . . It was Dante's Inferno. . . . It was Dante come to life. When I entered the camp and got out of the car on the square I stepped knee-deep into money; I didn't know which way to turn, where to go. I waded in notes, currency, precious stones, jewelry, clothes. They were everywhere, strewn all over the square. The smell was indescribable; the hundreds, no, the thousands of bodies everywhere, decomposing, putrefying."[27] Another compelling document comes from the American psychologist Gustave Gilbert. He had extensive conversations with the principal defendants at the Nuremberg trial and made these notes of their reaction to the screening of a Nazi film about concentration camps:

(Kelley and I were posted at either end of the defendants' dock and observed the prisoners during the showing of this film. Following are my notes jotted down during the showing of the film at about 1–2 minute intervals:)

Schacht objects to being made to look at the film as I ask him to move over; turns away, folds arms, gazes into gallery . . . (Film starts). Frank nods at authentication at introduction of film . . . Fritzsche (who had not seen any part of film before) already looks pale and sits aghast as it starts with scenes of prisoners burned alive in a barn . . . Keitel wipes brow, takes off headphones . . . Hess glares at screen, looking like a ghoul with sunken eyes over the footlamp . . . Keitel puts on headphone, glares at screen out of the corner of his eye . . . von Neurath has head bowed, doesn't look . . . Funk covers his eyes, looks away . . . Sauckel mops brow . . . Frank swallows hard, blinks eyes, trying to stifle tears . . . Fritzsche watches intensely with knitted brow, cramped at the end of his seat, evidently in agony . . . Goering keeps leaning on balustrade, not watching most of the time, looking droopy . . . Funk mumbles something under his breath . . . Streicher keeps watching, immobile except for an occasional squint . . . Funk now in tears, blows nose, wipes eyes, looks down . . . Frick shakes head at illustration of "violent death."—Frank mutters "Horrible!" . . . Rosenberg fidgets, peeks at screen, bows head, looks to see how others are reacting . . . Seyss-Inquart stoic throughout . . . Speer looks very sad, swallows hard . . . Defense attorneys are now muttering, "for God's sake—terrible." Raeder watches without budging . . . von Papen sits with hand over brow, looking down, has not looked at screen yet . . . Hess keeps looking bewildered . . . piles of dead are shown in a slave labor camp . . . von Schirach watching intently, gasps, whispers to Sauckel . . . Funk crying now . . . Goering looks sad, leaning on elbow . . . Doenitz has head bowed, no longer watching . . . Sauckel shudders at picture of Buchenwald crematorium oven . . . as human skin lampshade is shown, Streicher says, "I don't believe that" . . . Goering coughing . . . Attorneys gasping . . . Now Dachau . . . Schacht still not looking . . . Frank nods his head bitterly and says, "Horrible!" . . . Rosenberg still fidgeting, leans forward, looks around, leans back, hangs head . . . Fritzsche, pale biting lips, really seems in agony . . . Doenitz has head buried in his hands . . . Keitel now bowing head . . . Ribbentrop looks up at screen as British officer starts to speak, saying he has already buried 17,000 corpses . . . Frank biting his nails . . . Frick shakes his head incredulously at speech of female doctor describing treatment and experiments on female prisoners at Belsen . . . As Kramer is shown, Funk says with a choking voice, "The dirty swine!" . . . Ribbentrop sitting with pursed lips and blinking eyes, not looking at screen . . . Funk crying bitterly, claps hand over mouth as women's naked corpses are thrown into pit . . . Keitel and Ribbentrop look up at mention of tractor clearing corpses, see it, then hang their heads . . . Streicher shows signs of disturbance for the first time . . . Film ends.

After the showing of the film, Hess remarks, "I don't believe it." Goering whispers to him to keep quiet, his own cockiness quite gone. Streicher says something about "perhaps in the last days." Fritzsche retorts scornfully. "Million? in the last days—No." Otherwise there is gloomy silence as the prisoners file out of the courtroom.[28]

Even if the participants in the crimes did not always have a clear awareness of injustice, they did sense the inhumanity of their acts. The two primary reactions to such a situation are well known: silence and the consumption of large amounts of alcohol. This is how Christopher Browning has reconstructed the evening after the first mass executions carried out by the men of Police Battalion 101:

When the men arrived at the barracks in Bilgoraj, they were depressed, angered, embittered, and shaken. They ate little but drank heavily. Generous quantities of alcohol were provided, and many of the policemen got quite drunk. Major Trapp made the rounds, trying to console and reassure them, and again placing the responsibility on higher authorities. But neither the drink nor Trapp's consolation could wash away the sense of shame and horror that pervaded the barracks. Trapp asked the men not to talk about it, but they needed no encouragement in that direction. Those who had not been in the forest did not want to learn more. Those who had been there likewise had no desire to speak, either then or later. By silent consensus within Reserve Police Battalion 101, the Józefów massacre was simply not discussed. "The entire matter was a taboo." But repression during waking hours could not stop the nightmares. During the first night back from Józefów, one policeman awoke firing his gun into the ceiling of the barracks.[29]

Like many perpetrators, they had gotten caught up in this without knowing or suspecting what was to come. But once they had begun, most of them continued and did so with increasing brutality. In many cases, the brutalization took on a dynamic of its own once the critical threshold had been crossed. This dynamic following the gradual involvement in crimes has also been observed in other situations, such as the war in Vietnam. For instance, the American psychologist Kelman has speculated that the murder of civilians in My Lai had been "legitimized" by preceding acts of destruction and violence in response to orders.[30]

We can point to two motives behind this dynamic of brutalization.

First, every cessation of an immoral or criminal act once it has begun amounts to the admission—at least half-consciously—that one's prior conduct was immoral. This is a difficult admission to make, especially in stressful situations. Many carry on just so they won't have to make this admission. Second, and more importantly, however, is the tendency—frequently observed and analyzed—to "dehumanize" the victims, which should not simply be explained as bestiality or sadism.[31] Rather, this dehumanization was evidently "necessary" to carry on the murders without having to clearly think of oneself as a murderer. One had to rid oneself of the perception that these were human beings one was tormenting and driving to their deaths. Part of this process was the requirement that the victims had to strip down to the bare skin. This, as Stangl said, made them into a "commodity," into a "huge mass"; they lost their identity: "I rarely saw them as individuals. It was always a huge mass. I sometimes stood on the wall and saw them in the tube [the narrow passageway through which the victims were driven into the gas chambers]. But—how can I explain it—they were naked, packed together, running, being driven with whips like . . . " Stangl did not finish his sentence. The ghastly agonies were not to be changed "because it worked, it was irreversible." It is revealing that Stangl was not able to enter the places where the "transition" from person to "mass" took place, the barracks where victims were made to strip. They would have made him aware of this process of "dehumanization": "The undressing barracks . . . I avoided them from my innermost being; I couldn't confront them; I couldn't lie to them; I avoided at any price talking to those who were about to die: I couldn't stand it."[32] Time and again, it was above all the *eyes* of the victims—and sometimes the back of the neck bared for execution—that gave the perpetrators an unbearable scare: the eyes reveal the irrefutable humanity and individuality of the victims, and this makes it difficult or impossible for perpetrators to deceive themselves about the criminal nature of their act.

Kelman and Hamilton identify three conditions that play a role in pushing a person across the threshold into violence and crime: "authorization, routinization, and dehumanization." Individuals yield their responsibility to authority, routine stops them from asking questions, and dehumanization deprives an act of its moral quality. In addition, sociologists and psychologists have repeatedly noted bureaucratic or psychological "departmentalization." It creates physical or psychological distance to the victim and thus to the reprehensibility of the act, thereby helping to conceal one's own responsibility.[33] Reality is divided up or split off in such a way that moral problems can be blocked out. This process is also very well illustrated in Gitta Sereny's conversation with Franz Stangl: "It was a matter of survival—always of survival. What I had to do, while I continued my efforts to get out, was to limit my own actions to what I—in my own conscience—could answer for . . . ; the only way I could live was by compartmentalizing my thinking." And so the former policeman Stangl—even though he was now camp commander!—focused entirely on what could appear to be purely his police job of managing the valuables, paying attention that no "illegal trafficking" occurred. Gitta Sereny followed up: *"But these valuables wouldn't have been there but for the gassings. How could you isolate one from the other? Even in your own thinking?"* To which Stangl replied: "I could because my specific assignment from the start had been the responsibility for these effects." *"What if you had been specifically assigned to carry out the actual gassings?"* "'I wasn't,' he said dryly, and added in a reasonable and explanatory tone: 'That was done by two Russians—Ivan and Nicolau, under the command of a sub.'" [34] Shortly before his death, in his last conversation with Gitta Sereny, Stangl brought himself to give up this self-deception of compartmentalization and to admit his guilt: "The silent transition from falsehood to self-deception is useful," Primo Levi noted. [35]

In a study of Auschwitz doctors whom he interviewed, the American psychoanalyst Robert Jay Lifton used the concept of "doubling" to offer an even more subtle interpretation of their psychic state during their participation in these crimes. Lifton argues that these doctors, who after all had begun as healers and were now acting as murderers, had to "double" their self in order to survive psychologically in Auschwitz. The "healing self" was joined by a "killing self," which took over the "dirty work" of killing, as it were, thereby allowing the doctors to avoid seeing themselves as killers, even though they were engaged in murdering people. In this way, feelings of guilt could be avoided, not by simply eliminating conscience, but by "transferring" it:

"The requirements of conscience were transferred to the Auschwitz self, which placed it within its own criteria for good (duty, loyalty to group, "improving" Auschwitz conditions, etc.), thereby freeing the original self from responsibility for actions there."

The important thing is that this was not a sharp and clear split but that the "Auschwitz self" was at the same time both autonomous from the "healer self" and connected with it. For it is precisely this that led to the radicalization and brutalization of the killing. To prevent the reproaches of the "healer self" from growing louder, the murderous acts had to be reaffirmed as it were, and the "lethal power" of the potential sense of guilt had to be projected onto the external enemy, the Jews: "That same principle was active in the Nazi claim that every single Jew had to be killed, lest those remaining alive or their children kill Germans. The Auschwitz self, then, entered into a vicious circle of killing, threatened guilt and death anxiety, and more killing to fend off those perceived psychological threats." All this confirms the psychological principle that "cruelty begets cruelty." One kind of "selection" invariably followed upon a prior one.

Doubling is a universal human phenomenon. To some extent, we all practice it. But it becomes dangerous when we set loose the destructive self entirely and make others into our victims. Doubling is not the same as the radical splitting of a person suffering from multiple personalities who can no longer perceive her responsibility. It tends to be a temporary process of adjustment, not a lifelong character pattern. Accordingly, after the war the Auschwitz doctors were very concerned to find reconfirmation of their "healing self." This confirmation was also something they were looking for in their conversations with their colleague Lifton, which is why they eagerly agreed to them. Still, a person cannot simply mollify himself with this kind of "silent" return to the "healer self" because a repeat is possible at any time. As Lifton explains it: "Doubling is . . . the psychological means by which one invokes the evil potential of the self. That evil is neither inherent in the self nor foreign to it. To live out the doubling and call forth the evil is a moral choice for which one is responsible, whatever the level of consciousness involved. By means of doubling, Nazi doctors made a Faustian choice for evil: in the process of doubling, in fact, lies an overall key to human evil."[36]

From a psychoanalytical perspective, Lifton confirms basic theological and philosophical analyses of guilt and conscience: true guilt means no longer fulfilling the task of conscience, that of constantly reestablishing one's own personal identity.

One central way of carrying out crimes and later avoiding bringing them to the awareness of conscience is by splitting off, killing, or brutalizing one's *feeling*. Because of its special cultural and psychological significance, this phenomenon deserves a closer look.

The Cessation of Feeling

In (auto)biographical recollections, the brutalizing, deadening, and splitting off of emotions is regarded as especially important when it comes to explaining extreme crimes. It is often with utter incomprehension that historians, jurists, and contemporary witnesses confront the unbelievable lack of feeling with which countless Germans carried out the murderous orders, and their inability to imagine themselves in the victims' place and identify with them. Hanna Arendt summed it up in this disconcerting understatement: Eichmann "never imagined what he was actually doing."[37]

But even—and especially—in those places where people were intimately involved in the crimes (and not at a bureaucratic distance like Eichmann), there was an increasingly sealed-off lack of feeling: the workers in the crematoria of Treblinka were largely hardened against any stirrings of emotion. And when such stirrings were felt, the men got drunk. One of the Auschwitz doctors who talked with Lifton recognized in retrospect that the numbing of emotions was the "key to understanding what happened in Auschwitz." Höß, eager to acquire "a reputation for being tough," did not allow himself any display of emotion. When he watched the gassing (out of duty!), its criminal nature did not occur to him. He had expected the suffering to be even worse! A spontaneous identification with the victims, a comparison to his own situation as a father, did not enter his mind. By contrast, some of the men from Police Battalion 101 who did not or could not go on murdering Jews "pleaded that they too were fathers with children and could not continue." In this instance, the act of spontaneous emotional identification was still intact.[38]

The report of Lieutenant Fischmann, along with many others, shows how the very language of the writer expressed the fundamental lack of feeling for the fact that he was tormenting and murdering human beings: "The loading of the Jews into the special train waiting in the Aspang train station began at noon and went smoothly." SS-Obersturmführer Pohl "had 51 Jews capable of work between the ages of 15 and 50 removed from the train and taken to a work camp." Lieutenant Watermann reported that at the end of a trip by train, "most of the escaping Jews were eliminated that night or the next day by the railroad guard or other police units." In total, "at least two-thirds of the escaping Jews were shot or rendered harmless in some other way." Thousands of such reports could be cited, and their words can not simply be equated with the usual dryness of bureaucratic or proper civil servant dispatches.

The SS too knew how important it was to eliminate any feeling of compassion. We read this in the *Chief of Order Police Guidelines for Combating Partisans* (November 1941): "The enemy must be *totally de-*

stroyed. The continual decision over life and death posed by the partisans and suspects is difficult even for the toughest soldier. But it must be
done. He behaves correctly who, by setting aside all possible impulses of
personal feeling [*sic!*], proceeds ruthlessly and without mercy."[39] This is
how the American court psychologist Gilbert summed up his impression
of Höß: "In all of the discussions Hoess is quite matter-of-fact and apa-
thetic, shows some belated interest in the enormity of his crime, but
gives the impression that it never would have occurred to him if some-
body hadn't asked him. There is too much apathy to leave any suggestion of remorse and even the prospect of hanging does not unduly distress him. One gets the general impression of a man who is intellectually
normal but with the schizoid apathy, insensitivity, and lack of empathy
that could hardly be more extreme in a frank psychotic." The psychoanalyst Zeiler, in his own diagnosis on the basis of Höß's memoirs, speaks
of an "affective emptying" on the part of the author.[40]

This insensitivity was surely not only the *result* of the specific circumstances of the crimes, in the sense that one could interpret it merely
as the "natural" psychological reaction to the brutality of the crimes—
although that is undoubtedly also what it was. There are countless indications that many perpetrators had a prior disposition toward such insensitivity. We must now turn our attention to this disposition and its
persistence (still to be discussed), indeed its reinforcement, after 1945.

A number of children of famous Nazi parents have described the latter's
emotional frigidity and in many instances also the joylessness in their
homes. Vesper, the son of the Nazi poet Will Vesper, speaks about the
heartlessness, and especially the mercilessness, with which his parents
tormented their children. For weeks at a time they would not speak to
their son if he had done some mischief. Humiliation and shaming were the
primary pedagogical tools. The son of the SS doctor Gauch observed in
his father the basic quality of a cold and technical way of thinking. In the
biography of her father, Dörte von Westernhagen reconstructed as early
as the 1930s a "narrowing or blocking of his capacity for moral and emotional reaction." There are many indications that within the well-known
tradition of German authoritarianism (though authoritarian child-rearing
existed also in other countries), insensitivity and the tradition of hardness—not only as toughness but as hardening toward one's own human
impulses and those of others—played an important role. It promoted
the readiness to silence one's own conscience and *not* to follow moral impulses of compassion.[41]

This tendency may also have been due to an "elevated" philosophical-ethical tradition: the Kantian ethos of duty. At his trial in Jerusalem, Eichmann asserted during police questioning that throughout his life he had followed the Kantian ethos of duty. But he went on to say that "from the moment he was charged with carrying out the Final Solution, he had ceased to live according to Kantian principles . . . because he was no longer 'master of his own deeds.'" Hannah Arendt, however, interpreted his subsequent behavior to suggest that he now behaved in accordance with the categorical imperative as reformulated by Hans Frank: "Act in such a way that the Führer, if he knew your action, would approve it." In addition, Arendt traced Eichmann's painstaking thoroughness and intransigence in carrying out his murderous duties back to a misunderstood or amputated version of Kant. "A law was a law, there could be no exceptions"—this rigid maxim may have contributed to the deformation of his conscience. For Arendt it was quite clear: "No exceptions—this was the proof that he had always acted against his 'inclination,' whether they were sentimental or inspired by interest, that he had always done his 'duty.'"[42]

I will push these reflections a radical step further with the following speculation: the fact that hardness against oneself and others was seen, without further questioning, as ethically elevated has its roots in a long tradition in Germany. And this attitude persisted after 1945 in many German families, including those who had had nothing to do with the Nazis or had even resisted them. Kant's ethos of duty, in particular his stern refusal to ground ethical conduct merely in inclinations, is not without blame in the emergence of this tradition. There can be no doubt that a proper understanding of Kant's philosophy is diametrically opposed to Eichmann's murderous behavior. Although Kant defines the ethical will as being determined by reason and opposes all "sentimentality," he does acknowledge as well that "respect for the moral law is a feeling"; however, "it is produced by an intellectual ground" because it does not simply follow spontaneous impulses, but is tested by reason (that is, by the categorical imperative).[43] Still, his rigorous distinction between inclination (in principle suspected of being selfish) and moral law prepared the ground for eliminating spontaneous stirrings of compassion—or even purging them through systematic "training"—as being ethically irrelevant, in fact, possibly false because "immoral" in the higher sense. This becomes all the more plausible if one considers that complicated philosophies are always passed down in an abbreviated form in the mental realms to which they sink. If Himmler was able to find a receptive audience for his perverse idea that one could make the "self-sacrifice" of being a murderer and still remain "clean" in the process because the deadening of spontaneous feeling was right and necessary, the only possible explanation is that rigorism and hardness had traditionally been seen as possessing an ethical premium. And a sentence like the following one from Kant could certainly promote this tendency: "An action that is objectively practical in accordance with this law, with the exclusion of every determining ground of inclination, is called *duty*, which, because of that exclusion, contains in its concept practical *necessitation*, that is, determination to actions *however reluctantly they may be done*."[44] The essential aspect of the stunted handing down of the Kantian ethos of duty is the strict distinction between ethics and moral spontaneity. It attests to a deep distrust of—"corrupted"—human nature, a mistrust that Kant certainly shared.

It is not coincidence that an important representative of Anglo-Saxon thought, Adam Smith, who was not only an economist but primarily also a moral philosopher, titled his treatise on social ethics *Theory of Moral Sentiments*.[45] In his moral system, sentiment forms the basis of morality because it allows us to expand our limited self to the benefit of all others, to put ourselves in the place of others through empathy (something Kant wanted to achieve by means of reason). Both philosophers pursued the same goal, the development of a sustainable and viable sense of community, but Smith trusted that sentiment could lend crucial support to this process, while Kant mistrusted it.[46]

What finds expression here is a central difference between the German and the Anglo-Saxon traditions of political culture. Be that as it may, the disastrous consequences that the disdain of sentiment and the appreciation of hardness have had in Germany give reason to rethink once again the role that sentiment plays in an ethics of a sense of community. We must take seriously the observation by psychologists and psychoanalysts that sentiment is indispensable to an unconstrained perception of reality. Where sentiment is numbed or "eliminated," reality is perceived only selectively, especially from a moral point of view, because it allows a person to deny at first the meaning of events and later the facts themselves.[47]

Alfred Schöpf has called feelings "organs for perceiving our desire with respect to the desires of others." Without a grounding in sentiment we find no sure foundation from which to make a reasonable determination of ethical behavior. As an indication of the role that feelings play not only for the comprehensive perception of human reality but also as the foundation and indicator of personal integration, Schöpf notes that schizophrenics experience no feelings of guilt because no integration or personal identity is established. "Since the evil parts remain separated from the good parts, the affected person is torn between the two sides and cannot integrate them as feelings of guilt."[48] This also makes clear the difference between what Lifton has described as the "doubling" of Auschwitz doctors and true schizophrenics (i.e., split personalities). This is important especially for the question—still to be examined—of whether people who participated in the Nazi crimes did retain a feeling of their guilt in spite of all the fragmentation and vagueness of their thoughts and motives. If they did, we cannot simply speak of guiltlessness or the incapacity to incur guilt, but must speak about "silenced" guilt.

At any rate, these reflections reveal at the same time the importance that attaches to emotion not only for the perception of human reality, but also as the foundation of personal integration and identity and thus of conscience. And in this context, feeling does not refer to momentary or superficial sentimentality but precisely the opposite. We are talking about a feeling that encompasses the whole human being and informs her and her environment of her basic attitude (toward people and situations) and gives expression to it. Gitta Sereny has observed and elucidated in the case of Albert Speer the extent to which the numbing, suppression, or disciplined strangulation of feelings damages the capacity for love and for the morally sensitive perception of the suffering of others—that is, the capacity for conscience itself. In the process, it becomes clear that emotional frigidity as such—whether its cause is silenced guilt or something else—not only attests to a damaged personality but also continues to exert its destructive influence. Father Athanasius, with whom Albert Speer stayed on numerous occasions in his monastery in Maria Laach, summed up his impression of Speer this way: "I often wondered what happened to him as a child to make him into what he was, a brilliant man incapable of abstract thinking and, I think, incapable of sensual love and thus, finally, an incomplete man." Gitta Sereny offers this evaluation of Speer's moral behavior, which, the complexity of his personality notwithstanding, included the great lie that he had not known about the murder of the Jews:

Speer himself killed no one and felt no enmity, hatred, or even dislike for the millions in Eastern Europe, Christians, and Jews, who were systematically slaughtered: he felt nothing.

There was a dimension missing in him, a capacity to feel that his childhood had blotted out, allowing him to experience not love but only romanticized substitutes for love.

Pity, compassion, sympathy, and empathy were not part of his emotional vocabulary. He could feel deeply but only indirectly—through music, through landscapes, through art, eventually through visual hyperbole, often in settings of his own creation: his Cathedral of Light, the flags, the thousands of men at attention motionless like pillars, the blond children, rows upon rows of them with shining eyes and arms stiffly raised. This became beauty to him and, another substitute for love, allowed him to feel.[49]

A person's capacity for conscience and integration come together in deep and fundamental feelings. Without empathy we are incapable of reaching others as being in principle our equals and close to us. It is no coincidence that the Old Testament describes sin as "hardness of heart."

"But I only killed a louse, Sonia. A useless, nasty, harmful louse." With these words Dostoyevsky's Raskolnikov initially tried to justify his crime to Sonia. "A human being—a louse?," Sonia responded calmly and with certainty of feeling. "'I know—I know it wasn't a louse,' he replied, looking strangely at her. 'But I suppose I'm just talking a lot of rot, Sonia,' he added, 'I've been talking rot a long time. . . . It isn't that—you're quite right. There are quite, quite other motives here. . . . I haven't spoken to anyone for ages, Sonia. . . . I have an awful headache now.'" And later, while serving his sentence, Raskolnikov is amazed by the "enormous, unbridgeable gulf" that separates him in Siberia from all other people, while Sonia, who has followed him there out of love, soon wins the sympathy of all the inmates:

One other question that puzzled him was why they were all so fond of Sonia. She did not try to curry favor with them, and they met her only rarely, sometimes only when they were at work, when she came to see him for a moment. And yet they all knew her. . . . And when she used to visit Raskolnikov at work or met a party of prisoners on their way to work, they all took off their caps to her and greeted her: "You're good and kind to us, Miss! You're like a little mother to us!" Coarse, branded convicts used to say that to this frail little creature. She smiled and returned their greetings, and everyone was happy when she smiled at them.[50]

If emotional callousness is so important as a prerequisite for murderous action and for the numbing of the conscience in a criminal situation, we must inquire all the more carefully into what happened to this callousness after 1945 and what connection exists between it and the silencing of guilt. But it strikes me as sensible, first, to review the arguments and clues that point to the existence of "silenced guilt," that is, to the fact that people—even if they reject responsibility or a consciousness of guilt—still have a vague sense that their behavior was culpable.

WHAT DO WE MEAN BY "SILENCED" GUILT?

Defining "Silenced" Guilt

The murderous crimes of National Socialism had to be politically and psychologically prepared. Many indications attest that the core stock of traditional morality was certainly preserved in both private and public spheres alongside Nazi morality. In fact, there is evidence that it was in part renewed by National Socialist authorities themselves—even if they did so with an intent to instrumentalize and remodel it from a racist perspective. Just as numerous are the testimonies that many participants and onlookers recognized the criminal character of the acts at the time they were committed, that individuals had more latitude in their actions than they assumed or alleged, and that it was possible to recognize this—especially in retrospect.[51]

The following arguments are usually advanced by individuals to explain why they bear no guilt even if they participated directly or indirectly in crimes, supported them, or tolerated them tacitly: they didn't know anything, were ideologically blinded, were in a coercive situation and had no personal power to make decisions (obligation to obey, sense of duty, acting under binding orders), or simply didn't think about it—this last reason especially seems to have been applied with particular frequency.[52] What is denied then is guilt in the sense of responsibility for one's actions, the attribution of a crime to one's own conduct.

In this way, personal guilt is implicitly understood in a very restricted manner: as the voluntary and intentional infliction of harm, as doing evil, not as the failure to do something. The sphere of personal freedom, decision-making power, and responsibility is thus defined as a kind of remnant that is left after all other factors have been accounted for (orders from above, blindness, fear, indifference, the general tragic tangle of guilt). This line of reasoning rejects the notion that a person's sphere of action is not an objective given but can be influenced and that a person can—indeed, must—define freedom for himself. It denies that personal

responsibility is, in principle, unlimited because nobody can assume another person's conscience and that the determination of the boundaries
of freedom and responsibility is subject to a person's own test of conscience. Those who invoke these arguments to claim that they are guiltless therefore see themselves not as subjects but as objects and the
product of external conditions.

But all this involves a contradiction: any individual who denies his
guilt by arguing this way essentially upholds his capacity for incurring
guilt. For in the very moment when I describe myself as guiltless in a concrete case, I acknowledge that I am in principle capable of bearing guilt.
That being so, the burden of proof—or, to put it more mildly, the burden of justification—rests on me. I have to determine where my guilt
begins and where it ends. Avoiding this burden of justification, reflection, and clarification and proclaiming an understanding of responsibility
and guilt that—in its restrictive form—goes against all experience of
everyday life (it would exclude, for example, any liability for my children)
amounts in effect to a dishonest admission of one's own capacity for
guilt. It means that one does not really accept it and at the same time
tries to hide this fact from oneself and others.

This dissimulation occurs because hardly anybody is willing to declare herself openly the product of circumstance, that is, an object. The
English language has an expression for this self-deceiving half-hearted-
ness: doing something "in bad faith." It describes the situation in which I
know or suspect something without wanting to admit it. This is precisely
the condition of "silenced" guilt. In it, the gulf that exists between one's
own conduct and the norms that continue to be known and accepted
remains unspoken to oneself and others. What's more, I also forego an
examination of the question of how this gulf was possible, what room for
action I truly had (also in retrospect), why I neglected the opportunities
not to commit these crimes or not to support them. Thus, "silenced"
guilt is not only keeping silent about the clash between actions and
norms. It is also, and above all, keeping silent about the inner reasons
that gave rise to this clash. It is the refusal to subject myself to an honest self-examination, to bring to mind my freedom and my values and acknowledge my responsibility, to accept my principled capacity for guilt
not only rhetorically and half-heartedly but consciously, clearly, and with
respect to concrete cases. To put it pointedly: the true guilt lies in the
silencing after the fact: "Silenced" guilt is above all the "guilt of keeping
silent"—what Ralph Giordano, drawing on Jewish tradition (though the

idea is also in accord with Christian tradition), has called the "second" guilt.

How each specific instance of guilt should be judged *concretely* is subject to historical research and the individual test of conscience. However, given the essential openness of the situations in which crimes occurred, even under a totalitarian regime, we can speak of silenced guilt when any of those who lived during the Nazi period as responsible adults refuse to seek clarification of their share in what happened.

But is this not a far too all-embracing, denunciatory suspicion? Am I not judging from on top of my high horse, without having studied each situation historically (which I couldn't possibly do) and without having empirical evidence that silenced guilt is not merely a phenomenon postulated by me as normative, but is empirically experienced? Let me therefore bring in some evidence—or rather clues—that such a feeling or sense of guilt certainly existed after 1945 even in cases where individuals vehemently denied any guilt. These are clues that reveal the workings of an unquiet conscience that is left unexplained.

Clues and Empirical Evidence of Silenced Guilt

Theodor Reik, in his study *The Compulsion to Confess and the Need for Punishment*, writes that it sometimes takes criminals years to arrive at a confession, "until they know what they have done, what their deed *meant*." Criminals often conceal their crimes to themselves, and until they are capable of making a confession an inner process of confessional work takes place, in which the impulse to conceal clashes with the need to confess. This work is often done in silence, which can be "part of a negative confession"—but only if it ends up with the person speaking. The wish to speak in turn often follows a desire for punishment and includes a plea for love and absolution. However, too great a need for punishment can also counteract confession, for instance, if a person's hunch about her guilt is simply too much.[53] Although the need to confess indicates a feeling of guilt, silence can indicate both a defense against confession—which means defense against a personal engagement with one's own guilt and responsibility—as well as confessional work. This distinction is important in assessing the consequences of this behavior because destructive power lies above all in defensive silence. That is why the statement I made above—that the clues of a complex silence reveal an unquiet conscience, a sense of guilt that is not raised to the level of clarity of confession—calls for a more detailed explanation and justification.

One clue I have mentioned is the *physical rebellion*, as it were, against the crime—physical and psychic illnesses, suicide, and numbing through alcohol. Unlike Hannah Arendt, I interpret this physical revulsion against the horror not merely as a morally irrelevant, animalistic reaction but as the instinctive basis for a morality of reciprocity—though not a conscious morality, and in this instance certainly not one that guided conduct. It makes human beings sick to kill one of their own. Only in the case where this no longer happens has conscience been eliminated to such a degree that its place is taken by a sadistic euphoria of murder, possibly for pathological reasons or as a way of numbing oneself. Goldhagen assumes that the so-called demonic, eliminationist anti-Semitism was the attitude of the majority of the German "executioners." And there is no doubt that the willingness to engage in murder existed to a frightening degree. But that is why the physical counterreaction strikes me all the more as an indication that not all people had given up on themselves as moral subjects, at least not entirely. This is one clue that they did not feel "entitled" to committing murder, but that many did not make themselves aware of the horror of their actions, either at the time or in retrospect.

Many of the perpetrators had recurring *nightmares*. To see these as an indication of a profound disquiet of conscience it is probably not necessary to invoke psychoanalytic theories, which would recognize in them signs of a need for punishment and thus of a feeling of guilt. It is hard to imagine that people would suffer from nightmares without being driven by a great inner unrest. If such people in fact participated in murderous crimes, their nightmares make it plausible that they have a sense of guilt. The denial of any guilt when awake indicates that a person is still caught up in "silence."

The *urge to offer justifications* and *guilt projections* are interpreted, in psychological terms, as the result of feelings of guilt. (However, they can also be factually unjustified, that is, their cause could be a neurosis. Needless to say, in that situation they would not be seen as the result of guilt unjustly imposed from the outside but as an expression of subconscious or preconscious aspects of a person's psychic life.) Leaving aside all psychoanalytic assumptions, a justificatory urge aimed at specific acts (which means the urge is not vague) does not seem likely if there was no participation in a crime or if such participation took place but the person has reflected on it and come to terms with it. Jaspers's words seem appropriate here: "Then we are capable of unaggressive silence."[54] More-over, the *projection of guilt*, that is, *shifting the blame*, also makes little sense if a person does not feel any guilt. From whence would the need to shift guilt and blame onto others arise? Conversely, if we have truly looked at the burden of our own guilt, we hesitate to place it casually on others, for we are now humbled.

Drawing up a balance sheet of guilt—a type of behavior we are fa-miliar with from small children—also proceeds tacitly from a person's feelings of guilt. In this case, these feelings are at least tallied up, that is, they are included in the equation. But they are not included in such a way that the person assumes personal responsibility. Instead, the attempt is made to "equalize" guilt and make it disappear by pointing to the guilt of others, a move without any meaningful ethical justification.

Finally, the *denial* of reality, the *blocking out* of information, and *con-fusion* or *contradictions* in thinking make no sense unless one suspects that they are caused by strong emotional drives or resistance. That is probably all we can say beyond psychological and psychoanalytical the-ories. But if denial, blocking out, and contradictions concern crimes whose immoral nature a person cannot or does not wish to deny, it is rea-sonable to assume that this resistance to reality has something to do with his own direct or indirect participation in these acts, which he does not want to acknowledge. These responses give expression in equal measure to a feeling of guilt and a rejection of understanding.

In numerous conversations with the children of perpetrators, but also with the perpetrators themselves, the Israeli psychoanalyst Dan Bar-On has repeatedly observed that perpetrators will confess to *minor wrongdoings* and in return conceal their real acts from themselves and others. He interprets this as "paradoxical morality," a form of exculpatory suppression, but one that simultaneously indicates a deeper sense of guilt. It is a kind of unconscious compromise between the desire on the one hand to acknowledge and be able to present oneself as a moral sub-ject and on the other to defend against the confession of one's true guilt.[55] In Bernhard Schlink's novel *The Reader*, the old professor who has returned from emigration no longer invokes learnedness during a theo-retical seminar discussion of guilt in relation to the concentration camp trial: "Look at the defendants—you won't find a single one who really believes he had the dispensation to murder back then."[56]

Jäger's study of court records led him to conclude that many of the ac-cused were already suffering serious moral conflicts at the time they committed the acts. Historians, perpetrators, and victims have variously reported that at least an intimation, and frequently a recognizable awareness, of the criminal nature of the acts existed. According to Hilberg, the perpetrators tried to fend off the stirrings of guilt feelings with a number of rationalizations, although they could see that they were not valid: the murder of the Jews was reinterpreted as an act of preventive defense; some claimed that they had to subordinate their conscience to the order they were given and that they had to make a strict distinction between their own feelings and the duty imposed on them; some shifted their own responsibility onto subordinates—Höß couldn't launch enough accusations against brutal, evil block wardens (capos); people turned themselves into a small cog in the machine, a cog that was replaceable.[57] Common to all these rationalizations is the feeling that one's own behavior contributed to the crime but also the attempt either to reinterpret the content of the immorality one senses or to deny to oneself one's own sphere of power and freedom.

Other clues reveal that people knowingly did what was wrong, indeed, unbearable: the notoriously high rate of alcohol consumption; the destroying of evidence (Hanna Arendt, however, does not see in this a feeling of guilt but only the fact that the Nazis or the SS were aware that they clashed with the rest of the world and its morality, especially in the face of impending defeat); and serious illnesses suffered even by those Nazi representatives who were forceful ideological proponents. Among them was Erich von dem Bach-Zelewski, who fell ill after thousands of Jews had been killed under his command, or Captain Hoffmann, a strict and unapproachable SS man, who always suffered stomach cramps that confined him to his bed whenever executions by shooting were about to take place.[58] Depression and suicide were notorious afflictions, especially among high-ranking Nazis or SS men.

Browning recorded that the members of Police Battalion 101 moved off in a hurry after they had driven the Jews onto the trains. Niklas Frank notes with irony that his father did not keep a diary during ten crucial years of the Nazi era: "It would have been unbearable for you to write down what you had turned into: a foolish hypocrite." Nightmares too, not only at the time of the crime, attest to great internal unrest. Sigfrid Gauch remembers that his SS father, who was in Himmler's entourage, denied any guilt but suffered from severe nightmares.[59] Compensatory behavior at the time of the crime or as belated window dressing also points to a felt need to affirm one's own morality in the face of the crimes, something that would not have been necessary without a sensitivity to guilt.

Finally, there is the special form of silence one is tempted to call "eloquent silence." Here, we are dealing not merely with stillness: the person circles around the confrontation with his own guilt and surrounds it with a kind of wall. This approach includes what are often vehement, elaborate justifications; the balancing out of guilt; projections of guilt; denials; and a shutting off against irrefutable facts—all in all, a highly emotional and frequently aggressive fixation on the problem of guilt. In an experiment in 1955, various groups, whose members did not know each other, talked about the Nazi past for several weeks. The conversation was triggered by the fictitious speech of an Allied soldier. One noticeable fact was that those who resisted acknowledging personal guilt spoke about the problem in a much more irritated manner than the others, who also showed a clearly greater willingness to communicate about it.[60]

In their trials after the war, the members of Police Battalion 101 showed a strong exculpatory urge in their descriptions of German-Polish and German-Jewish relations. In contrast, their portrayal of Polish-Jewish relations was "extraordinarily damning." They painted the picture of "a rather benign German occupation of Poland" and accused the Poles of having "betrayed" many Jews to the Germans. It is significant that while the German policemen were fully aware of the moral category of "betrayal," they completely distorted the situation. They were silent about Poles who helped Jews in spite of the danger to their lives that came from the German side and who were often executed for their actions, silent about the fact that the mortal danger to the Jews came from the Germans and not the Poles, and silent about the fact that many Germans incited Poles to betray the Jews.[61]

Bergmann and Erb, in their study of postwar anti-Semitism, noted among the Germans an increasing mentality toward reckoning up guilt and blame as well as noticeable blockages among the older generation against digesting empirical data about concentration camps. Conversely, they report a clear connection between the acceptance of concentration camp accounts and the expression of shame as well as a connection between an emotional anti-Semitism and the willingness to give the Jews part of the blame for their murder.[62]

These mental constructs involving justification, projection, and a tallying up of guilt are usually very confused and contradictory. Their point is not to offer an objectively logical account or analysis but an apologia based on "psycho-logic." Bernward Vesper, the former fiancé of Gudrun Ensslin, has reconstructed from memory a typical defensive speech by his

father.[63] It contains all the elements we have indicated as bespeaking an
unresolved feeling of guilt:

*"The Allies wanted to keep Germany divided and prostrate for ever. For
that they needed evidence of our guilt. They did not shrink from any lie.
They invented the horror stories about the murder of partisans and civilians in Russia, even though every army in the world has to wage vigorous
war against unmarked combatants in the interest of the rest of the population. . . . And the lie about the six million murdered Jews. The billion-
dollar lie of the state of Israel. If there were concentration camps, it was
the ones in which the British in South Africa incarcerated the Boers," he
said. "So there weren't any concentration camps," I said, "but didn't
Goebbels threaten Hans Grimm that he would lock him up in a concentration camp?" "Those were improvement institutions, in a struggle like
this every nation has to protect itself from sexual offenders, mass murderers, defeatists." "What struggle?" I asked. "In 1933 you had all the
power." "There was cleanup work to be done," he shouted, "the Augean
stables had to be cleaned out, the people who were responsible for the
unemployed and the rot had to be protected from popular wrath for
their own good. Of course, a few Jews were also interned temporarily.
They were deported and were even able to take along the treasures they
had collected." "And a few died there," I said; "So what?," he replied,
"they would have died on the outside too. During the last years of the
war, the supply situation was perhaps also a little tight. Moreover, the
Kapos often exercised a cruel regime over their fellow inmates: if people
died, they are to blame for it."*

*"But the gas chambers?" No words could get him as riled up as
these: gas chamber. "We have evidence that all the pictures from the
concentration camps are fake, that the gold teeth were taken from the
safe of the German Reichsbank to Belsen, that the movies they are showing, in German prisoner-of-war camps, that everything is a huge fraud,
that the book The SS State is full of falsehoods. I really find it outrageous
that you, of all people, are reading something like this." "Women and
children were also killed; were they spies and saboteurs too?" I asked.
"That is not true!" he shouted, "Rosenberg and Frank are responsible for
that. The Führer knew nothing about it." "The government was built on
the Führer principle," I said, "if he didn't know, he should have known."
"Were you there?" he shouted, "did you see the unemployed, the starv-
ing; was the entire people supposed to go under, was the oak supposed
to fall because of the free-loading thistle; should all because of the few*

who were guilty?" ' "But were all Jews guilty?," I asked, "did not thousands die in the First World War fighting as German soldiers for Germany?" "Stop it," he yelled, "they're all back, what is it you really want?" [64]

Bernward Vester took his own life in 1971.

Not all remained in such a sealed-off silencing of their own guilt as did Bernward Vesper's father. Now and then, the wall of words opens up a crack, not to reveal everything, but still to take a small step in the direction of an admission of guilt. In the process, a person will admit to a relatively minor guilt in order to deny the real guilt with that much more vigor or treat it with silence. Höß may well have described an important psychological crossroads in his life when he described as "his guilt" that he did not muster the courage to admit to his superior, Eicke, that he was not suited for service in the camp "because I felt too much sympathy for the prisoners," and when he added that he did not want to make a laughingstock of himself by revealing his "weakness." However, this failure is of a ridiculously minor nature compared to the millions of murders for which he was responsible as the commander of Auschwitz. But that is all he could bring himself to say, knowing full well the horrible crimes that had been committed under his command. According to Hannah Arendt, Eichmann's conscience was troubled not so much by the mass murder as by the fact that he had lost his self-control and had slapped the president of the Viennese Jewish community. Stangl too, in his exhaustive conversations with Gitta Sereny, admitted at first relatively minor transgressions and harmless examples of moral corruption. A closer look at Eichmann and Stangl can help to flesh out the difficult complex of silence, which is usually not static but rather ongoing and dynamic, a process the psychoanalyst Theodor Reik has analyzed as "confessional work." [65]

The Case of Eichmann

Hannah Arendt thought it unlikely, though not impossible, that Eichmann felt devoid of any guilt, more precisely, that he had no *awareness* of guilt. But did he also not have any *feeling* of guilt? Did he feel free of any disquiet of conscience? Arendt makes it clear that he had not completely lost his conscience—even toward the persecution of the Jews, not only in his morally "compensatory" family life—by noting his rescue of twenty thousand Jews from the Rhineland and five thousand gypsies.

Here his conscience "functioned for four weeks in a way one would normally expect." Still, Eichmann consistently denied any guilt at his trial.

On the other hand, there is some evidence that Eichmann, despite having been kidnapped, came to Israel willingly, that perhaps he truly wanted to find peace—as the prepared statement from the Israeli authorities that he signed put it. Moreover, during the trial he admitted deeds that incriminated him but that would have been impossible to prove against him.[66] He admitted straight out—at least in retrospect—that the murder of the Jews was a crime. His desire to reconcile himself with the Jews and to see himself hanged as an expiatory sacrifice for the German youth, which—he found out—felt guilty, was something Hanna Arendt—understandably enough—regarded as rather tasteless. Still, it expresses the wish to be recognized as a moral person. The same is true of his claim—presumably false—that he had "continuously requested reassignment," which was not granted. He rebuffed the attempts by the Canadian pastor Hull to get him to confess his guilt: "I cannot allow you to sow doubts into my heart at this late stage." And he reported to Hull that his wife, in Argentina, always gave him answers from the Bible—it is not clear what the questions were. This made him very angry, and eventually he tore up the Bible in a fit of ill temper. He asserted vehemently that he didn't kill anyone: "Many others had to kill, but I didn't, I didn't have to kill." Guilt for the crimes did not lie with him but with the party.

Yes, he was remorseful, but he would not sign any paper that said as much. People would read it the wrong way and deduce from it an admission of guilt:

I mean: If I now say that I was remorseful, they will seize on that and say: "Where there is remorse there is also guilt." They will not admit that remorse and guilt are not the same thing. Whether I express my regret on a spiritual level or whether I admit guilt in court is a difference like day and night. But the lawyer only understands the word: guilty. *But I have no guilt." To which Hull replied: "But you said yourself that you made a mistake." Eichmann: "You asked me if I was remorseful, and I said yes." Hull: "You said you made a mistake." Eichmann: "In a general way, I said I regretted that I joined the party. That is what I said. It was a mistake to join the party. I would immediately sign a statement to that effect."[67]*

If Eichmann wanted to admit remorse without an admission of guilt, one reason was surely that he wanted to protect himself from the death penalty in court—unsuccessfully, as it would turn out. But beyond that, an admission of guilt that went beyond regret (which is probably what he understood by remorse) would have demanded a complete revision of his attitude toward life: he would have had to recognize that it was wrong to sacrifice his conscience to obedience (ambition, timidity, etc.) and that he had a choice or should have made it clear to himself that he did. This step toward recognizing his freedom and responsibility is one he would not or could not take. The fact that he was afraid of doubts that could be "sown in his heart at this late stage" suggests that he had an inkling of the true dimension of his guilt and genuine admission and shrank from it. At the same time, however, it also suggests that he had an inkling that the surrender of his responsibility had not made him incapable of incurring guilt. He shied away from complete clarification—he continued his "silent treatment."

The Case of Stangl

Unlike Eichmann, Stangl eventually took the step toward clarification. During his last hour of conversation with Gitta Sereny he admitted that the compartmentalization of his consciousness, in which he taken refuge in Treblinka, did not succeed in the end. He could no longer sustain the self-deception that he had to answer only for what he himself did intentionally—that is, on his own initiative—and could block out what he was de facto participating in. When Gitta Sereny asked whether the goal of these conversations for him might not have been the chance to face up to himself, his immediate response was

automatic, and automatically unyielding. "My conscience is clear about what I did myself," he said, in the same stiffly spoken words he had used countless times at his trial and in the past weeks when we had always come back to this subject, over and over again. But this time I said nothing. He paused and waited, but the room remained silent. "I have never myself intentionally hurt anyone, myself," he said, with a different, less incisive emphasis, and waited again—for a long time. For the first time, in all these many days, I had given him no help. There was no more time. He gripped the table with both hands as if he was holding on to it. "But I was there," he said then, in a curiously dry and tired tone of resignation. These few sentences had taken almost half an hour to pronounce. "So yes," he said finally, very quietly, "in reality I share the guilt . . . because my guilt . . . my guilt . . . only now in these talks . . . now that I have talked about it all for the first time. . . ." He stopped.

He had pronounced the words my guilt: *but more than the words, the finality of it was in the sagging of his body and on his face.*

After more than a minute he started again, a half-hearted attempt in a dull voice. "My guilt," he said, "is that I am still here. That is my guilt."

"Still here?"

"I should have died. That was my guilt."

"Do you mean you should have died, or you should have had the courage to die?"

"You can put it like that," he said vaguely, sounding tired now.

"Well, you say that now. But then?"

"That is *true," he said slowly, perhaps deliberately misinterpreting my question. "I did have another twenty years—twenty good years. But believe me, now I would have preferred to die rather than this. . . ." He looked around the little prison room. "I have no more hope," he said then in a factual tone of voice and continued, just as quietly: "And anyway— it is enough now. I want to carry through these talks we are having and then—let it be finished. Let there be an end."*[68]

After a brief, euphoric, almost exuberant good-bye to Gitta Sereny he died nineteen hours later in his cell from a heart attack.

Did the confession kill him? Was the previous silence essential for him to live? There are truths that are too terrible to live with, as Gitta Sereny commented. Mrs. Stangl acknowledged, indirectly and haltingly, her own share in her husband's guilt. On the other hand, Stangl had been seriously ill as early as 1955, and only in 1966, following a heart attack, did it occur to anyone that perhaps it had been his heart all along. "Perhaps it was finally the reaction to all those terrible years; I have always thought that his coronaries were the result of his terrible mental and spiritual stress"—that was Mrs. Stangl's interpretation. One could thus turn the whole thing around and say that silenced guilt had already manifested itself for decades as heart disease. Of course, this does not answer the question of whether there are truths so terrible that a person who admits to them will not survive.

Stangl himself kept silent for years—especially toward his wife and children. Still, the conversations with Gitta Sereny, once he had begun them, were very important to him. Once, after an interval of several weeks, he greeted her reproachfully: "'I've been expecting you every day; I've waited for you,' he said at once—instead of bowing or saying '*Grüss Gott*,' as had been his custom." Later, by way of explaining why he had kept silent in his family, he said: "I never talked to anyone like this."[69]

These conversations, and probably the confession as well, may have been the decisive step for him before he could die.

ORDINARY GERMANS:
DOUBLE MORALITY, PARTICIPATING, LOOKING AWAY

To shed light on the phenomenon of "silenced" guilt, the discussion so far has revealed the persistence of traditional moral values, which stood in opposition to the racist, and especially anti-Semitic, Nazi morality. My goal was to show the objective—but also the often demonstrably subjective—openness of the situation in which moral decisions were made. The perpetrators—and all people who did anything at the time—had the capacity for guilt and conscience even if, needless to say, it has not been possible to reconstruct in each individual case the motives or moral quality of the acts. Instead, I have used extreme cases to reveal and retrace the fact that the perpetrators did not act with a sealed-off lack of conscience—out of ideological blindness, habitual sadism, or increasing brutalization—and without any capacity for reflection.

"Report from the Reich":
Morality Had Not Been Forgotten

If this is true for high-ranking Nazi or SS representatives, there is much to suggest that the population that "went along," and was after all closer to "normal," traditional morality and was less ideologized, certainly did recognize the criminal character of the Nazi regime and was thus *able* to act in a moral way toward it. For instance, the "Reports from the Reich" supplied by the Security Service (SD) of the SS, which the political leadership used to inform itself about the mood of the population, document quite "normal" reactions shaped by the moral tradition. When the Nazi leaders were loudly expressing their outrage at the massacre in the Katyn forest, the population countered, for instance, by saying that they had "no right to become upset over the measures of the Soviets, because the German side had eliminated Poles and Jews on a much larger scale; moreover, the treatment of Poles, Jews, and Bolsheviks was not exactly scrupulous."[70]

The existence side by side of contrary moral values in German society, those of the Nazis and those of "tradition," becomes especially apparent in the reaction of the German population to the "Police Decree on the Identification of the Jews" (1 September 1941). The "Reports from the Reich" relate the following: "It is emphasized on all sides that this de-

cree was in accord with a long-held wish in many circles of the population, especially in places were there are still [*sic!*] relatively large numbers of Jews."

Discontent was aroused by the "half-hearted" nature of the exemp-
tions for "*Mischlinge*" [people of mixed race]and so on. This was not radical enough and caused confusion. Moreover, "it was now easy for malev-
olent people of German blood to have sexual relations with Jews without
being bothered." This was a defilement of the race. "The majority of the
available reports express the unanimous opinion that the measures taken
so far would not be seen as final. In particular, there is a general expectation that all special regulations in favor of Jews, Jewish *Mischlinge*,
and Aryans married to Jews, will be revoked as soon as possible. It was
also desirable that Jewish houses and apartments be given an appropriate identification. Most welcome, however, would be a speedy depor-
tation of all Jews from Germany."[71] But the SD also registered "attempts
by the churches to undermine the anti-Jewish attitude of the population
through pastoral work." Only the yellow star had made many Christian
aware of how many Jews attended Sunday services with them. Many of
them no longer wanted to have the Jews there because "one couldn't ask
them to receive the communion next to a Jew." The SD noted:

*The attitude of the clergy in the Confessional Front is characterized by
a leaflet that was written by a woman city-vicar in Breslau and circulated
in various parts of the Reich: 'It is a Christian duty not to exclude them
(the Jews) from the mass simply because of the badge. They have the
same right-of-domicile in the church as the other members of the con-
gregation and are especially in need of comfort from the Word of God.
There is a danger that the congregations will let themselves by led astray
by elements that are not genuinely Christian, that they will endanger the
Christian church through unchristian behavior. They need pastoral help
in this regard, with reference, for example, to Luke 10:25–37 ("Who is
my neighbor?") and Matthew 25:40 ("Anything you did for one of my
brothers here, however humble, you did for me.").*

The leaflet added the practical advice that faithful members of the con-
gregation should deliberately sit next to "non-Aryan Christians" and also
pick them up for mass.

In September of 1941, the chairman of the Fuldau Bishops' Confer-
ence, Cardinal Bertram, responded in a circular letter to the desire of

many Catholics not to be separated from their fellow congregants who were Jewish. In view of the police decree, the cardinal wrote:

One must avoid . . . hasty directives that could be seen as hurtful to Jewish Catholics, for example, the introduction of special Jewish pews, separation when administering the holy sacraments, introduction of special masses. 2. Orders for a separation of non-Aryans is [sic!] contrary to Christian love. . . . In view of the difficulties that have arisen for Jews living in Germany as a result of the Police Decree of Sept. 1, 1941, Catholics are admonished to show the consideration owed to all Christians, including Christians of Jewish background, in accordance with the principles that St. Paul proclaimed as the Christian duty: "All those who believe in Christ will not come to grief. For there is no distinction between Jews and Greeks; the Lord is one over all, answering all who appeal to him. All of you who have been baptized into Christ have put on the garment of Christ. There is no such thing as Jew and gentile, slave and freeman, for you are all one body in Jesus Christ."[72]

These documents suggest that anti-Semitic prejudice shaped the Germans much more strongly and broadly than anti-Slavic prejudice, for example, which was also racist. But the point is that there were also explicit and courageous actions against it. The Germans were not at the mercy of Nazi "morality." They were perfectly capable of remaining loyal to traditional morality, especially Christians.[73] And it is hard to imagine that people who followed the segregationist anti-Semitic policy should have remained without any feeling of guilt, at least after 1945, once they were forced to realize—in 1945, at the latest—what sort of crimes they had at least facilitated by segregating the Jews.

But did the majority of the German population even find itself in the obvious decision-making situation that formed the background to the examples I have cited (concentration camps, mass executions, euthanasia programs) and in which the criminal nature of the acts was undeniable? Was it possible as well to know or suspect in the "Reich" what sort of crimes one was permitting or facilitating?

Everyday Confrontations with Crimes

As of yet, we cannot know the precise number of people who were concretely involved in these murderous acts. Daniel Goldhagen is correct when he points out that we know little about this. And the effort to determine the precise number is perhaps an impossible undertaking, given the range of criminal situations that existed. But at least there is a series of facts that reveal how great a percentage of the population must have came into direct contact with the crimes, helped—quite consciously— to prepare them, or at the least was aware of them.[74]

Some ten years ago, Gudrun Schwarz, through painstaking and detailed research, recorded the number and type of Nazi concentration camps. According to her list, there were more than ten thousand camps inside and outside of Germany. They were assigned to sixteen different categories, from camps for prisoners of war and forced labor all the way to extermination camps. Many of the camps had numerous outside installations whose inmates worked in factories and service sectors: Buchenwald, for instance, had 129 such installations, Dachau 197, Flossenbürg 97, Groß-Rosen 118, Neuengamme 90, and so on.[75]

Germans were certainly aware of the abysmal conditions of the camp inmates, which often led to their deaths. Once again, the "Reports from the Reich" testify to this:

According to reports from Berlin, Frankfurt / Main, Dessau, Kassel, Kiel, and Münster, a larger number of industrial establishments have noted a continuing decline in productivity and an increase in illness and escape attempts among Russian civilian industrial workers. As before, the reasons given are inadequate rations, accommodations, and clothing; utterly inadequate health care; and allegedly false or misleading promises during recruitment.... For example, Kassel reports that the poor and insufficient food supply for the Russian civilian workers is strongly affecting their work output. Because of physical weakness, many workers simply can no longer stay on their feet, let alone do the least bit of work.... Many establishments in Berlin are also reporting a decline in the willingness to work and in the work effort because of insufficient food. At the AEG, Kabelwerke Oberspree, for instance, the Russian women working there are sometimes so weak that they collapse from hunger. About 20 percent of the workers are constantly absent. A falling-off in production is to be expected because of this situation. Similar observations have been made in Kiel. The food that is handed out in the common camps for Eastern workers is not sufficient to keep the workers healthy and fit for work.[76]

It is quite obvious that normal Germans in their working lives could not but see the misery created by a regime to which they nevertheless extended their loyalty. Individuals could—in fact, had—to recognize the contradiction between fundamental traditional notions of morality and the moral consequences of the Nazi policies they supported.

Between January and December of 1942, 303 ghettos were "liquidated" in Poland; in Transnistria (Romania) there were sixty locations with ghettos and camps, eight of them death camps. Between 1939 and 1941, six installations of mass murder were in operation in Germany and Austria, and in twenty-nine other institutions patients were poisoned with drugs. Forty penal camps were set up in the Emsland alone.[77] Because the names of some camps—Auschwitz or Treblinka—have taken on symbolic character, many hold the naive belief that there were only a few camps. But Germany during the Nazi period was littered with sites of murder and torture; Poland had 2,197 camps. The number of people who kept them running, or who could not but come into contact with the inmates during their daily work or when columns of prisoners were marched through the villages, must have run into the millions.

This whole question has been illuminated by a study of Kaltenkirchen "under the swastika." Kaltenkirchen is a small town north of Hamburg. Beginning at the end of 1941, transports with utterly exhausted Russian prisoners of war arrived regularly every few days at the nearby prisoner camp of "Heidkaten." There they "die en masse, before the eyes of the sailors and workers living in the adjoining barracks." A large number of eyewitnesses, whom the author of the study interviewed, remembered the evidently horrible scenes of seriously ill prisoners being brutally maltreated by German guards: "They were dragged like sacks out of the baggage cars and sometimes they were simply dropped on the ground. . . . Prisoners fit for work were used at various sites, especially at the airport installations. Their columns went every which way. One column regularly marched the long way from Alveslohe to the Kaden Estate. Others worked in Ulzburg and on laying cable on the Hamburg-Neumünster line. Many were employed in building the tracks to Krauser Baum and further on to Moorkaten. Especially here, in and around Kaltenkirchen, everyone saw how they were being mistreated." The transport of the dead by "horse-drawn carts" was a horrible and yet "daily affair" for the farmers, who were obligated to do it. In an "express letter," the Reich Minister of the Interior had decreed on 27 October 1941, that communities were obligated to bury the prisoners of war; a coffin was not absolutely required: "The corpse is to be entirely wrapped with strong paper (if possible oil, tar, or asphalt paper) or some other suitable material. Transport and burial is to be done inconspicuously."

But precisely that was not possible. Forty years later, these experiences still bore profound horror for the witnesses who spoke to the author.[78]

Scholars have calculated that somewhere between nine and ten million German soldiers took part in the war of annihilation against the Soviet Union. "More than half of all German soldiers were on the eastern front at any given time; in 1941/42 it was 70 percent, and toward the end of the war another 60 percent." In a representative survey in April 1956, 46 percent of men—as compared to 2 percent of women—admitted to having been in Russia, 23 percent in Poland. About three million Russian prisoners of war under the responsibility of the Wehrmacht died during the war against the Soviet Union. Most of the crimes were not committed at the front but behind the lines, and the ratio of frontline soldiers to soldiers behind the lines was about 1:6. "One part front, six parts behind the lines?" was the follow-up question from former chancellor Helmut Schmidt, who had been a soldier in that war, in an interview in *Die Zeit.* "Yes, that was about the ratio back then," the military historian Wolfram Wette responded. Upon returning from the front or during leave countless soldiers reported on the massacres, and some also about the gassings, they had witnessed.[79]

Moreover, a recent historical study has demonstrated in detail that the German Wehrmacht committed numerous crimes not only in the war against the Soviet Union, something that is now increasingly admitted, but also in Italy and in the Balkans. Soldiers and officers who had surrendered were shot, as were civilians, including women and children. In this context, Manfred Funke has pointed out that Maj. Helmuth Dobbrich and one of his company commanders, Hans G. Hennecke, refused to take part in the infamous execution of 335 hostages in the caves outside of Rome, without suffering any retaliatory measures. The hostages were subsequently murdered by Obersturmbannführer Kappler and Hauptsturmführer Priebke, who was acquitted by an Italian military court in 1996 on the grounds that he was "acting under orders."[80] Once again there is evidence that a moral and factual sphere for making ethical decisions certainly existed.

Moreover, recent historical scholarship has demonstrated that the initiative for the bureaucratic implementation of the policy of annihilation as well as for the concrete crimes in the camps did not always come from the top but also from the bottom. The National Socialists practiced a quite modern, "participatory" administrative policy. Civil servants were called upon to show initiative, active participation, and imagination, and they responded to the call with well-considered suggestions, whose outcomes they incorporated into their planning.[81] The mental and psychic threshold against murder proved terrifyingly low in this process.

Millions of Germans were thus involved in the crimes as perpetrators, as hangers-on, and as bystanders who did nothing against the glaring injustice. It should be noted, however, that acts of opposition—as individual cases of resistance, for example, in the strongly pro-Nazi town of Kaltenkirchen reveal—took a lot of courage. Revealingly enough, the people of Kaltenkirchen refused to rehire a teacher after 1945 who had been vocal about his opposition to the Nazis and had been arrested by the Gestapo in 1943: "His application was unanimously rejected by the municipal council."[82]

Because so few resisted, Norbert Frei has argued, most Germans after 1945 felt an inner bond when it came to warding off any confrontation with the crimes of the past. This was how he interpreted the beyond-rational level of support that demands for amnesty even for serious and convicted war criminals received from the German population in the early 1950s:

"Given the fact that the West Germans presented themselves as a weakly secularized folk community—especially in the hysteria surrounding the war criminals—and developed a need for amnesty so strong that it simply cannot be explained with the real interests of the vast majority, it seems permissible to suspect that this was also an indirect admission —confirmed by its denial, as it were—of the entire society's involvement in National Socialism."[83]

5

The Psychological and
Social Consequences of Silence

The destructive power of the silent treatment of guilt showed its primary effect in German families, radiating from there to society and politics, and especially to the political culture of the new German democracy after 1945.

THE GERMANS:
A PEOPLE WITHOUT WARMTH AND TRUST?

In 1987, Elisabeth Noelle-Neumann and Renate Köcher published a report about the attitudes and values of the Germans, based on an international study of values comprising Europe, the United States, and Japan. They titled their report *The Injured Nation*. The results of the survey—which was carried out in the early 1980s—revealed the Germans to be very different from other nations, indeed "isolated" and uniquely different from other Europeans and especially from the Americans. They "lack something like warmth, a spirit of enterprise, a zest for life." With little pride in their work or national identity they profess a special need for rest; "there is something depressing in many of the responses of the Germans." The Germans are subject to strong mood swings: they will feel very lonely one moment and elated the next. One could diagnose them as having a neurotic disposition, "a thin skin, testy, a broken pride." Individually, some of these symptoms are also found in other nations, but their cumulative presence is the specific problem of the Germans.[1] What they lack—and this answer is also meant as an indication of the cause of all of this—is "national pride." What precisely is this "pride?"

The authors of the report are at pains to emphasize that they are not talking about arrogance or conceit. Rather, we are dealing with a syndrome. "Pride" pervades all of a person's attitudes and feelings and is thus by no means limited to the nation: "Pride in one's nationality does not stand alone: this feeling of joy, of acknowledgment, of strength and vigor is linked and closely connected to pride in one's own family, one's children, and one's work. It is closely tied to the ability to look beyond oneself, to be selfless. . . . Pride has to do with the ability to establish bonds, to transfer the love for oneself to love for others, to 'identify,' as it is dryly described. In the process, self-confidence and selflessness establish a connection."[2]

In view of the complexity of this feeling and attitude—whose essential core seems to lie in a positive feeling of self and self-esteem as well as in trust in oneself and others as the basis of the ability to have relationships and form bonds—it is surprising that the authors pointedly direct this psychologically familiar syndrome at *national pride*.[3] The authors do not explicitly justify this move. Instead, they merely "support" it implicitly with suppositions about the causes of this German peculiarity, which in turn are neither justified nor substantiated in detail either theoretically or empirically. Since the authors go on to illustrate these German deficits by using the German family, in particular, as an example, one would expect them to shed light on the connection between the familial situation and the suggested causes. However, they do not do so, and we need to examine this discrepancy.

Isolating Oneself:
The Generation Gap and Coldness in German Families

How does the "isolation" of the Germans manifest itself in their families? To underscore the central place of the family in the analysis of a nation's society and culture, Renate Köcher invokes historical studies that point out that the decline of Western cultures always announced itself in the families. Moreover, it is a virtual truism in sociology that the family has a deep strategic significance for a person's individual, social, and political socialization. Even if we must pay very close attention to current shifts and new developments among so-called socialization agents, it appears that the central significance of the family remains beyond dispute. Attitudes and values are handed down and socially diffused primarily in and through the family.

The basic moral consensus of a society created in this way depends, in turn, on the emotional bonds within families and between the generations, and especially on whether a family lives in more or less sustainable relationships of trust. The moral consensus between the generations disintegrates "if the emotional bonds are not intact." This also has profound political significance, for one can observe throughout Europe, and not only in Germany, a close "connection between an intact transfer of values between the generations of a family and trust in the institutions" of society and politics in general.[4]

The most important vehicle for a society's basic consensus about its values is an *open and trusting dialogue* between the generations. When it comes to the passing on of experiences, parents must be emotionally and intellectually available to their children as models, as sources of inner strength, and as a place where they can experience integrity and truth. And this is precisely what children want from their parents, in the political realm especially (until now!) from their fathers. Even if children take a contrary stance toward their parents, they still want an encouraging parental model. If parents are not available to their children for orientation, self-affirmation, and identity-formation, it is very difficult for children to evolve a stable self and to find their own personal and political path. To develop a stable self, which is the foundation for assuming future roles in society and politics, children need the early experience that other human beings—today still primarily the mother—can enter into their emotional lives. This allows them to learn feelings for themselves and others, that is, empathy. They experience themselves as coherent, nonfractured selves who trust themselves and others. A warm familial atmosphere is important for this process, and liveliness and joy are part of it. Renate Köcher has noted that this emotional aspect of family life is becoming increasingly important. Since the family has largely lost its function as a place of work, family members increasingly look to the family to satisfy emotional needs and the need for meaning and security.[5]

What is the true situation in German families? In several respects it is strikingly different from that in other European and in American families. The first thing one observes is the gulf between the generations, a gulf of values, worldviews, and convictions. In the familial atmosphere it involves a weak sense of trust, an unusual degree of alienation between the parents and between the generations, and an extreme aloofness between the members of the family. Emotional satisfaction within families is notably lower in Germany. And since family members no longer have any great expectations of fundamental familial harmony, the generational gulf does not actually manifest itself as conflict; on the surface, relationships are often friendly.[6]

The relationship between children and their fathers is especially poor and distanced, not so much among the war generation, which often grew up without a father, but among the postwar generation, which had to deal with returning fathers. Weak emotional bonds and reservations about mutual obligations have a strikingly negative effect, not only on the family atmosphere but also on trust and confidence in the future. It is therefore likely that a connection exists between the difficulties of the second generation in making commitments and creating stable relationships and the fact that since 1965 the Germans have had the lowest birthrate in the world.[7]

The passing on of values is substantially impeded by the emotional distancing within families. German children accept their parents' claim to loyalty, respect, and love only with many reservations and qualifications. Authorities in Germany do not command respect from the outset; more so than in other countries they have to prove themselves in every case. Here it is interesting to note that the Americans, compared to the Germans, place a much higher priority on liberty and that their relationship to authority is much less complicated than that of the Germans. Renate Köcher appends to this finding an admonitory comment about the need for unquestioned authority and an implied critique of the questioning of authority in Germany. However, one could also suspect a connection between the lack of genuine—family-grounded—authority in Germany and a weaker appreciation of liberty, which was *not* handed down by persuasive authorities but was undermined by authoritarian forces.

A specific political consequence of this finding about the German family is that a particularly high degree of uncertainty exists in Germany when it comes to political judgment, along with a rather weak consensus about questions of value, both within as well as between generations and thus within society as a whole.[8] This would mean that the basic democratic consensus in Germany is fairly unstable.

Incidentally, the sociologist Friedrich Tenbruck already reached analogous conclusions in 1974, ten years before the survey by the two authors of the Allensbach Institute. He noted that in the years after 1945, people limited themselves to relationships within small, circumscribed spaces. Families and religious congregations were the most important places where people anchored themselves, while overarching social layers and norms were not yet visible. The family was of prime importance, for it alone promised stability. People looked to it for trust, reliability, and an affirmation of self-esteem. Political themes, however, were excluded within the family: people wanted to gain their psychological and moral orientation without them. As a consequence the past too was shrouded in silence: "A mute generation of parents was silent not only about the past, but about all questions concerning one's place in the political and historical landscape. In the process, the parents were left with the closed-off and irritating result of an incomprehensible and unreasonable discrepancy between their personal motives and the political outcomes; the children were at first left de facto and morally with the dull feeling of an unjust and dark legacy."[9]

The boundary between the private and the public, Tenbruck maintained, was a deep trench, and the public sphere showed cracks. People stayed within a small circle and built high walls. Forms of social encounter that bridged strangeness and created permeability were lacking. "Hunkering down," "walls of separation," and fundamental inhibitions toward what was new and toward spontaneous communication dominated the picture. Feelings of strangeness and insecurity were glossed over with seeming nonchalance and casualness. Elements of community could not arise in this atmosphere, which promoted neither a pronounced individuality nor agreement in and about public opinion. Arguments were dominated by self-righteousness, and distrust and accusations against the state and society were the norm. One could detect a good deal of ambiguity and a widespread uncertainty about norms and about how political judgments were arrived at. Other people—for example, in traffic—were experienced primarily as obstacles. "Insecurity turns into fear and distrust, at first of one another: the old of the young and the young of the old."[10]

Ten years before Noelle-Neumann and Köcher we thus encounter a very similar picture. It does not exactly confirm Hermann Lübbe's thesis on the transformation from Nazi supporters and hangers-on into citizens of the new democratic Federal Republic. The general climate of trust— or better distrust—is mirrored in a statistic from 1955: 61 percent of Germans believed at that time that a dishonest person would have more success in life and be better off than an honest person.[11]

The Causal "Analysis" of the Allensbach Pollsters

To what do Elisabeth Noelle-Neumann and Renate Köcher attribute the peculiarities of the Germans?—their melancholy, coldness, and emotional distance; the mistrust within families; the gap between the generations; the fractured transfer of values and a basic consensus; the lack of joy in one's work and optimism about life; the absence of pride in family, work, and nation? Although the authors do not make an emphatic and theoretically explicit attempt at explaining all of this, we can piece together their answer from various set pieces. First of all, there are "internal injuries," "nothing is visible from the outside; everything is whole and in order." We are thus dealing with something psychological, which is not immediately recognizable. The authors note that similar deficits of pride and joy can still be found above all in Japan and the Netherlands: "A depressing pattern: these are all countries that came out of the Second World War as losers or suffered the humiliation of occupation for many years during the war." Drawing on the work of the British social scientist Richard Rose, they point out that national pride can sometimes be traced back to liberation movements that occurred as much as two hundred years earlier.[12] For Noelle-Neumann and Köcher, military defeat and occupation emerge as primary causes, to which they add the frequent changes of government the Germans experienced in the twentieth century.

The authors become clearer still in talking about the comparison with Austria. Can one legitimately lament the Austrian's failure to engage their Nazi past, they ask, if one sees how much more pride the Austrians have in their nation and if one considers the connections between pride and performance? This would mean that, alongside military defeat, the engagement with the Nazi past is one reason why the Germans lack pride and have a feeble joie de vivre.

The authors go on to highlight with increasing emphasis the victim status of the Germans: "What are accepted values—religious, moral, political, human—if the system of government changes four times within a century? If not one, but two military defeats destroy the pride? If a brutal totalitarian state, perfectly organized in terms of mass psychology and techniques, creates a lasting situation in which idealism and fear are joined together? And if the only remaining decision at the end of the war is that between love of one's country and deliberate defeat?"[13] Throughout this entire passage the Germans do not appear as responsible actors, let alone as people who inflicted misfortune on others, but only as unfortunate victims and objects of outside influences. The authors continue rendering actors and responsibilities anonymous: "Total war had been pursued more seriously than probably ever before"—the authors quote a contemporary document.[14] Who pursued it seriously? Fate? And who else besides the Germans suffered from it?

And what was it, according to the pollsters, that the Germans experienced as a collapse in 1945? It was the collapse of "an army, a state, the cities, their own houses . . . their own convictions." Evidently, they did not experience the collapse as the end of the murders, the concentration camps, the exploitation of foreign workers. Thus, the Germans found themselves in 1945 quite "incomprehensibly" defeated and humiliated. They did their duty during the war and suffered a great deal, their homes were threatened from the air, and if that wasn't enough, the message they got after 1945 was "self-humiliation": "The population is kept from knowing that a majority never voted for Hitler in a free election." Did the pollsters ever read a German history book? Who was keeping this information from them? "And who would expect that a population living in a propaganda cage would be able to arrive at a correct judgment about the government that put out this propaganda?" According to the authors, the Germans simply could not know anything. And in the postwar period as well, victims once again, they "preferred keeping silent . . . to explaining in an atmosphere where there was no desire for understanding."[15]

The Germans as mistreated and misunderstood victims—no wonder they are so hurt. In an appendix of historical documents, meant to illustrate daily life in Germany prior to 1945, the report once again described the Germans only as victims. We read about conscripted Viennese women workers, but not about foreign workers from Poland or the Soviet Union. There is nothing about concentration camps, no daily life in the war the Germans waged beyond their borders. It is almost breathtaking that even at the end of the 1980s, one—if not *the*—reality of the Nazi period, namely, that of guilt and crimes, is blocked out and that the basic behavioral pattern of German parents after 1945, whereby they defined themselves not as responsible actors but as unfortunate victims, is repeated and continued!

It makes perfect sense that the implicit appeal of Noelle-Neumann and Köcher to the Germans—to finally give up their alleged "self-humiliation" and "destructive engagement with the past" and to find a "solid" national pride—was gratefully received and extended further by politically far-right authors such as Karlheinz Weißmann, for example, in his review of the book in *Criticon*.[16] Given the inadequacy of the causal analysis by the authors, which Weißmann does not bother to test, this affirmation of the "victim" thesis is not only politically and morally dubious; it is also quite counterproductive: de facto it amounts to a strategy of drawing a line under the discussion, and it cannot lead to a genuine national pride that is not loaded with chauvinism and resentment.

We must probe much more deeply into the reasons for these findings: Why do the authors attribute the coldness within German families, the mistrust, the aloofness, to the military defeat? Would there have been warmth if the Wehrmacht and the SS had subjugated all of Europe? What values would have been handed down in the families in that case? Did the postwar occupation (in the West!) damage German self-confidence after it had been healthy and intact before? Renate Köcher herself describes the tradition of distance and emotional frigidity that prevailed in German families already prior to the World War II.[17] And in her compelling study of Albert Speer, Hitler's confidant and later Reich Minister of Armaments and War Production, Gitta Sereny has made this observation about the family situation that had profoundly shaped Speer since his childhood: "His description of his home life, given in his customary deceptively nonchalant manner and tone, conveyed an overwhelming impression of cold: cold between the parents, cold between parents and children, cold between the mistress of the house and the staff. 'Now that I think of it,' he said, 'it's true: the only warmth I ever felt at home was from our French governess, Mademoiselle Blum. She was Jewish, you know.'"[18]

How then should we picture in detail the family dynamics that produced cold and distance? Renate Köcher at least raises the question cautiously. She points to the repeated, radical breaks in the German past: "So far the strain this has imposed on the family, the institution that guarantees continuity and the conversation between the generations, has remained completely unanalyzed."[19] Not so.

In the discussion that follows I will seek to analyze and illustrate this "strain," whose central empirical characteristic is the break between the generations, by looking at the silence of the parents, their "silent treatment" of their own participation in the crimes of the past. Of course, it would be methodologically naive and unjustifiable to argue that family dynamics can be traced back to a *single* cause or even to a bundle of causes. For my purposes, I must ignore the numerous factors that arise from the development of modern industrial and information society and affect the family—for example, the trend toward small and single-parent families. As a rule, these factors reinforce the destructive tendencies of silenced guilt. The analysis that follows is based primarily on autobiographies, interviews with members of the so-called generation of perpetrators (i.e., those born before 1925) and with their children and victims, on analytical reports in depth psychology, and on psychological and psychoanalytical theories.

DESTROYED FAMILIES AND DAMAGED OFFSPRING

By now, it is a widely accepted fact that there was consistent silence within families and to some extent in the schools, if not about the Nazi period in general, then certainly about personal participation in Nazi crimes, about the motivations that led to these crimes, and for the most part also about the brutal nature of these crimes.

Why Silence Does Not Help

Was silence a bad thing in the first place? Was there not something "soothing" and "protective" about it? "What I don't know can't hurt me," as the saying goes. Was that not also true for the German families? No, it was not: what was not known in the families, especially by the generation born between 1940 and 1950, did not leave them in peace. For what was shrouded in silence was not some insignificant, perhaps uncomfortable, triviality. Instead, it was sensed as something dark and ominous—one simple reason being that the parents mounted a massive and sometimes aggressive defense of the boundaries they drew against potential curiosity. What was left in the dark was unsettling and oppressive. The secrets thus had a presence that was both intense and frightening.[20] This silence in the families was not a friendly and relaxed silence, or one conducive to peacemaking.

But given the enormity of the crimes, was silence avoidable in the first place? Even Alexander and Margarete Mitscherlich, in the late 1960s, could hardly see a way in which the silence could have been overcome right after the war.[21] Moreover, it was often said that so many Germans had merely gone along, had perhaps even rejected the crimes. Could they even have a bad conscience in those circumstances? And wasn't there also a problem with the Allies, who ignored the differences among the Germans and accused them collectively?

It is along these lines that Manfred Kittel, in his 1993 book *The Legend of the "Second Guilt"*, lists the traditional reasons and justifications for the private silence after 1945. Although he does not wish to deny in principle the magnitude of the German crimes and the resulting guilt, he grants the Germans that it was entirely possible for them to feel guiltless because they had been subjectively "decent" or had merely been hangers-on. Kittel does not confront the contradiction between his justification of a subjective feeling of guiltlessness, on the one hand, and the undeniable guilt that was, allegedly, never denied or "suppressed," on the other. Instead, he offers more "good" reasons for the clean conscience of the Germans: Did the "millions of new, never punished crimes of expulsion [against ethnic Germans—Trans.]" not affect the Germans' consciousness of right and guilt as much as the failed process of denazification? Indeed, Kittel asks, did the Germans not engage in too much grieving? (Of course, that grieving was for their *own* losses, *not* for their victims!): "Grieving for family members killed or missing at the front, grieving over the lost homeland in the East. But perhaps it was precisely this sum of individual grieving in the 1950s that prevented an even stronger collective 'crestfallenness' over the suffering inflicted on other peoples, of the kind that later seemed appropriate to the '68 generation?"

If one has so much personal suffering, can one still think about the suffering of the others and the guilt of having inflicted it on them? What kind of conception of morality, justice, responsibility, and the universality of values lies behind this sort of question posed by Kittel, who is very typical in what he writes and whose reflections are aimed polemically at Giordano's notion of a "second guilt"? Must the world not simply allow us Germans to think only about ourselves and our suffering, regardless of what we perpetrated previously?

Still, even Kittel recognizes that the Germans sense a subterranean feeling of guilt. According to Kittel, one can see it in the fact that they have given up reunification and the eastern territories, "core pieces of their cultural sphere," precisely because the crimes of the Nazi period dominate history. Thus, the Germans come to terms with their Nazi past by means of their "often lamented, radical lack of memory and historical awareness." How so? Coming to terms through forgetting? Coming to terms through losing or "ravaging" one's awareness of history by equating all of German history with National Socialism, something Kittel both deeply regrets and rejects?: "And so one can say that the singular ravages in the German consciousness of history have to do with the mountain of guilt the Germans took on through the Holocaust—and which they subsequently did *not* 'suppress.'"[22]

But would the "mountain of guilt" really "devastate" the German historical consciousness if it did not weigh heavily on us undigested?—if the concrete faulty historical developments, responsibilities, and problematic German traditions and dispositions, and finally the personal developments and mistakes, which each person can admit only to him- or herself, did not rise up as impenetrable barriers? In fact, is it not possible that the path toward clarifying this guilt, toward overcoming what is dark and ominously impenetrable, toward recovering a human dimension, precisely also in guilt, could help remedy these lamented "ravages"? Would this not allow us to attain the inner freedom of recognizing our own suffering without having to block out the suffering of others, which was inflicted by our hands?

This would be the very opposite of the false alternative that has been frequently attacked (also by Kittel): that of "crestfallenness" or the so-called German self-hatred, both of which rest on dishonesty, falseness, lack of dignity, and destructiveness. Does clarifying one's own guilt mean losing dignity? Or is it not precisely a way of regaining dignity?

To be sure, apart from the reasons I have indicated, the terrible difficulties of daily life after the war, the all-too-human desire to have an easier life and live without worries, made it a natural response to push the past aside for the time being. Incidentally, an analogous phenomenon occurred in Israel after the terrible experiences of the Holocaust.[23] Still, the silence was not a benign and healing silence.

The following section will offer the destructive power of silenced guilt as a way of explaining and elucidating the glum diagnosis of the Germans with which this chapter opened, and in particular of their family situation. My intent in doing so is not to raise rigid moral claims but to illustrate the high psychological, social, moral, and political costs of this silence. Perhaps the silence was initially unavoidable—at least to a certain degree. But not everybody kept silent. Human beings are not automatons; they are not simply preprogrammed but have the ability to learn. And making ourselves aware of the damage that silence inflicts— and, even more importantly, the opportunities offered by overcoming it—may provide an incentive to act differently from our less fortunate predecessors.

I shall preface my reflections with a thesis about the destructive power and effect of treating guilt with silence:

The silent treatment in the families lays the foundation for a syndrome of attitudes and psychic dispositions and values whose effect is frequently destructive—destructive to the familial atmosphere; to the relationship of trust between parents and children; to the handing down of moral attitudes and values supportive of democracy; to the genuine and "harmonious" perception of reality as the basis for a normative and political "common sense"; to the sense of self and self-esteem; to trust in oneself and in strangers on the part of parents and—especially—the second and to some extent even the third generation; to the intellectual and emotional integrity of the second and third generations as autonomous persons; to their willingness and opportunities to assume responsibility and practice individuality as well as cooperation, nonconformism, and compromise; to their ability to enter into commitments that are lasting, reliable, and grounded in reciprocity and in this way develop a stable and affirmative relationship to the common good.

This is, indeed, a very complex and interconnected statement, and I will seek to make it more transparent. Needless to say, we are not talking about a strict determination of the nature of these phenomena but about tendencies that can be stronger or weaker and that countervailing factors can deflect in a positive way or redirect for the good. In other words, they are tendencies to which we certainly need not resign ourselves fatalistically. We are free also in situations in which external conditions affect us and push us into unwanted directions, and the more clearly we see these conditions, the freer we are.

This is not only my personal belief (and one I do not wish to conceal); it is also the basis of an approach to psychoanalysis or depth psychology that does not think of itself primarily in scientific but in humanistic-hermeneutic terms.[24] It is important to me to emphasize this point because some of my own discussion will draw on clinical psychoanalytical experiences and their theoretical systematizations. Though I am aware that there are many reservations about these theoretical constructs, I do not wish to dispense with their wealth of insights. However, I reject from the outset an interpretation that sees human beings merely as objects of external circumstances both in our psychic states and in the processes by which we become aware of these states. The Swiss psychoanalyst Gion Condrau once said that we are also responsible for our neuroses, and he was right.[25]

The Family Situation

The finding for this syndrome from which we start is thus the "silent treatment": not only of the period and circumstances of National Socialism but quite specifically of an individual's own behavior during that time, insofar as it could be seen as culpable. In general, the vast majority of the generation of the perpetrators denies feeling guilty, and one is tempted to believe them, were it not for clear signs that throw doubt on this sealed-off feeling of guiltlessness. To begin with, we find a noticeable and consistent avoidance of any possible personal share of guilt in the accounts about National Socialism and everything that happened in connection with it.[26] The parent generation in the families also avoided bringing out the brutal sides of National Socialism, for this could shed light on the implications that just going along or standing idly by had for letting the crimes happen.

The Israeli psychoanalyst Dan Bar-On, who has delved deeply into the consequences of the Holocaust for the children of perpetrators and victims and has conducted many in-depth conversations with both groups (sometimes jointly), identified a "double wall" of silence. It is erected by both sides, parents and children.[27] The parents didn't want to talk about it, and many children would rather not know about it, especially before they entered puberty. Children were reluctant to ask not only because many parents reacted strongly and threateningly to inquiries, shutting their children out, but also and primarily because they did not wish to put their parents on the spot. After all, they could feel that something dark was weighing on their parents. Perhaps it is therefore appropriate to examine the destructive family dynamics first of all from the perspective of the needs and desires of the children.

From early on, children approach their parents with a great need for affection, love, security, encouragement, trust, and happiness. No matter how unruly and insufferable children can sometimes be, they seek a sense of safety; they want to lean on their parents, experience guidance in the world from them, experience them fully "embodied." Emotionally too, a sphere in which we are most likely to be entirely ourselves, they want to get close to their parents. Children want "parents they can touch." They also want their parents to be happy and suffer if they are unhappy; they try to comfort them and make things better. And they want to admire their parents a little, to feel their strength, to be shown how to deal with the adversities of life. Moreover, they want to laugh a lot and be joyful; they are quick to sense subterranean sadness and depression, and these feelings take root in them too.

When children are young, much of the exchange between them and their parents takes place unconsciously and on an emotional level. Children need to experience that their parents can feel their way into their emotional world, otherwise they will find themselves alone. Through this emotional exchange and comparison to the more experienced parents, children must learn what their diffuse feelings really are and be able to show them, even if they occasionally do so in unpleasant ways and need to be corrected. Children must find in their perception of emotions and reality the confirmation that they are not entirely "off the mark," and they must be able to learn to frame their feelings a certain way so they won't be continuously at the mercy of moods and emotions. It is only the generational link as the continuity of experiences that offers them the ground on which they can gradually learn to live with a sense of confidence. Reality is not self-evident. It is highly confusing if one's own perception of it is not shared by others, whether it is the emotional component of reality, hard to define and beyond the cognitive grasp, or even the perception or confirmation of quite trivial facts or pieces of information. In such a situation, blue cannot simply be blue.

As children grow older, an open dialogue plays a increasingly important role in the transmission of norms, perceptions of reality, and basic attitudes in life such as trust and a sense of reality, persistence, and a sense of responsibility. This is not an easy task for parents because they must bring themselves into the dialogue and examine themselves in order to remain truthful. For truth and truthfulness offer the indispensable foundation for the trust without which moral convictions cannot be persuasively handed down. Finally, children also expect "missions" from their parents, challenges or offers for a meaningful composition of life that serve not only momentary pleasure. And children are proud if they can meet these challenges, even if they gradually separate from their parents and come up with their own vision of the goal of their lives.[28]

Of course, it is difficult, if not impossible, for parents to live up to all of their children's expectations and to meet all of their needs. Anybody who has children can attest to that. Parents are not supermen and superwomen (this too children must learn to accept). Today, mothers or fathers must often raise their children alone, under material and psychological conditions that don't make it very easy to convey a sense of the joy of life.

But beyond that, unspoken and unresolved guilt gives rise to particularly grave obstacles to a more or less successful generational transition. This is what I am concerned with in the present chapter. The experiences with National Socialism are my test case, but I believe that a number of the difficulties and "derailments" in the case of postwar West Germany can be applied to other situations of guilt.

The vast majority of parents in Germany after 1945 were seriously damaged: disappointed over the nation's defeat and their own illusions, beaten down in material and moral terms, denounced for the crimes the Germans had committed, crimes many had participated in directly or indirectly or at least had done nothing to stop. Many had lost their sense of self-esteem, their self-confidence, their very sense of orientation (especially from universal values), and they concentrated solely on surviving from day to day. Some were barely capable of still understanding the motives that had compelled them to go along with National Socialism.[29]

Alexander and Margarete Mitscherlich, in their famous book about the "inability to mourn," interpreted the disaster of the parents—following Freud—as a narcissistic insult from the loss of their ego ideal. Anita Eckstaedt (1992) agrees with that assessment in part, based on her own clinical findings. Elke Rottgart (1993) believes that the problem of self-devaluation is more likely grounded—at least empirically—in undigested feelings of guilt. All agree, however, in their diagnosis that the parents were physically and psychically defeated but kept quiet about it and were unable or also unwilling to ponder the discrepancy between their own—possibly justifiable—motives and the objective crimes of National Socialism, to articulate in a clarifying manner to themselves and their children their failure and moral guilt. They were probably afraid that they would not survive this process physically or psychologically or that they would lose their authority in the eyes of their children.[30] Yet some also continued to simply cling to their old ideas, out of conviction, in an act of defiance, or in a kind of "regression."

Splits, Vagueness, Hypocrisy, and Confusion

The silence that followed from this disorientation, loss of self-esteem, and sense of insult led to psychological splits, vagueness, hypocrisy, and confusion, with disastrous results.

Many families thus lived in a twofold, split reality. Parents continued to cling subconsciously not only to basic attitudes of National Socialism (e.g., "racial hygiene" and the condemnation of the weak and sick), but also to an explicitly positive assessment of National Socialism. At the same time, they adjusted outwardly (in the way Lübbe has described) to the new political reality and seemingly became "good democrats." In so doing, they offered their children what was often a very blunt example of a double morality and forced them—if they continued to be highly re-actionary—to decide in favor of the family position: "The Hitler greet-ing was still used at home [after 1945]. I was living between two worlds, and I chose my home so as not to get lost."[31]

On the outside, of course, one displayed a smooth, clean façade. Irene Anhalt recounts that the return of her father, a heavily compro-mised Nazi general, from Russian captivity caused her small home town to put on a celebration, at which the returning prisoner of war was lauded as a hero. As a small child, still ignorant of what her father had done, Irene had sought to share his punishment (de facto his guilt) "by kneeling on peas." Throughout his life her father denied his guilt, but on his deathbed he confided his secret to his daughter: "It was not right for the Spanish to take the land from the Incas and kill them." "My throat was choked with tears," the daughter adds in her story, "when I answered you: 'Yes, Daddy, thank you.'"[32]

In 1948, according to a poll by Noelle and Neumann, 57 percent of Germans considered National Socialism a good thing that had simply been badly implemented. In 1950, 25 percent of Germans believed that sabotage had led to their military defeat; in August of 1953, 53 percent of the men once again wanted to wear their medals from the Third Reich in public. In May of 1964 (!), about 30 percent of Germans believed that without the war Hitler would have been one of the greatest statesmen ever. At the same time, only about 50 percent of Germans clearly believed that Germany was responsible for the outbreak of the Second World War, and only about the same number were unequivocal in not regarding the German resistance to Hitler as "treason."[33]

In the postwar period, the widely circulating magazines *Quick* and *Stern* published long, memoiristic war novels in which the German soldiers were depicted as unblemished heroes. And the disastrous ideal of toughness, which eliminated all compassion, continued to be propagated as attractive and exemplary. In these fictionalized stories even French female spies succumbed to the attractiveness of these tough German men: "She saw his sharply profiled, noble, beautifully masculine head"— and, of course, took leave of her senses. In the face of his military duty, Captain Prien on the bridge of his submarine displayed an almost ascetic demeanor:

Suddenly, this face froze even more masklike, and his eyes lost their sparkle when he caught sight of the iron cables. . . . He was never one to give up quickly. He knew what his officers and each man of his boat thought of their captain. In their eyes, he was a tough guy. What they didn't know is that he hadn't always been that way. He had to learn it. Slowly and painfully, lesson by lesson. Life had begun early to teach him how to survive. He had suffered many wounds—but they had all healed over. They had broken open again and healed again. And every time the place where he had been hit had merely become tougher and more invulnerable.[34]

Not just war, but life itself was a battle in which one had to become increasingly hardened or be crushed: the message of this popular literature attested to the continuity of old mentalities. Although these mentalities stood in conflict with the official political understanding of the Federal Republic, they illustrate precisely the schizophrenia in the informal milieu of the new republic. The fate of displaced Germans and the fate of concentration camp inmates was placed on the same level; the victors were painted as soulless avengers with evil intentions. The recent war had been full of adventure; the real responsibility for war and death lay with the Allies and the partisans; Russians were Bolshevist subhumans;

Poles were dirty. There was great interest in the German prisoners of war in the Soviet Union, but none in the fate of former concentration camp inmates. From whence, indeed, asked a discouraged Michael Schornstheimer, should this generation draw the strength for an honest coming-to-terms with the past?[35]

Werner Schwan has vividly outlined the dishonest attempts at exoneration and the opportunism of many supporters and followers of National Socialism in the postwar period by examining a number of novels: Grass's *Tin Drum*, Lenz's *German Lesson*, Böll's *Group Picture with Lady*, and Meckel's *Searching Image*. As the title of his study he used the standard phrase of those who wanted to preserve their morality without being serious about moral principles: "I'm not a monster, you know." Walter Pelzer, the garden shop owner in Böll's *Group Picture with Lady*, uses this phrase, mantralike, to excuse his "opportunistic behavior during the Nazi period," along with "humble" hints that he also did some commendable things after all. He lived in the gray zone, was no criminal, yet he did not want to ask himself to undergo an honest self-examination. In Martin Walser's play *The Black Swan*, the son Rudi takes on the guilt of his father, who was a Nazi doctor and denies his past in favor of a fictitious present, and commits suicide.[36]

The inability of the generation of the parents to muster the strength to be honest had disastrous consequences: the children, who expected honesty and reliability from their parents and needed these qualities for their moral guidance, over long stretches experienced their parents instead as hypocrites. The split between public conformism and the private continuation of old ideals laid the groundwork for a massive dishonesty and uncertainty. It sapped the moral example of the parents of all its persuasive power. Children, after all, are acutely aware of hypocrisy, at least until they have found a way to live in this split reality. This split situation is promoted by the fact that the first split has a ripple effect, thus causing perceived reality to become on the whole uncertain, distorted, and truncated.

Suppression of Emotions

The splitting off and suppression of feelings takes on special significance. The war novels of popular literature are not alone in revealing that the memory of the recent past was not simply eradicated (memory, in any case, cannot simply be "destroyed"). And faced with the crimes that were so obvious and publicly invoked as a warning, it was not possible either to simply touch up this memory or eerily transform it into something heroic. The surest way, if not to eradicate this memory, then to prevent its painful parts from getting close, was to separate the facts from their attendant (painful) feelings.[37]

This is a general and well-known psychological process, one we are all familiar with from everyday life and without which we would probably not be able to cope. But there is a vast difference between an objective report, whose painful parts one has worked through and now does not wish to repeat over and over again, and a general and diffuse emotional tabooing of the past. Apart from suppressing emotions, this tabooing also excludes entire areas of events that happened in the past, making it possible to avoid pain one has not faced. Reality, too, is distorted by this process. At the same time, a person's own emotional life, which is burdened by the silenced guilt, becomes increasingly petrified; it withdraws to an inner "bunker." The sphere encompassed by this bunker is continuously expanded preemptively. The result is an increasingly distanced communication within the family, in which parents do not let the children get close, and children can no longer truly "reach" their parents.[38] In the end, the children no longer have parents they can touch.

Once this happens, the place of feeling is taken by sentimentality and self-pity. And so the functional suppression of their own emotional life on the part of the parents, intended chiefly to deflect feelings of guilt, continues the German tradition of education and child rearing (which was practiced not only by the National Socialists), in which feelings are regarded as a weakness and empathy tends to be rare and is, in any case, not cultivated.[39]

This persistent empathic refusal, which—as psychoanalytical theories tell us—makes it impossible or at least difficult for children to develop a good sense of self-esteem and a genuine empathic sense for the feelings of others, has been described by some as a "cumulative trauma" that is difficult to overcome. This is extremely destructive for familial communication: it creates an atmosphere in which only one's own feelings can provide reliable information about "who we are and in what kind of relationship we stand to others."[40]

The development of an attentive and subtle emotional life is also of vital importance in the formation of conscience as the foundation of all morality. Without attention to others, without empathy, without love for another person, the voice of conscience is mute or very quiet. Extensive interviews with children of the generation of perpetrators led the psychoanalyst Gertrud Hardtmann to this conclusion: the "genuine emo-

tional depth of a vibrant social conscience, which must be lifted out of
paralysis and deep freeze and brought back to life, is still far from having
been achieved in Germany." The ravages continue. One of the people
with whom Dan Bar-On spoke described the family that took him in, and
in which the mother underscored that she never kissed any of her seven
children, as a "deep freeze." [41] This sterility of emotional life and coldness
in many German families is destructive: I shall return later to the "second"
generation's notorious difficulty in forming relationships, more precisely,
its inability to love.

In connection with the basic idea that emotions, in particular, are
split off and separated from memory, we must first examine the negative
consequences this has for the perception of reality as such. Reality, after
all, is a complex and highly controversial thing. It is never unambiguous.
But if there is a basic tendency to block out emotions when looking at
reality, this produces further distortions: the meaning of words, gestures,
and event is truncated, shut out, or at least not openly talked about.
Anything that is unsettling, sad, or painful is "downplayed," and individuals for whom these meanings are important become confused and disappointed and are disparaged. This feeds a general doubt about the
trustworthiness of one's own perception and that of others — as it is, this
doubt already draws plenty of nourishment from the double morality of
the parents. The next generation finds no secure hold in reality and is
continuously shocked to discover that it does not understand the world
around it and its reaction to them, that it cannot find orientation or form
secure judgments about the world. According to an empirical poll in the
early 1970s, what German youths wanted most, compared to their British and American counterparts, was unambiguousness. What they feared
in politics was not so much a war of all against all, but anomie, a fear of
being lost, of being without orientation and assaulted by a Babylonian
confusion of tongues. [42]

These psychological splits, the moral double standard, the denial of
emotions in memory and in the present, and the dissociation of elements
of meaning and even of "crude" facts in the perception of reality led not
only to massive insecurities, especially among the second generation, and
to the compensatory need for clarity and unambiguousness—which often expressed itself in relentlessly harsh accusations against the parents.
On a very general level, these phenomena also undermine trust, be it
trust in oneself, in others, or in the future. They go hand in hand with a
symbiosis or intertwining of the generations, often painful for both sides,
in which the separation of the children seemed threatening to the par-

ents, who therefore made this separation very difficult and at times impossible. That is why psychoanalytical interpretations sometimes speak of "dependency relationships."

Dependency Relationships

From the intellectual and emotional perspective of the children, and to some extent also of the grandchildren, familial relations were burdened primarily by two problems: in some very diffuse and inexplicable way they felt guilty, and this often manifested itself in massive psychic and somatic symptoms. The most frequent symptoms were feelings of inferiority, fear, depression, sleep problems, and stomach complaints. The children were unhappy. (Incidentally, analogous complaints were experienced by many survivors of the Holocaust who suffered from so-called survivor's guilt, and who, in the horrible circumstances of persecution and the concentration camps, often had to violate moral norms for the sake of survival, which later weighed heavily on their conscience. Moreover, in the 1950s in Israel, many Holocaust survivors often encountered mistrust and implied imputations of guilt, simply because they had survived.) [43]

Then again, the children of the generation of perpetrators suffered from the fact that the older they got, the more they were forced to perceive their parents as split personalities. On the one hand, they saw them as nurturing mothers and fathers, which some of them certainly were, and the children needed them and loved them as such; on the other hand, they had been participants in or even initiators of crimes, murderers of defenseless human beings (that is, not merely soldiers in an "ordinary" war). The children often suffered severely from this division, and the attempt to reconcile and reunite the two halves of their parents was rarely successful. In a number of cases, that of Bernward Vesper comes to mind, despair over this situation led children to commit suicide.

We still know very little about the psychological processes that made children have feelings of guilt for acts committed, not by them, but by their parents. One obvious mechanism is "identification," which occurs between children and parents, but also quite generally between people who love each other. The phenomenon that people take on qualities or values from those to whom they are close or bound by feelings of love is such a common experience that it is not necessary to invoke theoretical explanations such as the Oedipus complex, the theory of the ego ideal, or specialized terminology such as "introjection" or "transmission." This identification with people one loves is strikingly evident on an emotional level in negative experiences, especially those of "borrowed" shame or guilt. One thing that can be empirically observed in this "transfer" of guilt is the children's tenacious demand for a confession of guilt from their parents. Many parents reacted sharply to this demand, threatening to terminate all communications or "expel" the child from the family.[44] Many times, these attacks by adolescents were also publicly criticized as arrogant or even inhuman and immodest, and in fact they sometimes assumed quite repellent, aggressive forms. But behind these attacks was, in the first place, merely the children's desire—often unconscious—to rediscover and acknowledge their parents as moral subjects. The truly terrible thing was not merely the crimes of the Nazi era. Children often felt that it was even more terrible and blameworthy that the parents were unable to admit to what they had done or failed to do. By admitting their guilt, parents could have undone—at least to some extent—the split between their nurturing and their irresponsible parts. Dan Bar-On found this assumption confirmed time and again in long and intense discussions with the children of perpetrators. A second motive behind these "attacks" of the children, their desire for an admission of guilt from the parents, was the hope—once again unconscious —that this would relieve their own, agonizing ("borrowed") feelings of guilt. The hope that they could begin to become independent and responsible beings, instead of remaining dependent on their parents in a blind wish for identification or an equally blind and aggressive act of rebellion against them.[45]

In this tense situation, parents, however, were unable or unwilling to understand that an admission of guilt would *not* have meant a loss of authority; quite the opposite, it would have allowed them to regain the respect of their children. It could have helped the children to find a new, shared reality and shared experience with the parents. And both, children and parents, could have discovered the old biblical wisdom about the joy created by the repentant sinner: the daughter of the Nazi general was moved to tears when her father admitted his crimes on his deathbed. Niklas Frank, whose book *The Father* drew too much attention for the insults he hurled at his father, was searching almost pleadingly for any stirring of moral sentiment in his father. Laboriously, he deciphered the handwriting in his father's diary, "always with the hope of discovering in you something that spoke to me, that lets me love you, that explains you to me; in vain, what emerged for the most part was only shallowness . . . "[46]

Evidently, parents did not have sufficient trust in themselves and in the love of their children, thereby hampering a possible restoration of the basis of trust between them. And the children—once again, unknowingly or unwillingly—often made life difficult, indeed, unbearable, for their parents. For they repeated the hardness, humiliation, and emotional frigidity they had often experienced from their parents, especially their fathers (whom we shall discuss in more detail later). This could be clearly seen in the 1968 student rebellion. According to the psychoanalyst Werner Bohleber, we know today

that opposition to and turning away from the parents does not eliminate subterranean continuities of thought patterns and behavioral patterns. We, as members of the student movement, still believed that it did. At the initiative of the students an examination of the fascist past was forced through at the universities, and the uncovering of the Nazi developments of the generation of perpetrators was an important step in lifting the general amnesia. But this . . . opposition toward the generation of the fathers had an unrecognized flip side: by attacking the fathers so vehemently, unmasking them, in part mocking or ridiculing them, we, for our part, brought out those identifications with our fathers in which were manifested their destructiveness and arrogance. The hatred for our fathers promoted and solidified the feeling of being different from them, rendering us incapable of discovering connections with them and similarities in ourselves and acknowledging them as part of one's own self. Only this acknowledgment can set in motion a fruitful process of examining these identifications.

We must take a closer look at this unknowing and unintended dependency of children on their parents and, conversely, of parents on their children. To do so, we shall return to theoretical and clinical analyses and findings from psychoanalysis whose premises, while certainly controversial, are useful for an insightful approach to this issue. They can help us gain a better empirical understanding of the often noted difficulty of the second and third generation in detaching itself psychologically from the generation of perpetrators and in developing into individuals and citizens who are independent and capable of taking on responsibility, forming relationships, and loving.[47]

The existence of nonrational, unconscious emotional bonds between the generations, in particular between parents and children, is not only well known and self-evident but also quite positive. Such ties are the foundation of mutual love and obligation as well as of the transmission of culture and of social cohesion in general. They become destructive, however, when they damage or entirely prevent the personal independence of the next generation. This is most likely to happen when the parents themselves, out of weakness, disappointment, unprocessed guilt, as well as fear of guilt and punishment, are dependent on their children to prop up their own identity, their sense of self-esteem, and their self-confidence. The roles between children and parents are reversed; children are "parentalized" into consoling, protective, supportive parents. They function as a kind of crutch, without which the parents would collapse. They are unable to develop their own self, their own idea of what they want to make of their lives by themselves and to follow their own thoughts. A variety of specialized terms and phrases have generally been used in psychoanalytical literature to describe these false bonds and dependent relationships: "delegation" (Stierlin 1980, 1982); "self-syntonic object manipulation" (Eckstaedt 1992); "telescoping" (Faimberg 1985); and "transmission," "transposition," or "time tunnel" (Kestenberg 1995).[48]

We have already mentioned that children like to be sent out into the world by their parents with a "mission," to look for and find meaning and happiness in the world. But this mission becomes a negative delegation if the parents impose it on their children only for their own "narcissistic purposes." For in that case, they don't truly let go of their children, but bind them as "delegates" to their tasks. At the same time, they use their children to compensate for what they themselves did not achieve, did not allow themselves, or despise in themselves. It is above all negative, traumatic experiences that they all but push onto their children, who then have to "drag" them around. This makes it so difficult for the children to develop their own self, and they suffer from this unconscious "occupation" that alienates them from their own selves. If children wish to free themselves from this delegation, they experience this desire as a lack of loyalty and develop guilt feelings.[49] The parents, in turn, because they feel dependent on their children, look with suspicion upon their desire for independence.

Stierlin has also interpreted the attempts at atonement by many children of perpetrators as delegation. The children face up to the guilt and restitution that the parents push away. Such efforts at atonement *can* be seen as an entirely positive mission and carried out as such—but only if the children do it consciously and out of their own sense of responsibility, not because they are driven by the burden of the unrecognized "borrowed" guilt of their parents, and if they are free to form their own judgments about their parents as well as the victims (e.g., the citizens of the state of Israel). This requires that the silenced guilt be overcome, talked about, and clarified. Conversely, the delegation caused by silence blocks children from developing into independent personalities, leading the false self that evolves to act in a manner that is not constructive and creative, but compulsive, dependent, rebellious, and unhappy.

Anita Eckstaedt's "self-syntonic object manipulation" has encountered some sharp, almost hostile, criticism in the professional literature, but less for psychoanalytical and theoretical than for political and—in my view, partly misunderstood—reasons. The criticism implies that she simply tried to direct attention to the victim role of the Germans while ignoring the true victims of National Socialism.[50] To be sure, there is a real problem in the fact that Eckstaedt includes very different cases: not only the children of perpetrators but in general the child victims of the war and the postwar turmoil. I will limit my discussion to her interpretation of the situation of the children of "perpetrators."

According to Eckstaedt, the destructiveness of the "self-syntonic object manipulation" lies in the fact that the children are used to confirm the parents' own distorted reality, and this manipulation in turn renders them unfit to function within reality. In addition, children become "hosts" for what has become unbearable for the parents (in terms of negative experiences, disappointments, guilt feelings) and they have pushed away from themselves: "The object relationships [in the self-syntonic object manipulation] turns into . . . a dependency relationship; it is abused openly or in a concealed way. One person is impregnated with the wish of the other and is allowed to grow only to the extent that he or she fulfills the function of the bearer for this wish."

However, in the "recipient" this process triggers conflicts with her own desire to develop autonomously; the recipient becomes unhappy. This is one explanation for the latent depressiveness of the second generation and the frequent weakness of their sense of self. And often the "recipients" defend themselves defiantly, which again leads them to develop, not an independent stance, but merely a "contrarian stance" and sometimes a (negatively) dependent and false self. Disastrously enough, this manipulation or instrumentalization of people in their immediate or wider environment continues also in the second generation and triggers hostility and aggression:

The "second generation" borrowed this modality from their parents'
generation, who used the children for their own adornment. It was over-
loaded, burdened, and the space for its inner development—the fu-
ture—was predetermined. Inevitably, there occurs the same modality of
laying claim to some other nearby object, which is used to realize one's
goals. In both cases, we are dealing with a narcissistic and destructive di-
rection of the human drive, which first seeks to use an essential part of
the other and then all of him, thereby destroying him; we are thus deal-
ing with life and death.

One of the clinical cases that Eckstaedt interprets in this way was an individual who came to her for chronic, incurable stomach pains. The pa-
tient had tried to cure the pains with a regimen of "water and bread," un-
aware of the symbolic meaning of this regimen and its connection with
the guilt he had taken on for his father.[51]

At present, little work has been done to examine and clarify whether
and to what extent this destructive attitude is passed on to the third
generation. As it is, such acts of "passing something on" become increasingly difficult to discern clearly given the influence of a broad array
of real-life factors. Thus, the danger lies not so much in a simple repetition but in impenetrable deformations that are increasingly difficult to
heal. In any case, National Socialism, under the aspect of the burden
of guilt, continues to play an important—though certainly not a uniform—role in the self-definition of the "third" generation. But even if we
leave the deep psychological context aside, clarity especially about the
moral dimension of the events is of great significance: "At present, the
more problematic the relationship to National Socialism, the more uncertain the expression of national affiliation and the more unstable a national self-identification."[52]

In view of the poll findings by Elisabeth Noelle-Neumann and Renate
Köcher, it makes perfect sense to ask, in the words of Anita Eckstaedt,
"whether relationships today, including those between the generations,
are not increasingly hostile toward the other person, and whether behavior in everyday life is not increasingly antagonistic. This behavior is
shaped by the fact that the strategy of the other person forces me into
a relationship in which my disadvantage guarantees the other's advantage, my insecurity the other's security, my not-having the other's having,
and my misfortune the other's happiness, as becomes apparent in the
transmission forms of narcissistic neuroses."[53] Did Noelle-Neumann and

Köcher not ascertain a particularly neurotic disposition on the part of the Germans?

The two other interpretative models of a destructive symbiosis between the generations—"telescoping" and the "time tunnel"—were developed by analyzing the stories of the sufferings of Holocaust victims and their children. In this case as well, it is difficult for the second generation to develop an autonomous self. The reasons, however, are different: not so much silenced guilt (although feelings of guilt tragically persist even among the victims) but rather the continuation of traumatic experiences and silence about them, as well as the natural desire of the second generation to console their parents and to compensate them psychologically for what they suffered. Much like the children of perpetrators, this second generation also has a difficult time building independent, reliable relationships.[54]

The Split Image of the Parents

The fractured image of the parents further reinforces the destructive effect of the silent treatment of guilt on the development of autonomous personalities able to muster trust in themselves, in others, and in their perception of reality. To be sure, as adults all of us must recognize that our parents were neither the "angels" nor the "heroes" we may have wanted to see in them. Still, if people evolve into independent individuals under reasonable conditions it is possible in the end to integrate and reconcile negative and positive elements, thereby making peace with our parents and with what we require of them. We have then become independent persons who are not dependent on the "purity" of their models and who can also look at their own weaknesses and integrate them ethically as best as possible. In doing so, we can build on the positive elements of our parents with which we first identified.

All this is incomparably more difficult for the children of perpetrators who were directly or indirectly involved in murder. Especially against the background of a handicapped development of self-strength and an autonomous self, these children wrestle with the question of which inherited murderous elements they may harbor in themselves. This often creates a profound fear and a paralyzing distrust toward oneself, which makes the courageous assumption of responsibility more difficult—accompanied by the distress of not really being able to love one's parents. For that reason, many children also avoid finding out in greater detail what their parents did during National Socialism, with the result that they remain for them vague and diffuse figures who cannot serve as supportive models. For many others, conversely, the mysterious lack of clarity about their parents' past is much more agonizing than the truth—however bitter—about their participation in murder and crimes could ever be.[55]

Some children must imagine the hour of their birth or conception as a ghostly scene. One daughter recounted this to the psychoanalyst Gertrud Hardtmann: "I was born in 1943 and was an eagerly awaited child; what madness—in Lemberg, my father had just sent the trains on their way; the ghetto had just been cleared."[56] The ability to make decisions and to take pleasure in doing so, not only in political but also and especially in personal matters, suffers from this. And this is another reason for the widespread inability of the second generation to form relationships and to love, and for their often only semiconscious decision not to have children.

Incidentally, the deep uneasiness evoked by the Nazi crimes—"How could that happen?", "Would I have participated?"—affects not only the children of perpetrators, who after all are more intimately bound to their parents than to anyone else. Studies of the effect of school lessons about the Nazi period on adolescents, especially if they are confronted with gruesome scenes from the concentration and death camps, have shown that they often leave behind a profound distress and lasting doubts about oneself and the moral integrity of humanity.

Teachers generally fail to raise or address questions about motives; the psychological dispositions of the perpetrators; the concrete circumstances of the crimes; the space for free decision that existed; and the dangerous, seemingly insignificant, beginnings. As a result, a paralyzing bewilderment settles over the children, an existential uncertainty about what human beings are capable of, and a loss of trust that saps the life force. The more sensitive youths are seized by helplessness and fear of a recurrence. The others simply resist, deny what they have seen, and at the same time fail to find any access to the perspective of the victims.[57] A pedagogy of silent, frightening confrontation, which de facto uses the tools of fear and intimidation, does not help to prevent a repeat of violence. Instead, it distresses children and has a destructive effect on a helpful, clarifying insight into the concrete mechanisms of criminal events and on an ethos of responsibility.

Peculiarities of Father and Mother Relationships

Against the background of the particularly deep chasm between the generations in Germany, which Noelle-Neumann and Köcher brought out in
their comparative study, we have so far been concerned with the general
relationship between parents and children. Yet the two pollsters also underscored the especially bad relationship between children and their *fathers* in Germany. To shed some more light on this finding, we shall therefore take a look at some experiences from family observations and family
counseling, as well as from biographies and autobiographies, that address the special role of the father or mother and their reciprocal relationship to each other.

The literature conveys the impression of an atmosphere of external
toughness on the one hand and internal weakness and anxiety on the
other, especially among fathers. On the whole, family life is characterized
by a lack of joy, implacability, disappointment, and mutual denigration—
between the parents and above all between fathers and sons. The fathers
returned—often years after 1945—as physically, psychologically, and
morally defeated individuals, to the disappointment of their frustrated
wives who were after all in the prime of their lives, and at times as unsettling strangers to the children. They were greeted not with warmth, compassion, and joy but often with distance and even contempt. They had
been imagined or presented to the children as distant heroes, and now
they came back ragged and "small." This is how Anita Eckstaedt has described the return of a "great" SS father on the basis of an analysis:
"There was neither joy nor compassion with the father, who, when he returned, sat on a small handcart, emaciated and ill." [58]

But this situation, which might strike outsiders as rather pitiful, did
not by any means make the fathers de facto more sympathetic or evoke
compassion on their part. On the contrary, many, like some form of compensation, tried to demonstrate toughness, especially toward their sons.
From a psychoanalytical perspective, all the softness and suffering they
scorned or refused to acknowledge in themselves they sought to fight
against vehemently in their sons and, moreover, to "displace" their own
failure onto them. [59]

They often rebuffed the children's need for intimacy and tenderness,
in particular their sons, and frequently displayed a shocking lack of sensitivity. And it was not only Nazi fathers who behaved this way. This is

how Dan Bar-On has summarized his experiences with the many family stories he recorded:

Insensitivity as the result of a doctrine of toughness manifests itself in all our stories. Anneliese's father, himself not a Nazi but conscripted in Germany, burned all of his little daughter's beloved dolls, which he considered dirty, in front of her eyes, ignoring her tears. The little girl had just heard about the horrors of Auschwitz, and she thought of her dolls as her children. Konstant's father had not actively participated in the activities of the Nazi system. But evidently he too was a "child of his time": he treated his son like he was nothing. Trivial occasions brought harsh punishments. The son himself always had to go get the stick with which he was beaten.[60]

Punishment was often extra harsh, as though the fathers were attempting to uphold in their children a morality they themselves had not practiced. This created a discrepancy that caused considerable damage to the relationship between fathers and their children, especially sons, and to the latter's sensitivity of their experience of guilt. As the children perceived the anxiety of their fathers, their lack of courage in facing up to themselves and their acts and reflecting on them conscientiously, they felt all the more unjustly treated by the—often very harsh—paternal punishments, which were aimed at humiliating and belittling them. This led the sons for their part to refuse an honest assessment of guilt. They reacted to these injured feelings with additional contempt for their fathers because they were cowardly *and* unjust. As a result, fathers lost all the more completely the very authority they had tried to reassert through their harshness.[61]

This situation is an almost classic demonstration of the difference— no, the stark contrast—between authority and authoritarianism. Authority is tied to truth, truthfulness, justice, and competence, and its true goal should be to increase (from Latin *augere*, to increase)—by setting an example—the strength and independence of the "subordinates."[62] To this day, one can observe the effectiveness of genuine authority— and even the desire for it—not only among the young. By contrast, the behavior of most fathers produced the exact opposite. On the outside, they were hard, unapproachable, unrelenting, and irritable, but on the inside they were soft, hurt, and vulnerable. They timidly shied from their children's questions because they could not muster the courage to take a clear-eyed look at themselves, to dispel the fog, to overcome the silencing of their past and their guilt. Such a lack of courage does not give rise to authority but turns into authoritarianism. It is no surprise that Noelle-Neumann and Köcher noted that the Germans in general, including the emerging generation, are particularly distanced from "authorities." Genuine authorities were simply very rare in German families, and to this day we must search hard for them in private and public life in Germany, to the detriment of our liberal democracy.

Many fathers also earned scorn for the conformism the children observed in them. While voicing strong criticism in private, in public they often behaved in a conformist manner and advised their children that they would be better off being spectators on the stage of life.[63] This truly did not make fathers into useful authority figures or models!

Moreover, contempt for the father was often disastrously heightened by the dynamics of the marital relationships. In general, National Socialism with its potential for threats and guilt was frequently instrumentalized for personal conflicts, including in marriage. In addition to personal misconduct, spouses would also confront each other about their failure under National Socialism or suggest as much in front of others. What's more, many mothers transferred their disappointment over the returned father and their contempt for him to one of their children, preferably a son (as "substitute husband"). That son became in a sense the delegated "despiser," which allowed the mother to seemingly avoid the moral reprehensibility of such contempt for her husband.[64]

Under these circumstances, it was very hard for a beneficial relationship to take shape between fathers and sons, a relationship that has always been fraught with difficulties to begin with. Sons also need warm and admiring feelings for their fathers in order to construct a secure male identity.[65] Here is presumably one source for the noticeable insecurity of the male identity in the second generation. (Of course, this insecurity has a wide variety of causes, and it is also quite understandable given the increasing emancipatory tendencies of women and the difficult redefinition of the gender relationships this has entailed for both men and women.) The tradition of German masculinity is not quite as "magnificent" as the magazines of the 1950 were still suggesting in their novels about ordinary soldiers.

Finally, after 1945 many children associated a vague experience of destruction and death with their fathers. Contrary to the public declarations of normality and the euphoria of rebuilding the country, the hope for a life that was also successful inwardly had died in many fathers. The overwhelming majority of men did *not* speak with their wives about their terrible experiences, so they had no outlet here for unburdening themselves, and the children sensed this nonliving hopelessness. In interviews, the children's experiences are expressed like this:

The hope of still finding something alive in the fathers shows how terrible the feeling is if, wherever you touch, there is nothing alive there, there is only death, and nothing alive can be made from it. . . . This is one phenomenon of National Socialism: you encounter death in a naked, pure form. There is not a spark of life you can get out of it. Does it make sense to continue dwelling on it? Can you get more out of death than death? It is the death of every society, all cohabitation, every joy of life; it is the end of the life, a dead end. This road does not go any further. No matter how much you dig, you always run into death. Living? That takes you in a different direction.[66]

What about *mothers*? So far we know very little about them, but their behavior was not uniform either. Delegating their contempt was by no means all they did. On the contrary, the majority of them "protected" their husbands. However, and this is the point, they did not do so by speaking or getting things off their chest but by further reinforcing the wall of silence. Many displayed a noticeable mania for cleanliness (though this must also be attributed to the traditional German fixation on cleanliness and to the difficult circumstances at the time). Their strength and vigor in mastering everyday life, a skill in which they usually outdid their husbands, contrasted with their nervousness and emotional insecurity. The latter made it difficult for them to approach their children in an emotionally protective way and to offer them the sense of security they needed and surely longed for.[67]

Both fathers and mothers defined themselves in their own minds and to their children as *victims*. Given their sufferings and misfortune, it is understandable that they should do so, but it was only half the truth and therefore dishonest. For they knew that it was not the Poles, Russians, or French who had attacked the Germans, but the Germans who had attacked them; that it was not Jews who put Germans into concentration camps and killed them, but Germans who did this to the Jews. This is a very simple, very bitter, and very necessary realization. But very few could summon up the courage for it, the courage to not see oneself simply as a suffering victim but of defining oneself—also temporally—as a responsible actor and perpetrator. They did not pass this example on to their children, and many of the latter continued and continue—this, too, an act of unconscious continuity—to define themselves once again as victims, all their political rebellion notwithstanding. And in part they are indeed victims. But at the same time they become once again perpetrators, frequently continuing, especially in their personal relationships, the thoughtless egocentrism and ruthlessness of the parents they criticized, without the ability to sense the suffering they impose on their immediate and wider environment in the process.

And so in German families after 1945 we find considerable material improvement, a successful functioning, seeming normality—a smooth façade on the outside. After 1945, many parents wanted to offer their children a "proper home." But what the children truly needed they very often did *not* experience: affection, warmth, reliability, inner strength, honesty, trustworthiness, and genuine joy.[68] As Elisabeth Noelle-Neumann put it: "nothing is visible from the outside, everything is whole and all right"—but the Germans "lack something like warmth, a spirit of enterprise, joie de vivre." No surprise.

Is there a way out of this destruction? A way out of the inability to summon up responsibility, trust, love? Out of the narcissistic tendency to misuse others for one's own material or psychic well-being? I believe that way out lies in overcoming the silence:

Experience has taught us that silence in human life is never "mute," but contains specific statements. "Eloquent silence" can contain approbation as well as rejection and disparagement. Especially in conflict-laden situations, it can develop intrusive [invasive and domineering] powers. By way of projective identifications and re-introjections, these effects can lead to profound changes in the capacity of perception and thought and the willingness to communicate, not only in the individuals keeping silent but also in those exposed to this silence. [For example, the disparagement of the self is "handed on" to the other person, who takes it and "gives it back."] Apart from shielding the self from the confrontation with unbearable conflicts, silence evidently has a further virulent effect, which secretly infiltrates the defensive mechanisms of other people as well, takes hold of them and purposefully influences them.[69]

Silence, especially punishment through silence, has a long tradition in German families.[70] It can have deadly effects, and often that is its very intent.

But can one dare to break through this silence? Would it not mean lancing an "abscess" (Hecker 1992), not knowing what would happen, whether the wound would heal again? What are the prospects for speaking, and what can one hope to gain from it?

THE PROSPECTS FOR OVERCOMING SILENCE

The opportunities exist because the well-known psychological "law" that evil deeds trigger a "compulsion to confess" (Theodor Reik) finds confirmation in the family situations of the postwar era. Confession frequently occurs only shortly before a person's death, yet this in itself shows that previously there was a feeling of guilt that weighed on the individual. In those rare cases in which parents were willing to talk and children to show understanding and compassion, the process was beneficial for both sides. The sensitive son, who allowed his father to admit and reconstruct his motives and misdeeds, was able to rediscover the longed-for integrity and humanity that was *also* part of the father. He could help his father find a new sense of self-respect, a comforting experience for both. Talking about something is not the entire process, but it can facilitate or initiate mutual understanding and a change of ways.[71]

To heal the disruptions within the families of perpetrators and especially between the generations, Dan Bar-On, drawing on his extensive experience, has formulated five stages of "processing" that make it possible to overcome the destructive silence:

1. *Recognizing the facts*: Knowing what happened in the annihilation process and, specifically, what role the parents had in it. . . .

2. *Understanding the moral significance*: Understanding not only the facts but their moral significance for the parents as well as for one's own moral responsibility. . . .

3. *Emotional participation*: Reacting emotionally when one knows the details and understands their significance with regard to moral responsibility. . . .

4. *Emotional conflict*: Feeling the conflict between the newly experienced emotions and the positive feelings toward or good relationship with the perpetrators-parents. . . .

5. *Integration*: Integrating knowledge, meaning, and conflicting emotional reactions into one's own moral system.[72]

Experience has shown that if the children embark on this challenging path, they are able to regain their autonomy and self-esteem and overcome the fear of the vagueness of evil, which has made it so difficult from them to take on political responsibility. Negating the fathers and destroying them inside does not help. It would not be a decision for life. Help for a change of ways and the simultaneous incorporation of diverse parental and personal psychic elements into one's own sensibility and their ethical evaluation offer a way out, a way that overcomes evil, which is the very embodiment of isolation.

In a brief essay, Claus Leggewie has offered a sensitive description of the feeling of "resentful compassion," which does not push the Nazi crimes aside but maintains a balance between a natural compassion with the perpetrators and fathers, on the one hand, and a rejection of their acts, on the other. It could be the beginning of the path outlined by Bar-On, though the path itself would still need to be taken. The promise of standing by the perpetrator-father, of not turning one's back on him, helps his chances for a change of ways. To change themselves radically, human beings need "significant others" who support them, above all objectively but also emotionally. What is needed are emotional convulsion and support at the same time. Loneliness can prepare the process, but generally human beings do not achieve an inner conversion alone. From the perspective of the perpetrator, the experience of guilt supported in this way can open the chance for a new self-encounter. Atonement and a genuine encounter with guilt seem possible only without fear—not because one is hoping to avoid punishment but rather because one can discover new possibilities in confronting one's own guilt, possibilities that do not take the form of a depressive self-accusation but "make an offer of a relationship to oneself, to others, to my people, to nature, to God, to everything."[73]

Overcoming silence is important not only to heal the social core of society—the family—and the psychic and moral condition of individuals from the ravages inflicted by silence. In the social and political sphere as well, talking and providing clarification is the precondition for regaining and keeping alive the psychic dispositions and communally affirmed values that are necessary for democracy. The coming generation especially must find a way that leads out of the paralyzing "uncertainty of diffuse horror," on the one hand, and the narcissistic defense of complete emotional frigidity, on the other, which lets nothing, including responsibility, get close to the person. That which is unknown and covered in silence instills fear, creates a paralyzing distrust of the self, and makes people susceptible to slights that—in perpetrators as well as their children and grandchildren—can turn into resentment against those who, as victims, trigger this unexplained feeling of guilt. What needs to be done, instead, is to reconstruct the decision-making situations in detail, to recognize and name the concrete failure of perpetrators or onlookers, and to understand the mechanisms that led to these acts. Obscuring the events of the Nazi period in an all-embracing guilty past prevents us from seeing the concrete spheres of action that can encourage us to take a stand against an all-encompassing despair for the world or humanity. Only in this way can we regain a moral sensibility and, above all, the energy for moral commitments and realistic assessments. At the same time, we are no longer open to manipulation or blackmail through false accusations of guilt or vague guilt feelings.[74]

The consequences of silence, as we have discovered, are destructive for the family, which is the central locus of personal and political socialization. They undermine the fundamental abilities and values of the individuals, on which their well-being, social behavior, and trusting communal life depend. They cut the ground from under a basic moral consensus over a shared experience of reality, which we need to live together in a democratic way. To what extent and why they also damage and endanger our democracy will be discussed in the following chapter.

6

Damage to Democracy

There is a long and venerable tradition of philosophical reflection on what holds together a polity and what destroys it, a tradition whose roots go back to Plato and Aristotle in ancient Greece. This tradition argues (and presents a good deal of evidence) that political systems remain stable when the objective political institutions correspond to the subjective attitudes of the citizens. Despotism can maintain itself only if fear rules its subjects; a monarchy, if its subjects are guided by honor in their actions; a republic or liberal state, if its citizens love freedom and equality, respect these values for their fellow citizens, and act accordingly. If those conditions are not met, the respective political regimes and their institutions lose their effectiveness. Despotism collapses (fortunately) if people are not afraid; a monarchy perishes if people no longer strive to excel in honor before the crown and exert themselves on its behalf; a liberal republic is destroyed by corruption, ambition, the absence of communal feeling, and a lack of responsibility.

This, more or less, is the broad scheme of how political institutions and so-called political cultures are situated. In the twentieth century this venerable tradition has given rise to the idea of "political culture." It describes the subjective attitudes, values, conscious or unconscious mentalities, and psychic dispositions one finds distributed—not always in equal measure—within a population, and which are the subjective "motor," as it were, that keeps the network of institutions running.

The field of study within political science devoted to "political culture" grew after World War II, especially in the United States. Its goal was to investigate why, in the period between the wars, in spite of the fact that many industrial countries were rattled by very similar socioeconomic crises, some states (above all the Anglo-Saxon countries) were able to preserve their democracies, while others, especially Nazi Germany and fascist Italy, saw their democracies collapse.

Economic crisis and unemployment could not have been the sole causes. The subjective attitudes of citizens, their values, their basic assumptions—in short, their cognitive *and* affective identification with their respective political systems—must have played a role. Identifying and unraveling this identification in its various dimensions and components was the methodological goal of the postwar doyens in this field, Gabriel Almond and Sidney Verba. Their comparative study included five countries—the United States, Great Britain, Italy, Germany, and Mexico—and was based on polls and quantitative analyses. Entitled *The Civic Culture*, it became the "Bible," as it were, of the study of political culture, with a corresponding number of critics and exegetes.

The Civic Culture, published in 1963 and based on polls from the second half of the 1950s, stood at the beginning of a flood of studies on German political culture. These studies began with findings that were rather negative for German democracy. Today, after almost euphoric interludes, they have arrived at a sense of guarded optimism.

This raises the question of whether the critical assessments by Elisabeth Noelle-Neumann and Renate Köcher, which I tried to explain in the previous chapter by looking at the family dynamics shaped by silenced guilt, have any relevance at all for the continuation and quality of our democracy. For if the political culture of our democracy seems to be in fairly good condition, if it is strong, stable, and dynamic, why should we care about the sadness in the familial atmosphere, the cold personal relationships, the lack of trust the Germans have in themselves and in others? Was Hermann Lübbe perhaps right in concentrating on and limiting himself to the public and undisputed dimensions of our democracy, disregarding the subjective "internal conditions" because they are irrelevant to democratic politics?

HOW STABLE IS GERMAN DEMOCRACY?

The discussion that follows seeks to define the specific *political* importance of the "internal conditions." It will start from a brief survey of a few diagnoses of (West) German political culture. These diagnoses are accentuated differently depending on the year in which they were made, and, needless to say, they are not exhaustive.

In 1963, Gabriel Almond and Sidney Verba arrived at a negative finding with respect to the prospects of German democracy: Although the Germans were quite satisfied with the output of their political system, that did not mean they were truly committed to it. In contrast to their intense commitment to the previous regime, they were keeping an almost cynical distance from democratic politics. The supporters of various parties were often hostile to each other, with no bond of trust between them. The Germans were barely able to cooperate on the political level. It was highly questionable whether they would continue to support the system if it ceased to offer them so many material benefits. The stability of German democracy was therefore certainly in doubt. Moreover, political participation in the social sphere was not something the Germans pursued, expecting solutions from a hierarchical leadership. In sum: "Though the formal political institutions of democracy exist in Germany and though there is a well-developed political infrastructure—a system of political parties and pressure groups—the underlying set of political attitudes that would regulate the operation of these institutions in a democratic direction is missing."[1]

About twenty years later, Almond and Verba published *The Civic Culture Revisited* (1980), a "revision" of their pioneering study in the form of a collection of essays that discussed the theoretical concept behind it and presented new empirical findings. This study was intended therefore as a theoretical and empirical evaluation of the original findings. The diagnosis of German political culture at the end of the 1970s was almost euphoric. The Germans had learned an enormous amount, professing strong support for their new democratic institutions. While only 7 percent of Germans had been proud of their political system in 1959, that number had risen to 31 percent by 1978! And they trusted their system as well as the possibility of public speech; however, trust in the latter declined again in the late 1970s (in all likelihood especially among the more educated Germans). Still, democratic values—such as political competition, freedom of speech, and civic freedoms and democratic representation as such—had found increasing acceptance among the Germans, who were less inclined to authoritarian styles of upbringing and education. They isolated themselves less and no longer simply withdrew into their private lives, as they had done in the 1950s.[2]

Moreover, according to Conradt, the author of the essay on Germany, the German family had not been as antidemocratic as had previously been believed. During the period of National Socialism, which—contrary to its "ideology of motherhood"—had had a modernizing effect on the family especially through the increasing employment of women outside the home, the family had become more, not less, "democratic"! The atmosphere in the families, so Conradt maintained, had little to do with the regime. For this assessment, the American author drew on secondary literature that he did not discuss or examine in detail. On the whole, Germany in the late 1970s presented itself as a model of democratic stability. Challenges to the system came, if at all, from the left, and these critics were pushing for more democracy or a different kind of democracy, not against it. The legitimacy of the system in the consciousness of the population and its identification with it had grown clearly and markedly. Overall, it was no longer the stability of German democracy that was in question, only its quality.[3]

A decade later, in 1989, Max Kaase took stock, and his conclusion was more cautious. On the whole, he accepted the finding that there was an increase in democratic stability. By highlighting more strongly both National Socialist continuities and the clear German aloofness toward democracy until the beginning of the 1950s, he did reveal the impressive progress in democratic matters: in 1952, 42 percent of Germans still considered the period between 1933 and 1939 the best of times, only 2 percent opted for the Federal Republic (as compared to the high number of 81 percent who did so in 1971). Up until 1948, more than 65 percent still wanted nothing to do with politics, and 70 percent of the population felt that the Germans bore no overall responsibility for World War II. Forty percent identified superiorities of race, and two-thirds of Germans were concerned primarily with economic security, not political liberty.

At the same time, Kaase pointed out that the Germans had not truly wrestled with National Socialism internally. Thanks to the economic miracle and the integration into the West they didn't have to. For the most part, they had suppressed their guilt. Still, a change in consciousness and in their guiding images had occurred. The Germans approved of democracy, but they retained an ambivalent feeling about the German state. Studies in the 1980s recorded a strong "fluidity" in the attitudes toward security and defense policy. Values showed both continuity and change: traditional values such as achievement, duty, and punctuality were still strongly supported in the mid-1980s. At the same time, beginning in the late 1960s, there was a trend away from conformism and convention toward independence and liberal approaches to education and child rearing.[4]

A striking and a little problematic fact for Kaase was something that Noelle-Neumann and Köcher also highlighted: the strong emphasis on the goal of independence and self-sufficiency, which put the Germans almost in a class by themselves; only the Danes display a similar attitude. Kaase, however, attributed this to the general trend toward individualization in modern societies.

Germans now took a much stronger interest in politics. They also felt subjectively more competent, that is, they believed they could influence politics (an important indicator in democratic theory). However, Kaase saw it as an open question whether the Germans had also become objectively more competent. On the whole, the assessment of democratic stability was positive, though the loss suffered by the established democratic institutions as models and carriers of trust indicated that this stability was subject to erosionary tendencies.[5]

A year later, at the outset of the German process of unification, Dirk Berg-Schlosser formulated his review of German democracy even more cautiously. Once again, the issue concerned the core question of the "inner" identification of the citizens with their polity. "Pride" is an important indicator of this identification. When it comes to "pride" (this is the term used in the internal comparative study, which Noelle-Neumann and Köcher also draw on), the Germans are in last place. And economic achievements are no longer so clearly the object of pride as they were in the 1950s (which would indicate that political liberty was taking a backseat); instead, the political system and the achievements of the welfare state are also increasingly the focus of pride. However, from the perspective of identification with the political system, pride in the achievements of the welfare state is an ambivalent indicator because it is based not on civic liberties but on material security. In principle, material security can also be promoted by undemocratic regimes, and it was one important basis of German support for the Nazi regime. In fact, as a value it has a long tradition in Germany, reaching back to the authoritarian state of the nineteenth century. Accordingly, Berg-Schlosser detects a wavering within the strong general support for the democratic system when it comes to the *motives* for this support: the pendulum swings back and forth between political and economic achievements. Moreover, while it is theoretically possible (and common in research on "political culture") to draw a distinction between so-called specific support (for a certain government) and so-called diffuse support (which extends to the entire political system independent of the preferences for a particular government or party), empirically it cannot be so clearly done. Furthermore, since the mid-1970s, two trends—already noted by Kaase—have been running counter to the generally strong support for democracy: first, the so-called leftist postmaterialists (according to Ronald Inglehart, they are less interested in material security than in individual self-realization, expression, and participation) are not very satisfied with the democracy of the Federal Republic; second, the established parties—as central mediators of the formation of the political will—are finding less support. But the crucial "open flank" for German political culture is found, according to Berg-Schlosser, "in their communal system." Is what holds the Germans together merely a "prosperity patriotism," which would not be genuinely liberal and democratic, or is it a "constitutional patriotism" (Sternberger), which many consider too dry and intellectual and therefore not sufficiently capable of binding people to one another and to their polity? In this sense, the identification of the Germans with the German Federal Republic—that is, precisely the *republican,* the *democratic,* aspect of that identity—remains "fragile." [6]

In the early 1990s, Felix Philipp Lutz investigated German attitudes toward values (as part of another comparative international study of values conducted by Helmut Klages, Hans-Jürgen Hippler, and Willi Herbert). His primary methodology was qualitative interviews. The study was therefore not based on set questions and quantitative analyses but on open interviews, which offer a greater likelihood of reaching the level of motivations and feelings and of reconstructing how values arise. Values rest on personal experience, that is, on contextualized reflections on personal actions and experiences, and are therefore more clearly expressed in these kinds of interviews. Invariably, biographical reflection always refers simultaneously to the present, the past, and the future. Such reflection is never finished but continues for a lifetime in a continuous process of creating individual identity or personality. The qualitative interviews revealed that the existential experiences under National Socialism constitute a crucial factor in the formation of the values of the Germans, both in East and West Germany and across generations. Unlike Noelle-Neumann and Köcher (though the contrast may be more apparent than real), Lutz concludes that the difference between the generations with regard to values and attitudes and their conceptions of history is not all that substantial. (For methodological reasons, however, his conclusion can not claim to be representative). But given the "dramatically different experiences" of the respective age groups, the "nature of the contextual assimilation of these values" diverges profoundly. On an abstract level, we find the same values, understood as goals or desires: a peaceful world,

familial security; happiness in the sense of contentment; personal freedom and the possibilities of personal choice in the broadest sense; the feeling of having accomplished something; a pleasant life (prosperity) and self-respect, which rest chiefly on pride, the country's economic capabilities, and the social safety net of the Federal Republic. Behind these desires are instrumental values . . . such as ambition in the sense of industriousness, personal qualities such as competent/effective, clean/ orderly, responsible/reliable, self-controlled/self-disciplined, and ambitious/success-oriented.

Looking at this abstract continuity of values, we note that all of them — with the exception of "responsible/reliable"—are aimed at satisfying individual desires. In any case, they do not express an interest in the contentment of others, let alone in emotional, communal, and warm bonds with others. These values are more about restrained, disciplined advancement; individual contentment in search of prosperity; liberty as individual choice; and the satisfaction of individual needs than about action on behalf of the political community. Here, we can thus detect convergences with the diagnosis of Noelle-Neumann and Köcher, with the difference that these authors interpreted the egocentric trait of these values as "dissolution" and "decline" compared (also) to the Nazi past, while Lutz detects continuities. Incidentally, the continuities extend much further. Like their parents or grandparents, many of the younger people Lutz interviewed echoed the positive clichés of National Socialism without having examined them: National Socialism got rid of unemployment, it promoted the construction of the highway system, and it guaranteed general security. It is not part of the clichés to ask at whose expense and in what inhumane manner all this was done.[7]

Lutz confirms and decries (as do Noelle-Neumann and Köcher) the "decline of values of duty and acceptance," though at the same time he notes a willingness to become involved in large groups (social movements), which contradicts the thesis of a general trend toward disconnecting oneself. As for the satisfaction with the political system of the Federal Republic, though it rests also "on the economic successes and the methods by which social benefits are distributed, which is largely regarded as fair, that is not all it rests on."[8] Personal liberty is part of it.

This last aspect in particular once again raises the question of whether a change in the methods of distributing benefits, which would then be seen as less fair, would substantially impair the loyalty to the system. This is not an academic question since democratic politics of the future — as we shall explore—will increasingly confront the challenge of not letting justice and fairness fall by the wayside in the face of growing material problems. In spite of these constraints, democratic politics must seek to further strengthen the feeling of solidarity among citizens and the general trust in the system in order to prevent an insidious dissolution of communality. This dissolution does not invariably lead to civil war, though potentially to more crime, all kinds of addictions, illnesses, aggression, and hopelessness. We can already detect trends in this direction in our society today. It could all end in another turn toward authoritarian politics.

On the whole, the findings after more than fifty years of democratic political culture in the Federal Republic are mixed. On the one hand, we note a clear increase of declarations of approval and support for democracy and clearly more commitment and willingness to participate than existed at the beginning. Democratic values are accepted; the models for behavior, education, and child rearing (though not necessarily the practice) have become less authoritarian; and democracy has produced universally respected economic, social, and political achievements and is regarded as stable. Moreover, no alternative proposed in any serious way is in sight, especially after the collapse of the communist systems.

This part of the findings confirms Hermann Lübbe's expectation that people can learn democracy by conforming to it outwardly. It also lends support to the expectation of all democratic theorists that democratic institutions can develop their own "integrative" effect. Institutions can channel the behavior of people and thereby genuinely change them. And it is possible that people will not simply function as reprogrammed puppets but will have new experiences: for example, successful cooperation, conflicts well resolved, problems jointly solved, and the discovery that one cannot elbow one's way through life. In this way, citizens can evolve new democratic motivations and attitudes. These observable changes are not simply a new version of old insincerity and self-deception, as Hannah Arendt was still noting with such irritation at the beginning of the 1960s.

But this is only half the story. For there are also continuities in the historical perceptions of National Socialism that repeat the opinions of its supporters and followers. And the continuity of values also points more to egocentrism and an emphasis on personal material security than it does to solidarity and a willingness to participate and take responsibility that is not grounded in materialism. Overall, the degree to which individuals relate democratically to the wider community remains uncertain. "Pride" as an expression of self-esteem continues to be weak, a traditional German problem with the well-known consequences of potential chauvinistic overcompensation. The identity of the Germans, that which holds them together normatively and as a motivator, remains vague: is it economic prosperity and security or—possibly even among victims—a "good" life with political freedom and social justice? Support for the established democratic institutions in the Federal Republic, chiefly the large parties, is steadily eroding (news reports regularly reveal that their membership is continuously and noticeably declining). And less clear is the internal condition of the Germans, which becomes all the more important as the objective institutions become less significant in formulating the political will and making decisions. That condition is also very difficult to ascertain in principle because qualitative methods, which are more suited for that purpose, "dig deep" but are able to evaluate only a few cases and simply cannot be generalized. (This difficulty also besets my own approach, as I attempted in the previous chapter to reconstruct family dynamics and use them as an explanation. This method is convincing only if the individual cases in aggregate speak not only for themselves but for a large number of others as well.) One indication that a method is relevant and representative might be that many people find their own experiences reflected in it.

Finally, statements about political culture based on representative polling can document only values, attitudes, and intentions (quite honest ones!), but not more deeply buried motives. Moreover, whether actual behavior—especially in times of crises—will in fact correspond to these statements is an open question. As a rule, we assume that it will. But it is not only the experience of 1968 that has shown us that declarations of intent and actual behavior can be quite contrary. One is struck by the authoritarian way in which *anti*-authoritarianism was called for back then!

It is certainly true that German democracy is presently not in danger of imminent collapse and that its stability is not acutely threatened. Looked at from the outside, it has attained stability in spite of silenced guilt. And one could also raise the question of whether we really have to attribute the present often-discussed shortcomings in political involvement and orientation toward the common good to such subtle causes as the subterraneously destructive silencing of guilt. Should we not attach greater weight to the declining credibility of political promises, the anonymity of the large established organizations, the complexity of the political problems, the confusion about the truly relevant levels of decision making (communities? federal states? the Federal Republic? Europe? regions?) and above all the growing social and material uncertainties? Why revert to such a complex and not easily identified phenomenon as silenced guilt, with all its controversial psychoanalytical and psychological implications, if we have much more concrete factors at hand with which to explain the shortcomings?

But this brings us precisely to the problem we have already identified, and that the research on political culture triggered in the first place, because the experience of the period between the wars casts doubt on the close causal connection between economic prosperity and democratic reliability or identity. The basic attitudes of people—their political culture, their psychic dispositions beyond material well-being—evidently played a central role for the perseverance of democracy in the United States and in Great Britain. Political behavior could not and cannot be traced back simply to the economic situation, especially in times of crisis.

Moreover, everyday political experiences show that there is considerable room for constructive solutions even in times of difficult economic conditions—at least if the capacity for cooperation, trust, and trustworthiness are present and if people think problems through and develop creative initiatives with greater empathy and a greater sense of responsibility that embraces society as a whole. In such a situation, the pursuit of politics through the mechanisms of the law, which can pose a considerable obstacle to initiative and innovation, would not have to go as far as it has in Germany.[9]

I believe that the qualitative shortcomings identified in these analyses of (West) German political culture can undoubtedly be traced back to silenced guilt. The reason is this: on the whole, they indicate that the difficulties and conditions that caused or favored the culpable behavior under National Socialism were carried over in the generational transfer—even if at times they were changed, shifted, and circumscribed. Up until now they have prevented unambiguous and stable democratic attitudes and motivations—that is, attitudes and motivations oriented toward liberty, justice, and solidarity—from putting down solid roots. But this should not lead us to jump to conclusions, for example, that the present-day radical right can simply be traced back to National Socialism.[10] The interconnections are much more complicated.

It is an important argument for my thesis that as we look toward the future, these interconnections will become increasingly important—at least if we take the diagnoses of the contemporary discussion of democratic theory seriously. These diagnoses see significant challenges arising for the Western democracies, which we can only meet if we recognize the weight of the subjective psychic and moral attitudes on which we shall have to depend more than ever to preserve freedom and solidarity within democracy.

THE CONTEMPORARY DISCUSSION
OF DEMOCRATIC THEORY

During the past few years, many observers have pointed to the paradox that democracy is facing a growing crisis precisely after communism's fall. The reasons for this are the increase in normative, social, and political conflicts; the growing insecurity in the analysis and normative assessment of pressing problems and decisions; and the increasingly embarrassing and noticeable helplessness of democratic politics, which is confronted with higher and higher demands placed on it.

New Potential for Conflicts and Uncertainties

The constant expansion of political spheres—from regional unions (European Union) to the globalization of the economy, which encompass a growing number of interests, social groups, cultural traditions, and economic linkups—increases the potential for conflict and the complexity of reciprocal interconnections and demands political answers and decisions. In the wake of the great migration movements, different cultures, ethnic or national traditions, and demands for independence clash. National societies are becoming less uniform in their models, in their experiences and sense of belonging, and in their dreams and fears. Widespread and rampant mass unemployment, for which no solution is yet in sight, heightens this potential for conflict, as does the scaling back—already carried out or imminent—of the safety net of the social welfare state. Political liberalism, at least in the eyes of its critics, sanctions selfishness and the shameless pursuit of individual interests, thereby promoting a society of egotists. If the emblem of the modern person is emptiness, so the critics say, liberalism is its peculiar political form because it does not provide for the richness of human communality but undermines it. The reaction to the emergence of new and large spheres is a return to circumscribed localities, to ethnic roots, to particularisms, which sometimes leads to ghettoization and self-ghettoization and creates additional obstacles for bringing together competing interests.[11]

This increase in conflicts and in the potential for conflicts is accompanied by a growing insecurity: insecurity about the psychic well-being of citizens, who no longer feel cradled but uprooted and who develop fears and aggression; insecurity about normative orientations, which, given the cultural diversity and postmodern reservations about uniform standards, are difficult to reconcile or at least demand a considerable

willingness to communicate and "translate"; insecurity about the information that is needed for reasonably confident political decisions since
the large scale and complexity of the issues no longer permit us to fall
back on our own experiences in making judgments. The experts are often
worse (or in a worse situation): as experts they only look at pieces of the
larger picture and no longer integrate them into the larger contexts (or
are unable to do so) and thereby de facto distort reality as a basis for
making decisions.[12]

These insecurities are exacerbated by a growing distance between
political representatives and citizens. This promotes cynicism on the part
of the citizens, alienates them from politics, and helps explain why they
feel less and less inclined to become politically involved, and why they
vote in shrinking numbers.

While conflicts and insecurities thus increase and reinforce each
other, the democratic state finds itself confronted with rising demands to
implement solutions at a time when it is increasingly unable to do so. Because of the complexity of regulations and the way in which organized interests and social subsystems close themselves off against each other
and display a lack of understanding, democratic politics has less and less
room to maneuver in. Democratic politics is suffering a "loss of sovereignty" and is less and less able to have its way. Political institutions are
growing weaker and thereby losing their trustworthiness. People are becoming increasingly dependent on the benefits of the social welfare state
while at the same feeling increasingly, and often justifiably, disappointed
by the state.[13] The future of democracy does not look all that agreeable.
What to do?

The hope has proved illusory that one could broaden democratic
participation, allowing more and more citizens to participate in political
decisions and thereby mobilizing them and raising their competence (to
correctly analyze the present issues and arrive at a correct moral assessment of what should be done). The experiences of the past twenty years
have shown as much.[14] (Committed democratizers like Claus Offe and
Ulrich Preuss are impressive on this point in their courageous critique
and self-criticism, though they may have gone a bit too far. In any case,
the strategy of invigorating, strengthening, and stabilizing democracy
through changes in the structures and institutions of democracy seems
"exhausted" at this time.)

The traditional alternative to better institutions has been better citizens. During the past few decades it has been largely ignored in the discussions on democratic theory because the appeal to morality, which is

what reflections on the better citizen often amount to, do not seem particularly convincing and realistic either. But now political theory is striking out again in this direction. And as always happens in cases like this, the discussion picks up on older themes.

Good Citizens Are Once Again in Demand

How can we defuse the potential for conflict? How can we make decisions in a climate of uncertainty? How can we recover the capacity for political action in democracy?

Democratic politics is inconceivable without conflict and equally so without compromise and decision making. How to unite conflict and consensus is one of the fundamental and original questions of political science. Ernst Fraenkel is the German doyen of the theory of pluralistic politics, and his book *Germany and the Western Democracies* has remained a classic on the topic. He emphatically underscored the need for both a basic consensus about the norms of coexistence and the rules of conflict resolution and an arena in which political differences and alternatives are in fact sharply articulated and thoroughly investigated. He reminded us forcefully of the dangers a democracy faces from two sides: too little consensus but also too little conflict.[15]

Conflict is therefore not a priori bad for democratic politics, and there is no general need to contain or even suppress it. It all depends on *how* one deals with it. In a nutshell, the question is whether we have the courage to get to the bottom of conflict, that is, to identify clearly the underlying interests, demands, and expectations, rather than assign them hastily to different camps and in the process cement them into polarized positions. Fraenkel, observing the Federal Republic in the 1950s, noted rather too little conflict and saw in this a threat of stagnation and rigidification. By contrast, the traditional concern in political theory was aimed primarily at the spread and explosive power of conflicts, in other words, at the ways in which one could strengthen the sense of community. To this extent, current democratic theory is certainly part of that trend. The two traditional answers to the question about the cohesive political communality in conflict-ridden, pluralistic societies are as follows:

1. *Citizens* must practice *virtues* or *attitudes* that curb conflict.

2. Society must develop and hold fast to a *basic consensus* about common values, from which one can derive the specific rules for engaging in conflict as well as behavioral patterns and policies. Since the French

Revolution, the three core norms of such a basic consensus have been liberty, equality, fraternity—in more contemporary terms liberty, justice, and solidarity.

Since these principles are affirmed not only by German political parties but practically by all democratic states in the world, one might think that things could not be any better. But that is not so. These norms need to be manifested in concrete, day-to-day politics and in the declared and—especially—practiced values or attitudes of individual citizens, otherwise they remain mere rhetoric. And as a rule, they remain mere rhetoric rather than becoming vibrant, powerful moral guides in the hearts and minds of the citizens. Therein lies the crux of the problem, and thus the theoretical discussion revolves around a return to the necessary civic ethos and, if need be, its redefinition or readjustment in view of specific new challenges. A skillful institutional setup of checks and balances, or a cleverly devised strategy of institutional democratization where one could do without moral postulates, is simply not enough in and of itself. As Herfried Münkler summed it up: the "approach of unburdening the public realm morally . . . must be seen as having failed."[16]

But what kind of morality do we need in the "public sphere"? What kind of democratic ethos? What kind of civic virtues? In the history of political ideas, the specific answers to these questions have varied, and even in the liberal or political traditions they depend on how the respective political systems are defined in detail.[17] This is reflected in the contemporary debates between supporters of liberalism, republicanism, or communitarianism, all of whom consider themselves democrats. However, at times it appears that the disagreements are artificially inflated in order to stake out one's own position more prominently within the public discourse. For the virtues of the citizen in a liberal democracy or a republic as described by the various authors definitely share certain features.

The two central structural characteristics of a political system from which the virtues are derived are, to begin with, liberty and equality. Human beings are free, that is, they possess—by nature, divine decree, as children or partners of God, by social convention, by the linguistic-logical analysis of the so-called communicative act, or by virtue of all of the above—the same rights, the same claim to self-determination, and the right to determine their life within society (precisely within society) in accord with their own goals and with what they regard as meaningful. Citizens are individual bearers of rights but in a community in which all members share these rights.

This gives rise to obligations, unless one simply wants to be an egotistical freeloader—which one can choose to be, of course, and de facto often does, but which is difficult to justify unless one wants to shamelessly deny to others the right to freedom that one claims for oneself. No democratic, republican, or liberal theory of democracy denies that individual liberty is linked to obligations toward the other members of the community. But the extent of that link, whether citizens must simply respect other people and not bother or harm them or whether they must actively look after them, is a question to which there are many different answers. Contemporary communitarian critics of the theory of liberalism, who at times reduce it to a caricature of egotism, overlook the fact that John Locke, the founding father of the "property-owning," "individualistic," egotistical" liberalism they decry, specifically emphasized that individual citizens have a duty to look after not only their close neighbors, but all of humanity. The "state of nature" provided the theoretical foundation of society and of political union, which meant that its basic ethical and psychological dispositions could not simply be "left behind" but should continue to be practiced in the political community. This is how Locke described this state of nature:

But though this be a state of liberty, yet it is not a state of license; though man in that state have an uncontrollable liberty to dispose of his person or possessions, yet he has not liberty to destroy himself, or so much as any creature in his possession, but where some nobler use than its bare preservation calls for it. The state of nature has a law of nature to govern it, which obliges every one; and reason, which is that law, teaches all mankind who will but consult it, that being all equal and independent no one ought to harm another in his life, health, liberty, or possessions. For men being all the workmanship of one omnipotent and infinitely wise Maker—all the servants of one sovereign Master, sent into the world by His order, and about His business—they are His property, whose workmanship they are, made to last during His, not one another's pleasure; and being furnished with like faculties, sharing all in one community of nature, there cannot be supposed any such subordination among us, that may authorize us to destroy one another, as if we were made for one another's uses, as the inferior ranks of creatures are for ours. Every one, as he is bound to preserve himself, and not to quit his station willfully, so by the like reason when his own preservation comes not in competition, ought as much as he can to preserve the rest of mankind and not, unless it be to do justice on an offender, take away or im-

*pair the life, or what tends to the preservation of the life, the liberty,
health, limb, or goods of another.*[18]

It is important not only for academic and historical reasons to point
out that political liberalism in no way represents a justification of particularistic private interest and of a narrow-minded conception of the civic
individual. Hegel, in his philosophy of law, offered just such a one-sided
depiction, which allowed him to use this truncated liberalism as a foil for
his authoritarian justification of a metaphysically superelevated state and
bureaucracy—with disastrous consequences for the German consciousness of liberty and citizenship. Locke's liberalism can most definitely not
be used to justify Manchester capitalism and all the acts of economic
ruthlessness and fraud that accompanied the process of German reunification, for example. On the contrary, it offers a basis for vigorous
criticism. Galson has rightly rejected the overdrawn charges of selfishness and atomism brought against liberalism—at times also by American
communitarians—in favor of a more differentiated understanding of liberal virtues.[19]

On the other hand, one cannot ignore that Locke's main emphasis is
in fact on the idea that individuals ought not to harm one another. Drawing boundaries and the safety of personal space are important, not solidarity above all else. Early liberal theory, after all, took aim at the impo-
sitions and interferences of the absolutist state. Moreover, as observers
from Karl Marx to Max Weber have realized, the dynamic of the capitalist economy, nascent in Liberalism and justified by it, has increasingly destroyed the moral and customary ethical bonds among people. As a result, today we face the problem of a disjunction: on the one side are the
community-destroying effects of capitalist economies and social and
sociopsychological individualization, atomization, and disintegration; on
the other side is the need—for the sake of social cohesion, not to mention the "good life"—to find community-creating sources, impulses, and
driving forces that counteract the erosion of community and are able to
hold and secure the balance of a democratic polity.

To find these forces it is important, first, to identify briefly the
specifically *republican* tenor of Locke's discourse on virtue, which has often additionally discredited it in contemporary eyes and is markedly different from the *liberal* tenor of his discourse. The republican tradition,
which returned to the idea of ancient Sparta, is found among Roman
thinkers, later in Rousseau, in a radicalized form in Robespierre during
the French Revolution, and today among rather conservative theoreti-

cians and politicians, who decry the loss of values, the hedonism, and the dissoluteness of contemporary society (especially among the young). Here egotism and weakness, luxury and pleasure, are the main enemies, which must be opposed with toughness and resoluteness in favor of the common good. Republican virtues are based on *suppression*: of personal evil impulses, of external and internal temptations, of the personal and motivational enemies of everything that is labeled, rather abstractly, the common good. The common good is the primary concern; orientation toward that goal must be maintained through constant training, while habit must make toughness and frugality second nature. That is also why perpetual peace is not useful: it promotes weakness, whereas war challenges us to show courage. This republican conception of virtue is militant, has repressive tendencies, is not particularly joyful, and in its extreme form provides a dangerous basis for fanaticism and "democratic" totalitarianism. Instead of stimulating, inspiring, and encouraging people, its aim is to restrain and curb them (it has a rather pessimistic picture of humanity), and it has decidedly illiberal and nonpeaceful characteristics.[20] In psychological terms, it is not all that far removed from a compulsive authoritarian character.

The liberal conception of virtue, by recognizing equal liberty for all citizens, for its part entails a host of virtues and basic attitudes. Here, the accent is less on repression and frugality and more on activity and communication: tolerance (not indifference or the grudging acceptance of the other person but the affirmation of his personal dignity, even if you reject his opinion), respect for others, self-distance, self-discipline, moderation, friendliness (Montesquieu), responsible and active participation in political decisions (Tocqueville), a sense of justice or fairness (Mill), the capacity for discernment and a willingness to engage in debate (the "Federalists"), the capacity for conflict and compromise (Fraenkel), independence and nonconformity, love of truth, the ability to trust strangers and oneself, as well as criticism—on the whole: autonomy and sociability as rational and reasonable conduct.[21]

The Psychic Preconditions for the Civic Ethos

This catalogue of values has undergone further theoretical elaboration since the beginning of the century—especially in the United States—under the theoretical influence of depth psychology, empirical developmental psychology, and later in response to the traumatic experience of National Socialism. Leading thinkers included Harold Lasswell, Alex Inkeles, Abraham Maslow, Gordon W. Allport, Robert E. Lane, and in Germany Alfred Adler and Karl Mannheim.[22] They all sought to define so-called democratic personalities or characteristics as the psychological "underlining" of these values and attitudes, in the process often amalgamating "democracy" and "health."

Politically, these thinkers and medical practitioners understood themselves to be defenders of liberal democracy. But in terms of theoretical science, they developed their concepts on the basis of the pathologies they encountered in their clinical experiences and from what they perceived to be successful treatments. The healthy personality was now indistinguishable from the democratic personality, which is why Maslow wanted to abandon the term *democratic personality* altogether in favor of "healthy" personality.[23]

It must be said that the equation of health and democracy is dangerous because it can seduce people into defaming political opponents as ill (the political abuse of psychiatry comes to mind). Moreover, it does not offer a way out of the dilemma that there are no unequivocal or even compelling criteria for assessing and establishing this kind of personality. After all, definitions of health and democracy are, in the final analysis, always based on normative and philosophical blueprints, which one can elucidate and make plausible but cannot prove. On the other hand, it is not irrelevant that patients with psychological pathologies, that is, painful experiences, change even in the eyes of the democratic theorist when they find healing or at least experience it subjectively: in their psychic constitutions they often assimilate themselves to what one could see as the psychological type or psychic basis for values and attitudes that promote liberal democracy.

There are a few classic formulations of this type, which are essentially very similar. I shall return later to the question of whether we are dealing with "closed" types, ideal types, or only a (loose) complex of character traits (though their grouping is not accidental). Here, as one example, are the words of the American social psychologist Alex Inkeles:

The citizen of a democracy should be accepting of others rather than alienated and harshly rejecting; open to new experience, to ideas and impulses rather than excessively timid, fearful, or extremely conventional with regard to new ideas and ways of acting; able to be responsible with constituted authority even though always watchful, rather than blindly submissive to or hostilely rejecting of all authority; tolerant of differences and of ambiguity rather than rigid and inflexible; able to recognize, control, and channel his emotions, rather than immaturely projecting hostility and other impulses on to others.[24]

Controversy surrounds the question of whether there are psychological or psychoanalytical "core dispositions" for this collection of psychic qualities (e.g., in the Freudian tripartite model the ego strength, which then essentially creates the ability to love and work; or cardinal dispositions such as the feeling of self-esteem, self-confidence, and the ability to love). Presumably, there is no need to clarify this unequivocally since there is much to indicate that we are dealing with a coherent — though not hermetically closed or inflexible, unchangeable, or clearly definable — syndrome of psychic dispositions, resources, and abilities. These traits cannot be derived from one another in a straight line but influence each other. As we shall see, the feeling of guilt plays a major part in this syndrome.

Alongside the psychic dispositions we have mentioned so far and which continue to be important, there are a few others that deserve our attention given the current challenges to democracy. On the whole, the importance of active solidarity, emphatic empathy, and conscious initiatives at creating community is now greater than it was in early liberalism or in the civic societies of the nineteenth and early twentieth centuries. Moreover, today we often find ourselves confronted with new kinds of conflicts. The issue is no longer merely the opposition between individual and society (particularistic interests versus the interests of the whole) or the dichotomous model of class (or gender) conflicts. Conflicts have become so differentiated that a good deal of mediation is necessary. As a result, what is most in demand is the subtle ability and willingness to perceive differences and the skill to focus argumentative discussions on the common elements instead of allowing them to degenerate into an exchange of verbal blows. This entails an acute sense of justice, by which is meant primarily an understanding of what the other side means and of the intentions and interests that are expressed, perhaps not always skillfully or in a cool and rational way. *The ability to listen* is becoming a very critical skill that we need to build community.[25] All-around sensors are required and above all the development of sensitivity, empathy, and wise self-observation, which makes it easier to understand others more accurately.

The seemingly rational, often hasty intensification of conflicts into clashes of principle, which must then be fought out in a hard struggle where only one side can win and which are seen as a zero-sum game, is of no use to constructive conflict management under present-day conditions. In these situations, the imagination often no longer exerts itself to search for alternatives and new solutions. A conception of ethics that thinks not only in terms of principles but is animated by the goal of preserving personal relationships intact whenever possible, develops more creativity and finds a third, fourth, or fifth way to circumvent avoidable difficulties.[26] Or at least it remembers the negative consequences if hurtful decisions have to be made, in order to compensate for them later on in a kind of "post facto" justice. This attitude does not render steadfastness superfluous but supplements it with imagination and creativity, thus setting it apart constructively from stubbornness. Firm adherence to principles and a pedantic insistence on them are two very different qualities.

Finally, it is not enough to restrain oneself so as not to harm others (although this is difficult enough and often violated). We need an attitude of active, "offensive" responsibility and solicitude, an attitude that understands better than before that we live de facto in and from relationships that we need to cultivate psychically and socially. As the well-known American social philosopher Michael Walzer has said, until now we have spent too much time thinking about competition and social formations and too little time thinking about solidarity and trust.[27]

EXPANDING THE LIBERAL CONCEPTION OF AUTONOMY

Our conception of autonomy and self-understanding must change and broaden: from what Pamela Conover calls an "I identity" to a "we identity." This need not remain a moralizing postulate. Conover's comparative empirical studies—representative polls in Great Britain and the United States—have shown that the ideal type of the "I identity," the extreme case that emphasizes independence and is not concerned with overall responsibility, accounts for less than 15 percent of the population in both countries, while more than 40 percent tends to assign itself to a "we identity." Those in the latter group experience themselves as "interdependent," which means that they live in relationships on which they depend and toward which they are oriented. As a result, they tend to emphasize an attitude of responsibility and solicitude. They consider it important to have some feeling for those around them. Personal experiences are very important to the development of such a self-conception (though a self-conception is not yet that same thing as acting accordingly). In a "healthy community" these experiences promote civic behavior that is also emotionally linked to the community and practices sympathy, helpfulness, a sense of duty, civic courage, and personal responsibility. Anyone who has followed the discussion about feminist theories in political science will not be surprised that this "we identity" is found more frequently among women than men, just as the new accents in civic virtues in general seem to be the result of female rather than male socialization. Yet one must not turn this into a dogma. Even Carol Gilligan, the "high priestess" of the female revolt against a narrow-minded male conception of ethics and morality, has emphasized that while the "different" view of responsible behavior and social ethics tends to arise from female experience, that is not always or necessarily the case, and it is therefore not bound to gender.[28]

The goal in defining a contemporary civic ethos and its psychic "underlining" is to expand and thereby change the outmoded conception of autonomy. Until now, civic virtue tended to revolve around individual independence and rationality. Now it needs to be broadened by including the insight (already found in Aristotle) that our basic dependence on society is necessary and valuable and by recognizing that emotions have value in providing understanding and motivation. The more male tendencies toward separation and individuality must absorb the more female appreciation for bonds and differentiated emotionality (and overcome their fear of these qualities, which is to some extent evidently created in early childhood). Dependence need not be negative: as a sense of personal belonging it can bestow on us a precious feeling of security and fulfillment.[29]

Conversely, women must learn to contain their fears of independence and the loss of personal ties and recognize the benefits of independence and rational argumentation, both in personal communication and in public debate. What we are talking about is a reciprocal supplementation and enrichment of different experiences of socialization. This would benefit not only a new political ethos of communality (without the loss of individual self-determination!) but also a better understanding in personal relations between the sexes, which are not doing so well.[30]

Because it would facilitate communication and understanding and because the orientation toward relationships could occur more spontaneously, such an integration of the two types of socialization would be one possible way of freeing the necessary new civic virtues of their repressive and "preachy" character ("You don't just have rights, you also have duties!"—well, of course, but perhaps one might even like to fulfill them). Instead of people being oppressed, they would be encouraged and liberated to engage in spontaneous communality. This does not render superfluous self-discipline and moderation, the deferral of pleasure, and a tolerance for frustration. We must continue to work hard, life will not become easier simply because we see it through new glasses, or better, through two new glasses simultaneously. But oppressive fire-and-brimstone sermons could be replaced with encouragement and warmth, not least if it is possible to rediscover and revive emotion as the basis of spontaneous communality and mutual enrichment.

I would next like to take a closer look at the special role that feeling, "empathy," has in formulating a contemporary civic virtue and corresponding psychic dispositions.

The Value of Empathy
in Containing the Increasing Potential for Conflict

In the mid-1920s, the German philosopher Max Scheler examined the *Nature and Forms of Sympathy* and undertook a subtle analysis of "empathy," especially from the perspective of its significance for ethics and morality. He began by drawing some sharp boundaries against false expectations placed on empathy and against vague generalizations. Empathy, according to Scheler, is a spontaneous emotion, an inborn capacity, a primal phenomenon, which cannot be causally derived from anything else, let alone anything mental. In this primal nature lie its limitations but also its possibilities, its value. Empathy cannot take the place of a well-thought-out ethical system, of reflection on moral criteria. In itself, it contains no moral criteria; on the contrary, it can lead to false sympathy or cause individuals to be pulled into a false direction through suggestion (especially in a group). Moreover, empathy does not mean that one feels "one" with the object of one's feelings. On the contrary, genuine empathy feels with the person as *the other*; it feels the distinction and at the same time bridges it spontaneously. We can examine this more closely by looking at a special form of empathy, compassion: it only becomes genuine compassion (from Latin, *com* = "with" and *passio* = "suffering") if it overcomes the self-reference toward one's own suffering and turns toward the other person, if it takes the suffering of the other seriously as *her* suffering, especially if the unreflected self-experience of this suffering would not experience it as being all that painful.

Empathy, which is strongly present in genuine compassion, overcomes this egocentrism.[31]

Even though empathy is inborn and happens spontaneously, it does arise as a *reaction* and is not self-initiated. Empathy is truly practiced only if behind it stands an intention that itself must go back to a self-active, initial emotion: *love*. Love is not only reaction but action: it approaches the other person and wants to give itself to him. Although compassion, as a spontaneous reaction, cannot simply be derived from love, it depends on love's underlying strength (and thus also on the *capacity for love*) so it may be addressed at the other person not only verbally but genuinely and with consequences. On this basis, empathy can also be "expanded" beyond one's immediate circle of experience to the degree to which a person develops and seeks an understanding of the "grammar" of psychic experiences. Without love, empathy—especially beyond the most intimate sphere—does not become active, and human egocentrism cannot be overcome if empathy is not activated:

The complete overcoming of autoerotism, of egocentrism, real solipsism, and egotism, occurs only in the act of empathy. The emotional "realization" of humanity as a genus must therefore already have taken place in empathy for human love in this specific sense to be possible. That love and empathy are closely connected is also apparent from the fact that neither depends on prior distinctions between the positive or negative value of people with respect to the value of the emotions that one feels for the other. True love of humanity does not distinguish between Volk comrades and foreigners, criminals and good people, between racial worth and nonworth, education or the lack thereof, nor between good and evil and so on. Like compassion it embraces all people simply because they are human beings—but in specific distinction from animals and God.

Empathy, as compassion that is *not self-referential*, is a crucial source of the willingness to help others, which in turn is an indication that compassion is genuine.[32]

The American developmental psychologist Martin L. Hoffmann, using an empirical perspective, arrives at similar conclusions. He differentiates and breaks these conclusions down psychologically. In his systematic observations he has identified a number of developmental stages (six in all), reaching from earliest infancy to adulthood. The logic of these stages lies in the differentiation—not separation!—of feelings and understanding and of the self and the other. The older I get, but also the greater the sophistication with which I develop empathy and am encouraged to do so through my upbringing (for example, by showing concern for the suffering of others), the more reflective my empathy becomes. This means that I don't simply go along with the other person. Instead, I let empathy motivate and stimulate my judgment and actions but not guide them directly. Moreover, I am capable of extending my imagination from the present into the past and the future, so my compassion for the other person does not simply impel me to recommend the "most convenient" path to quickly alleviate her (or my own) suffering. For while empathy can motivate a person, it cannot dispense with cognitive moral judgment. In the full development of empathy, my own self-observation, in particular my careful processing of past experiences, their mental reconstruction and moral evaluation, plays a decisive role. Only this will enable me to have feelings for a great variety of people and to reconstruct their ambivalence: after all, feelings are not "logical" but often quite contradictory. Only in this way can I assume a stance toward others that is free of arrogance and characterized instead by both sympathy and distance.[33]

As we have seen (see "Without Conscience There Is No Free Society" in chapter 2), the sociologist Lothar Krappmann had already recognized a clear connection between personal and social integration from a sociological and sociopsychological perspective. The better human beings integrate themselves — that is, process their experiences and thus form a differentiated personal identity — the better they are able to understand others and bring them together.

The American sociologist and political scientist Daniel Lerner, in a classic pioneering work on the end of traditional societies (*The Passing of Traditional Society*), demonstrated several decades ago that empathy is an important skill for understanding other people and being able to orient oneself in complex situations that are not easily grasped or instantly familiar. To him, empathy meant neither sympathy nor antipathy, but the ability to put oneself in the place of others in unaccustomed situations and create a consensus.[34]

My *feelings* are important in this in order to awaken my sensitivity to others in the first place, which then triggers my sense of responsibility and desire to help. However, feeling will do this only if it is not stuck in the "intermediate stage" of compassion as self-pity but returns to the other person and thereby reveals both the shared elements and the differences. The kind of "role taking" that is often called for, the ability "to think from the standpoint of everyone else" that Kant demanded in his *Critique of Judgment* (characteristically enough on a cognitive level!) and that Hannah Arendt takes further in her reflections *On Judging*, requires compassion, both as a motivation and to gain a differentiated understanding of the situation of the other person. If this empathy has not been deadened but nourished, bystanders are also more likely to feel that their sense of responsibility and willingness is activated, and they themselves are prevented from simply looking the other way.[35]

Empathy motivates feelings of guilt, encourages a person to act fairly, and invigorates the sense of justice, which suffers if others are worse off. We know this from the experience of "survivor's guilt." But the feeling of guilt does not always have such a positive and constructive effect. It can also confuse a person (e.g., when small children are overloaded and overwhelmed with guilt feelings), degenerate into egocentric pleasure, paralyze a person if it is not clarified, trigger fear, and expose the bearer to manipulation. This happens much more readily if there is no opportunity to clarify guilt and to "work it off." Observations in nursery schools have shown that guilt feelings are prolonged if children are not given the opportunity to repair the harm they did.[36]

If human beings are unable to rid themselves of guilt they feel "worthless" and weak. This also makes it hard for them to recognize themselves as the cause of harm inflicted on others, and they are tempted to push the guilt onto their victims in order to cast off their own burden. Empathy will thus trigger compassion, a sense of responsibility, and helpful behavior. The resultant guilt feelings will be constructive and strengthen human bonds only if these feelings are clarified and do not confuse, overwhelm, or paralyze people. If they remain unclarified and cannot be resolved or "redeemed," they promote aggression against oneself and others. They turn empathy from its orientation toward fellow human beings into the opposite.

There is much to support the notion that the destruction of the emotions in Germany—the emotional frigidity in familial socialization since the Empire [1871–1914] (emotions were suppressed and not cultivated into refined feelings) as well as vague guilt feelings imposed by a culture of a rigid, hostile conscience—was one important prerequisite for the fact that so many Germans allowed themselves to be manipulated by communal demagoguery in the interwar period. Similarly, the destruction of the emotions was a precondition of the fact that some years later the threshold for participation in crimes was low and that many at first watched and then, when they noticed the suffering caused by the regime they supported, looked the other way. For individuals who are trying to "endure" criminal situations (a very plausible psychological interpretation, which I tried to outline in chapter 4), separating the emotions plays a central role. And this act of separation was further reinforced by this experience. The silencing of guilt after 1945 once again promoted the separation of feelings among the generation of perpetrators, with comparable destructive consequences for the next generation. Empathy as a central source of personal relationships as well as democratic responsibility and solidarity has a difficult time in Germany. The silencing of guilt has damaged empathy further, in many people destroying it beyond recognition.

And yet we need empathy more than ever—not only in Germany—to disentangle the increasing and ever more complex conflicts and to preserve human cohesion in liberty. To be sure, empathy is tied to individual experiences, which makes the famous American political scientist Robert Dahl skeptical that it can be "universalized" beyond small social units, especially when outsiders are felt to be threatening. Empathy is therefore not simply a secure resource or a technical device that is always ready for use. It needs to be nurtured, developed, and carefully promoted, which makes it all the more important to indicate very clearly the structural or attitudinal obstacles that are in its way and threaten to crush it. Silenced guilt is such an obstacle, a very troublesome and oppressive one.

We must try to overcome this silence. We must reawaken, in our language and in public debate, the sense that language can promote or destroy empathy, thereby supporting or harming communality, as the American political scientist Benjamin Barber has emphasized. We can observe this every day in concrete decision-making procedures and especially in the manner in which they are prepared. Anyone who has ever held a management position knows that decisions are made in the most harmonious way, and then actually implemented, in a climate that is characterized by mutual empathy, by an inherent fairness sensed by all parties, and by the trust that grows out of this.[37]

Before I examine this second central source for contemporary civic virtue, trust as trust in oneself and others, I shall address the significance of the basic normative consensus in solving political conflicts.

Politics in a Climate of
Growing Uncertainties: The Renewal of Trust

In theory there is no problem: who would publicly contradict the fundamental values of our democracy, "liberty, justice, and solidarity"? Who would deny that our policies should be measured against them? But who really cares? Who conforms to these statements?

The basic problem of this consensus on values is not in the theory but in the fact that it is not really alive in the consciousness and feel-ings of the citizens, that there are many whose actions it does not guide. Instead, it degenerates into a rhetorical ornament, even if it is regularly invoked, especially against political opponents. We know that we cannot simply postulate the consensus theoretically since a compelling cross-cultural, theoretical, or metaphysical legitimation no longer exists. In-stead, we must come together time and again in this consensus, per-haps even finding our way there through conflicts, and we must do so publicly. This consensus will act as a "living convention" only if we "come together" in it genuinely and out of conviction.[38] Preaching does not help and threats do not help. What does help?

One answer is awakening and preserving common experiences, for example, experiences of (or myths about) the establishment of the po-litical community. This could also be strengthened through symbolic acts, ceremonies, and the ritual recollection of community-building insti-tutions (e.g., Constitution Days). Joint political activities and agreements could also promote solidarity about basic values, even — or especially — if conflicts have to be overcome in the process. But this is easy only if the experiences are pleasant or the conflicts are resolved well.[39]

Much more difficult and necessary is the communal processing and evaluation of painful experiences, especially if they were culpable experi-ences. In those cases, people want nothing more to do with them. Yet if one could muster the strength to confront them in spite of this it would offer special opportunities for a truly vibrant basic consensus. For the agreement over the basic consensus would have passed through the "acid test" of personal insults, hurt feelings, and self-examination. It would have required honesty and would go deeper and motivate more strongly. This agreement, first and foremost, would make us once again aware of the meaning of responsibility and, if it came about, would make us capable of assuming responsibility. The final chapter of this book will examine the conditions that can promote it. It will focus on this question: how can we together overcome the silencing of guilt?

To return to our opening question: how can we defuse the potential for conflict? Although we must have traditional institutions of conflict reso-lution and must participate in them, more importantly we need "better" citizens, that is, a renewal and broadening of the civic ethos and a re-vitalization of our basic normative consensus. What this implies is not so much the morally rigid virtues of the republican tradition, but a strength-ening of the understanding of liberal autonomy. At the same time, autonomy must be broadened and changed: we must incorporate the capacity to enter into relationships and empathy into the notion of autonomy and transcend the traditionally restricted focus on individuality and rationality.

The increasing uncertainties that make political decisions ever more difficult affect our information, our criteria of judgment, and our psychic well-being. These uncertainties are interwoven with the growing potential for conflict in modern, pluralistic societies. It is nothing new to politics that we must make decisions and act under conditions of uncertainty. But the situation is much worse now. The traditional remedy against the paralysis that can be caused by uncertainty is trust. In the wake of the modernization of society and the resultant complexity and lack of clarity, the importance of trust has been increasingly recognized on an analytical level. Niklas Luhmann attributes to trust the function of "reducing complexity," and he is right: trust makes the stage on which we must act easier to survey and it facilitates decision making.

Trust has fulfilled this function since time immemorial, as faith in God or the gods. In the Judeo-Christian tradition, faith in God means trust in the personal pledge of His love, His truthfulness, His care, and, finally, our redemption through Him. Faith as trust thus describes a personal attitude in a personal relationship—trust is, first of all, a personal category. Even in earliest times, trust as faith served to reduce complexity and uncertainty: anxiety about the unforeseeable, vague fears, a lack of orientation, a sense of being lost, the feeling of being at the mercy of the powers of nature and fate.

In the worldly realm of human interaction, trust also described a personal ability and the quality of a personal relationship, which—speaking as a political scientist—can extend to institutions as the solidification of relationships. In the interpersonal realm as well, trust builds on the voluntary dependability of the other person or persons, their truthfulness, rectitude, competence, loyalty, willingness to engage others, and solicitude. Some believe that the root source of the capacity for trust is a so-called primal trust, which is often attributed to healthy mother-child relationships.[40] It appears that children who grow up with reliable, loving parents are in turn challenged and encouraged to engage in reciprocity and for their part develop the capacity for trust and trustworthiness. In other words, they become reliable, genuine partners. We are not entirely certain about this theory, but there does appear to be a clear genetic and systematic connection—in the sense of a positive loop—between trust in others and trust in oneself.

In the history of ideas (e.g., in John Locke), trust is simultaneously a theoretical and practical pillar of liberal democracy. However, trust must not be blind, it needs to be combined with control that is based on personal experience and is institutionally secured. Still, trust plays an eminent and foundational role. Its counterpart, mistrust, leads not to liberal democracy but to the Leviathan of Thomas Hobbes, who is entitled to rule over individuals with absolute power.[41] In Locke too, we find a combination of trust in persons and trust in institutions. Mustering trust was less of a problem back then: in Locke's day, politics was territorial and its effective sphere and tasks were manageable. The goal and duty of politics was to achieve a peaceful coordination of private interests rather than satisfy the needs of highly differentiated and interdependent societies.

Where in our present times of insecurity can we find the trust to act? In other words, how can we regain the capacity for political action?

"Social Capital" as the Foundation of Democratic Cooperation

Two interesting and recent empirical studies demonstrate the systematic connection between trust and the capacity for political action. At the same time, they pursue the question of how trust, especially trust in institutions, can be regained in those places where it does not exist or has been lost. Ellinor Ostrom studied the creation of a number of small communal institutions, primarily irrigation systems and fisheries, all over the world—in Switzerland, Spain, the Philippines, Sri Lanka, California, and Nova Scotia. She discovered that the personal experiences of the participants, their personal contributions to solving problems, and the shared norms that evolved on their own and "horizontally" in the process (and were not handed down from the top) were a constructive and valuable part of the functioning of these institutions and that a dictate "from the top" had a very dysfunctional and destructive effect. Continual cooperation—that is, secure, mutually advantageous, and trustworthy engagement—created a "social capital" whose yield is impossible to overestimate.

Ellinor Ostrom tried to discover the conditions under which this kind of social capital can be created: the participants are clearly identified (not everybody can take part sometimes and drop out at other times); the spheres of action are clearly defined; the participants live in a common neighborhood, which means they can observe and supervise what is going on; the violation of agreements is punished. Cooperation is introduced gradually, and the "surrounding political regime" plays a significant role. The personal contribution of reliability and the monitoring of reciprocal behavior go hand in hand and lead to conditions of trust, which in turn promote cooperation. Without control, without monitoring, and without sanctions it wouldn't work.[42]

Robert D. Putnam chose Italy as his "laboratory" and studied the highly diverse political, social, and economic developments of the region in conjunction with all possible factors influencing them. Inspired by Ellinor Ostrom, he too arrived at the conclusion that a given political culture, and within it especially the "social capital," are especially significant. In essence, the difference revolves around a culture of trust or a culture of mistrust. The accomplishments of the political, social, and economic institutions depend crucially on the nature of the culture. Why is that the Italians—and societies in general—do not learn from the insight that trusting cooperation is to everyone's advantage? In a culture of distrust, according to Putnam, it is entirely rational to pursue personal, short-term advantage and to not muster the patience that is necessary for an investment of trust that would only "pay off" over the long term.[43] And strict authority from the top cannot replace, let alone create, trust. How then do we arrive at Ostrom's "social capital," at trusting cooperation, at small but highly productive networks?

The critical element is the reputation for honesty and reliability of those engaged in cooperation: to start cooperative politics, one has to muster trust in trust, that is, in the trustworthiness of the partners as well as in oneself. Anybody who knows himself to be unreliable and accepts himself as such will not be able to trust others and will not receive any trust for his own part.

Even though one does not or cannot know all participants in cooperative actions, it is possible to arrive at trusting collaboration. This is achieved through "third parties" whom all participants trust. That is why a few personalities of integrity can often achieve a remarkable amount, and why it "pays off" to develop oneself into a person of integrity if one is interested in constructive democratic politics. For there is a double mystery about trust: one cannot force, extort, or manipulate it. One cannot buy it. It has to arise and be freely given. And if it is wisely—and not naively—practiced, it grows and becomes stronger. Trust reinforces trust, and the "social capital," whose core it forms and which becomes productive through it, is the only capital that increases rather than diminishes through use. Trust "lubricates" cooperation and expands the available resources because participants lay the information openly on the table. Put in technical terms, social trust lowers "transaction costs." In this situation, individuals approach new challenges with more courage and try innovations.[44]

But the flip side of this positive loop is the negative loop created by a breach of trust, and even more so by a tradition of mistrust. Such negative traditions often have long-term consequences: for it is especially when people must face up to something new, unknown, and uncertain that they will instinctively fall back on past experiences, and then it becomes important what elements went into the making of these experiences. Putnam (borrowing from Douglas North) calls this the "path dependence" of political action. It shows the degree to which institutions depend on the attitudes and the past of those who manage institutions or work within them. In North's words: "Path dependence means that history matters. . . . We need to know much more about culturally derived norms of behavior and how they interact with formal rules to get better answers to such issues. We are just beginning the serious study of institutions."

Once again we find that the past is important. When it comes to the creation and formation of trust as the condition of successful political institutions, there is no "zero hour" from which we can start all over at will. If we want to reverse the negative circle—which is almost daily our cardinal task in the personal and the political spheres—then we must attempt "to have trust in trust." Since this cannot be achieved blindly, we must clarify and consciously and convincingly free ourselves from those parts of the past that have destroyed trust or are doing so to this day, instead of treating them with silence. And so, as we seek to answer the question of how we can make decisions in a climate of uncertainty and how we can regain the capacity for political action, the past catches up with us again: we must summon up the courage to confront it to regain trust in ourselves and in others, thereby accumulating "social capital" for our democracy. This is how Putnam sums up his study of Italy: "Building social capital will not be easy, but it is the key to making democracy work."[45]

Robert Dahl, like Michael Walzer, remains skeptical about whether it is possible to make trust active in geographically large polities and large-scale organizations. Dahl does recognize its central importance and hopes that it will be institutionally supported through "trusted surrogates," for example, citizen assemblies. Yet on the whole his institutional suggestions in that direction remain very general. They point to the need to advance participation step by step, oppose hierarchical and centralized solutions, and call for smaller entities and the decentralization of decision making.[46]

But these vague institutional suggestions offer us no answers to the challenges of the large scale of contemporary politics. That is the reason why Michael Walzer in the end rejects the general dissolution of state politics in favor of small cooperative networks of "civil society," even though he is sympathetic toward them. We still need the state as an institution in order to provide a valid and binding framework and to implement politics in an international context. In addition, we must not overtax people's willingness to participate politically or overburden it with illusory expectations.[47] If state politics must continue, and if the established institutions, at least insofar as they were created to represent or settle conflicts of interest, have clearly suffered a loss of trust then the critical resource that must be reinjected is "personal trust," what Robert Putnam calls the "reputation for honesty and trustworthiness." Where and how can personal trust be newly created and brought to bear?

THE POLITICAL SIGNIFICANCE
OF SUCCESSFUL FAMILY LIFE

The problem we have outlined has led liberals to reflect anew on the meaning of the family, not only its significance for personal well-being but also its role as the wellspring of social and democratic civic behavior. As Galston has pointed out: "A growing body of evidence suggests that in a liberal society the family is the critical arena in which independence and a host of other virtues must be engendered. The weakening of families is thus fraught with danger for liberal societies." It is the task of parents to help their children to become secure, independent young people who learn moderation, solidarity, and outward orientation along with tolerance, truthfulness, and an enterprising spirit. Voluntary organizations like the family, Galston maintains, are where these attitudes and this sense of responsibility can be practiced.[48]

This kind of language is unusual from the mouth of liberals. Praise for the family is part of the domain of the conservatives, whose views are often—and with some justification—dismissed since contemporary families are, in fact, frequently not the place where these virtues are being "cultivated." And when they are not such a place, the internal dynamics of the family often lead in the opposite direction. The structural conditions of family life are very bad today. I am thinking especially about the problem of reconciling family life with the demands placed on two working parents and the question of whether the family can be a genuine community of parents and children and not merely the technical and often rudimentary organization of a household. Yet if the family remains a "strategic" place to raise independent individuals and citizens, there is much that needs to change. Under these conditions, the call for a new appreciation of the family and for supportive policies is not "conservative," let alone reactionary, but very timely, innovative, and urgent. Yet it is exceedingly difficult to spell this out in detail and put it into practice because it entails a host of institutional as well as psychic and cultural transformations: from a change of the life cycle; of gender relations; of priorities (career or personal relationships? Which at what point?); all the way to insurance, housing, education, and social policies. This is not the place to examine all this in detail; suffice it to say that there is no way to avoid this task if we genuinely wish to improve the whole matter of "civic virtue."

From a theoretical and analytical perspective, it would seem appropriate at this point to summarize and clarify once again the connection between silenced guilt and the psychic dispositions and shared normative values that are essential for democracy. After all, the quality, and over the long term perhaps even the stability, of our democracy depends on the civic ethos and the basic normative consensus within society.

SILENCED GUILT AND DEMOCRACY

A conception of liberal autonomy that has been expanded to include a strong emphasis on communality and empathy is the foundation of the civic ethos we need for a liberal and reasonably just social democracy. Democrats must be able to act on their own initiative and out of their own conviction and to lead self-determined lives in private and public contexts. They must not only grant this same right of self-determination to their fellow citizens in the spirit of tolerance but actively promote it. They must be able to assume responsibility. No only must they interact with others in a spirit of moderation born from distancing personal interests, they must actively engage their fellow citizens, feel with them, and trust them in the same way they must be able to trust themselves. Only in this way can they be trustworthy, make and keep promises, understand others, and find constructive solutions or compromises for the many and varied conflicts we face.[49] The capacity for cooperation and communication, self-distance, friendliness, empathy, and the recognition of mutuality and mutual acceptance are all part of this attitude. We must have the courage to publicly advocate our opinions in a nonconformist way, which means we must not simply accommodate ourselves. We must listen and at the same time be able to take on challenges, uncertainties, and risks. We need a solid sense of self-esteem, one that includes self-criticism as well as an appreciation of and respect for others. Like us, our fellow citizens are neither angels nor devils.

Trust in our fellow citizens must not and should not be blind; control has to be possible. But the basic democratic attitude toward ourselves and others is not hostility but benevolence. The capacity for empathy and trust, which has always been a principled component of a democratic civic ethos, requires special nurturance and support because communality and security are increasingly threatened. Citizens must feel competent, that is, they must be able to take care of their private and political affairs. The feeling of powerlessness and worthlessness is diametrically opposed to a successful civic ethos.[50]

What then is the effect of silenced guilt on the psychic dispositions, values, and basis attitudes of individuals and thus on the civic ethos we are calling for?

Psychic Consequences
of Silenced Guilt: Sigmund Freud

Freud believed that guilt feelings whose causes, origins, and sometimes very existence patients were not consciously aware of constituted the core of neurotic suffering. He saw the genesis of these feelings primarily in an unsuccessful processing of the Oedipus complex. This is not the place to discuss the validity of his assumption. However, useful insights come from Freud's repeated empirical observation and theoretical articulation of a fundamental connection between unrecognized or unprocessed guilt feelings and a pathological reduction of self-esteem or self-confidence, and of the consequences that this reduction has for the psychic attitude of individuals. We read the following in the thirty-first introductory lecture on psychoanalysis (written between 1932 and 1933): "But the major part of the sense of inferiority derives from the ego's relation to its superego; like the sense of guilt, it is an expression of the tension between them. Altogether, it is hard to separate the sense of inferiority and the sense of guilt."[51]

If an individual does not observe the norms, the superego punishes the ego "with tense feelings of inferiority and of guilt." The primary result of this is anxiety: "If the ego is obliged to admit its weakness, it breaks out in anxiety—realistic anxiety regarding the external world, moral anxiety regarding the superego, and neurotic anxiety regarding the strength of the passions in the id." In his explanation of masochism, Freud further noted an almost identical closeness between unconscious guilt feelings and the desire for punishment, which he also offered as an explanation for "expectant anxiety" or "expectation of misfortune." The desire for punishment arises from the aggressiveness of conscience or the superego and is turned against the self in the form of masochism and against others in the form of sadism. Accordingly, nightmares are "wish-fulfillment by the consciousness of guilt reacting to the reprobate drive-impulse." [52] If the desire for punishment turns outward, it leads to a mechanism whereby one's own disparaged qualities or intentions are projected onto others and to the resultant search for scapegoats.

On the whole, the neurotic effects of unconscious guilt feelings—the reduction of the feeling of self-esteem, the triggering of fear, the desire for punishment, aggression toward oneself and others, and projection onto others—leads to a serious impairment of the self, which is no longer able to fulfill its function of reconciling the demands of the id and the superego in a way that is appropriate to reality. To ward off this overload, the self denies the demands of the id and segments of experienced or newly encountered reality; it splits off the unbearable demands, experiences, or components of itself. According to Freud, a person hounded by unconscious guilt feelings is therefore not "fit for reality."

Mitscherlich's "Inability to Mourn" and Other Interpretations

On the basis of the Freudian theory, Alexander and Margarete Mitscherlich further developed these notions of an unfitness for reality or "derealization" in their famous book *The Inability to Mourn* (originally published in 1970). Once again, this is not the place to present their theoretical ideas in context or give them the attention they deserve. (Briefly, the central argument is the identification of the Germans with Hitler as their ego ideal and the resultant approval of National Socialist crimes). Important for the question we are pursuing is the Mitscherlichs' assumption that the Germans did not dare wrestle with their guilt after 1945 and that they were perhaps unable to do so. The full realization that their ego ideal had deceived them and had collapsed would have invariably thrown them into depression. To avoid all of this they did not process their guilt, denying or "derealizing" the experiences of reality connected with it. As a result, after 1945 they were also fearful and selective in their engagement with new experiences of reality, which made them, right up into the 1960s, closed and unreceptive to new problems—in other words, incapable of innovation.

As a result of silenced guilt, the behavior of the West Germans is therefore shaped by denials operating on the level of the unconscious, with grave political consequences. For there is "a determining connection between the political and social immobilism and provincialism prevailing in West Germany and the stubbornly maintained rejection of memories, in particular the blocking of any sense of involvement in the events of the Nazi past that are now being so strenuously denied."

This denial impairs not only the perception of reality but also imaginative and creative solutions to conflicts, and this in turn reinforces the denial. Denial strengthens the feeling of incompetence or lack of influence and promotes prejudice. Turning one's back on an inner concern and sympathy for "one's own behavior" produces a psychological immobility "in the face of the acute problems confronting German society."[53] Nor was an emotional reconciliation with the enemies of the war possible in this climate. Instead, the lost ego ideal, Hitler, was replaced with an uncritical idealization of the Americans combined with a continuing, subliminal contempt, while an equally uncritical, racist-anti-Bolshevist image of the enemy was carried on.

Twenty-five years after their original study, Margarete Mitscherlich, following encounters with young people from the former East Germany who wanted to publicly declare their allegiance to their Hitler ideal, continued her theoretical reflections on derealization and brought them up to date. In the process, she underlined the compulsive repetition that one can observe in situations of denial and repression.[54]

Tilmann Moser, who comes from the school of the Mitscherlichs, criticized their theory on the basis of his own experiences as a psychoanalyst. Moser found fault with the conflation of psychoanalytical and morally judgmental statements as well as with the unreflective transition from insights derived from individual psychology to sociopsychological statements about "national character." Regarding our question about the consequences of silenced guilt, he not only rejects the Mitscherlichs' call for grief (one cannot morally demand grief) but also doubts that grief over the murder of the Jew was something one could have expected psychologically. After all, even before the Holocaust the Germans had expelled the Jews from their "environment of fellow human beings." More likely, shame and despair would have been the appropriate reactions, but empirically the capacity for grief and shame was presumably exhausted in the vast majority of Germans by grief for their family members.

One should also bear in mind, Moser argues, that the "archaic guilt feeling" over the Holocaust and the war against the Soviet Union had the effect that the Germans saw the bombings, the collapse of their country, the expulsions from eastern territories, and the many dead "as an equally archaic punishment" that they "had just barely survived." However, all of this was a largely unconscious process, in the same way that the accusations by the Allies were taken as punishment. The Mitscherlichs did not mention these dimensions of the punishment. And Moser does not "tally them up" against the guilt of the Germans (especially since they were not preceded by any remorse and atonement on their part). His critique, however, does relativize the Mitscherlichs' clear-cut interpretation of the rejection of guilt, though Moser himself offers no theory of his own. Moser also points out that in therapeutic terms—and thus implicitly also in analytical and diagnostic terms—the Freudian approach offers little help for dealing with denial and derealization as a result of unprocessed guilt. After 1945, Freudian psychoanalysis saw itself, rightfully, on the side of the persecuted, and it was not prepared "to offer the petrified perpetrators room for changes in their identity of victimhood and justification." [55]

On a theoretical level, one could conclude from Moser's therapeutic experiences and reflections that unprocessed, silenced guilt, as an unconscious "compensatory feeling" of archaic guilt and punishment, *does* entail a "petrifaction" of the perpetrators, that is, a lack of empathic ability.

Once Again: Damaged Offspring

In his rich and thoughtful book *The Mask of Shame*, León Wurmser, once again on the basis of Freudian theory, has pointed urgently to the connection between guilt and shame and the quality of political life: "Shame and guilt cause direct conflicts; they themselves can be seen as the result of the struggle of inner forces; they play a decisively important role in all unconscious internal struggles, and we cannot imagine the unceasing play of external, conscious conflicts without them, not only on an individual level, but in the life of entire cultures, societies, and political forces." [56] To distinguish guilt and shame, Wurmser defines guilt as "the fear of inner condemnation" and shame as "the fear of external condemnation." One aspect that is important to our question of democratic theory is the thought, only hinted at by Wurmser, that guilt creates a fear of shame, which can give rise to a tendency to concealment or conformism. Moreover, through the shame effect, guilt burdens not only those who are themselves guilty but also those close to them and who identify with them, especially their children: "One becomes ashamed not merely of one's own personality but also of one's family, of a friend, or of one's ethnic group or nation, very akin to 'borrowed guilt.' 'Because of the pervasive and specifically unalterable character of experiences of shame, shame for one's parents can pierce deeper than shame for oneself, and a sense of continuity with one's parents is correspondingly important.'"[57] Of theoretical importance are also Tilman Moser's observations concerning the continuation of the guilt effect in the generation following the perpetrators. Rage, a desire for persecution, shame with regard to the parents, and the wish (in the words of Gabriele von Arnim) "not to be the offspring of guilty parents"—all this strikes Moser as noticeable and plausible. The "pressure of suffering" that Mitscherlich found lacking was "at least handed down to the second generation," which was often incapable of facing up to its family past without therapeutic help. Moser then adds the "conjecture that the present-day psychotherapeutization of society may very well have something to do with the subterranean processes by which the Holocaust guilt was handed on, as well as with the responsibility for war and the collapse of the nation."[58] So far, Moser believes, psychoanalysis has been unable to acquire the competency to grasp this theoretically with greater clarity. Only the 1980s saw the emergence of a climate in which it was possible to speak publicly about fear, shame, and guilt and to systematically evaluate the findings by looking at test cases of therapies with children and grandchildren of victims and perpetrators. Theoretical work in this regard is therefore in its infancy. It can only develop if the silence is overcome.

Still, it is quite obvious how important for the political culture of democracy is this continuation of guilt in the next generations. Feelings of shame not only follow from guilt feelings; they also exert an important influence on the attitudes of individuals because—like guilt—they induce feelings of inferiority, in particular, feelings of failure, helplessness, and weakness. Wurmser has noted that "shame emerges particularly in those family relationships that are involved in mutual power struggles and degradation."[59] That being the case, it is reasonable to surmise that silenced guilt—with its consequences of feelings of inferiority, a desire for punishment, and projection onto others—further intensifies such power struggles and attempts at degradation within families, and qualitative empirical studies have in fact confirmed this (see chapter 4).

Moreover, the identification with guilty parents can also have other consequences in the next generation. According to Paul Parin, children have essentially two ways of reacting: identifying with the soul-blindness of the parents or rebelling. Identification with the parents, as Rolf Vogt has also noted, urges children to defend against everything that could deeply upset the parents or people who are close because of the burden of their barbaric deeds. New and vague anti-Semitic emotions, for example, are based on a corresponding "narcissistic protection against having one's feelings hurt."[60] This is only one of the reasons why there are serious doubts about Daniel Goldhagen's assertion that the Germans underwent a radical change after 1945.

But even rebellion as an alternative reaction does not guarantee an end to guilt and shame if it gets stuck in moralizing reproaches that do not express critical solidarity but, once again, "rejection. In that case, it prevents self-reflection and turns the other into a scapegoat who should be driven into the desert."

"The sons no longer want to live with the shame that hides itself behind their backs." And we have not yet found the "son who acknowledges that this is how it was, whether the father is silent, lies, or cries. The kind of son who has grown up and seeks his own way does not seem to exist, or not yet."[61] As we have seen, the effects of unprocessed guilt on the next generation are shame as a feeling of helplessness, false identification, and dependence on the parents, even in rebellion against them.

Empirical psychologists, who do not base themselves on Freudian theory, have also noted a connection between the sense of self-esteem and guilt feelings. Erich Witte, invoking Ickes and Layden, notes that human beings tend to reject responsibility in a situation of negative experiences in order to maintain a positive sense of self-esteem. Conversely, psychic wholeness and the development of a positive sense of self-esteem depend "on the positive evaluation of one's own person as measured by criteria such as just, helpful, smart, and so on." Geppert and Heckhausen maintain that "guilt feelings stimulate many thoughts about the crime. Plans are devised to set everything right again." Evidently, they were thinking about conscious guilt feelings. For elsewhere the authors present observations in which one can hardly detect evidence for a link between guilt feelings and altruistic behavior. With reference to Lynd, they see a connection between "shame and feelings of helplessness and a loss of control," which would promote a rather passive and even depressive behavior.[62]

In distinguishing between guilt and shame, Geppert and Heckhausen offer this elaboration of the concept of loss of self-esteem through guilt feelings: "While guilt feelings lead to self-contempt and self-hatred, shame leads to social anxiety." Since guilt is a matter of personal conscience, there is "no escape" from it, unlike shame, which is tied to external perceptions. However, culpable behavior does not always trigger *feelings* of guilt, namely, if empathy for the victims is lacking. This observation is important from the perspective of democratic theory because a person who has no feelings of guilt after culpable actions is evidently not capable of empathy.[63]

Finally, there is another finding of empirical-psychological observations that is illuminating for our purposes: individuals who reject their guilt have a tendency to associate with rigid groups that are built on the moral justification of their members and to close themselves off against the outside world.

If we summarize the observations and theories presented here, they all share a number of salient insights: unprocessed (unconscious, suppressed, or causally misunderstood) guilt feelings, what I call "silenced" guilt, damage a person's sense of self-esteem and self-respect. They produce anxiety, aggression, a desire for punishment, projection, and a search for scapegoats. They promote expectations of misfortune, make people unfit for reality, and further denial and derealization. They block empathy, creativity, and conflict management that is capable of compromise, and they close off a person's sensitivity to new problems, in part because he or she is unconsciously absorbed in the past. Through open or latent feelings of shame, they provoke—especially among the next generation—a sense of helplessness, depression, blind identification, or nonindependent rebellion. The contrast to the democratic civic ethos is clear: damage to or loss of self-esteem and self-respect contrast sharply with trust in oneself; fear, aggression, projection, the search for scapegoats, and the desire for punishment are set off from trust in others, sympathy, openness, and tolerance; expectations of misfortune contrast with confidence in the future; a lack of fitness for reality, denial, and derealization oppose openness toward new experiences, mental flexibility, and the willingness to innovate; the blocking of empathy, creativity, and conflict management capable of compromise contrast with partnership, friendliness, peaceableness, and the willingness to engage in debate; feelings of helplessness and depression are set against a sense of competence and confidence; blind identification and nonindependent rebellion oppose psychic independence and a reflective distance towards one's own position; and closing oneself off in homogeneous groups based on self-justification contrasts with an open, pluralistic society, whose cohesion also requires overlapping loyalties.

Democracy and "Self-Esteem"

These findings are corroborated by a very different realm of experiences, those of the United States. In 1975, the psychologist and democratic theorist Paul M. Sniderman published a comprehensive theoretical and empirical study entitled *Personality and Democratic Politics*. In it, he subjected the link between personal character traits and political attitudes or values to a searching examination. Sniderman stands, and sees himself as standing, in the tradition of American research on "democratic personality" and its opposite, the authoritarian personality (Adorno). But he goes far beyond that tradition in his integration of various theoretical approaches and in the subtle and comprehensive nature of his empirical observations.

In the process, the very concept of "personality" itself is repeatedly questioned conceptually, specified, and reformulated. For in empirical terms, so-called psychological personalities are not closed off, definitive, and internally homogeneous types who are fundamentally or entirely different from one another. That is why Sniderman tries to analyze the interplay of traits, their interdependencies, openness, and gradualism, but also their not entirely coincidental concurrence. Personalities as hermetic, stereotyped types do not exist. Psychic dispositions are created by an interplay of internal propensities and drives, social constellations, and personal—often idiosyncratic—experiences. We humans can be influenced when it comes to our character; we are subject to changes and do not follow a straightforward causality of factors or characteristics.[64]

But the combination of basic attitudes that we develop is by no means purely arbitrary. That is why Sniderman speaks of a complex, an interwoven context of individual attitudes and dispositions, all of which together do create a specific picture and influence or reinforce each other.[65] This gives rise to the superficial impression of a type.

The questions that guided Sniderman's study are these: Why do so many people take on democratic values? Why do they participate politically in democracy (possibly even in leadership positions)? What stands in the way of this kind of democratic participation? In answering these questions, he points to either a supportive or an obstructive complex of character traits, whose strategic center he locates in "self-esteem." Self-esteem is defined through the cluster of traits that it infuses and from which it receives influences. It includes these very important qualities: self-respect, a sense of self-worth, self-confidence, confidence in the future, the ability to learn, tolerance, a feeling of competence, and the basic attitude of perceiving and approaching obstacles as positive challenges and not as threats.[66]

Interesting in our context is Sniderman's finding on the relationship to guilt that a person who is "endowed" with these qualities and a positive self-image has. While this person will not be free of feelings of guilt, she develops a tolerance toward a fundamental guilt feeling she can never get rid of. She accepts guilt as an unavoidable frustration because she always remains guilty of something. Yet this frustration (the equivalent of Karl Jaspers's "metaphysical guilt" or Martin Buber's "existential guilt") does not cause paralysis; instead, it stimulates its profitable translation into responsible behavior.[67]

Sniderman locates the strategic opposite to "self-esteem" in a vague feeling of guilt. It is central to a complex that includes—as a mirror image to the "self-esteem" complex—basic feelings of worthlessness and helplessness; of emptiness, fear, and self-contempt; of a quickness to take offense; of powerlessness and futility; and of a lack of self-control and hostility. People who live in this kind of emotional cage blame themselves for their failure, feel vaguely responsible for it, and therefore suffer from this guilt feeling—often unconsciously but decisively. In the process, reciprocal interactions occur in both complexes between the various self-attributions and feelings that reinforce one another. For example, worthlessness and failure can lead to guilt feelings, but guilt feelings can also lead to worthlessness, failure, and all the other negative emotions and self-assessments. Guilt is even closer as the causal center because in empirical terms there are more frequent direct connections between the vague feeling of guilt and the various other components of the complex than there are among the components themselves. This holds true not only for Sniderman's empirical study but also for other studies, some of which take different theoretical approaches.[68]

Incidentally, the central importance of "self-esteem" lies not merely in its significance for democracy, but also in the fact that every person has the cardinal wish to have a positive self-image. That is why "self-esteem" stands at the center of human self-understanding. What's more: *self*-understanding and with it self-assessment are closely tied to the understanding of *others*. As a general rule, if I appreciate, like, and trust *myself*, I will spontaneously appreciate, like, and trust other people.[69]

This reciprocal interconnection, a truism in psychology, is decisive in shaping the specific effects that a particular self-understanding and sense of being will have on social relationships, on politics, and on democracy. For the lower my self-esteem and so on is, the stronger is my distrust, hostility, helplessness, and vulnerability, and the greater my difficulties with personal relationships and democratic participation in politics.[70]

The Destruction of Empathy and
the Capacity for Trust by Vague Guilt Feelings

Individuals who are molded or "undermined" by guilt feelings, by feelings of worthlessness and futility, live at an emotional remove from others (out of a fear of being vulnerable). Their "personal relationships" are impersonal, they feel no warmth and cannot radiate it, they have problems with intimacy, and they keep everything on the surface—in fact, they live in isolation and in inner loneliness. Mere outward activity does not necessarily argue against this, for it represents neither genuine personal communication nor genuine political participation. We cannot prove a direct connection between the identified characteristics or attitudinal complexes, on the one hand, and the political attitudes toward values and most importantly actual behavior, on the other. Sniderman believes such a connection is highly plausible, but scientific honesty leads him to call it "an article of faith."[71] However, there is a good deal to support the notion that people who are afraid feel hostility, are vulnerable, and do not think much of solidarity or do not believe in it. They do not enter into committed political participation, let alone participation that is empathic, trusting, and communal, the sort of participation we have identified as a necessity for present-day democracies.

And there is no good reason to think that political participation as such will promote "self-esteem." Empirical findings, in any case, do not substantiate this hope, even though—under favorable conditions and given the positive and negative loop structure of the various components of the complexes—participation might nourish a cautiously sprouting self-confidence and trust and promote the establishment of a common stock of values.[72] But the reason for this does not lie in some kind of mechanical effect institutions have on attitudes. Rather, attitudes only change if the acting persons, within the framework of institutionally ordered behavior and participation, are able to learn something new and change their inner dispositions.

According to Sniderman, the capacity to learn is therefore an important prerequisite for our becoming democrats. For that reason, he examined the complexes not only from the point of view of their motivational power and the question of what the individual character traits encourage us or forbid us to do. He also analyzed their effect on the human capacity to learn. That capacity depends largely on our willingness to expose ourselves to information, on our ability to understand, and on our expectations of "reward."[73]

Even though learning also contains some measure of "accommodation" to reality and to the demands of the social and political environment, it makes a difference what exactly one is supposed to accommodate oneself to. To individuals with low self-confidence and so on, it is easier—"more appropriate," as it were—to conform to the demands of a dictatorship and a totalitarian system than to those of a pluralistic democracy. For such a democracy confronts us with demands for independence, decision making, courage, and choice, skills that are difficult to learn for a fearful person, or more difficult than doing what one is told.[74] The transition from dictatorship to democracy is more difficult than the reverse.

To that extent, there is evidently a specific affinity between self-esteem and democracy; conversely, there is a specific and stark opposition between vague guilt feelings or silenced guilt and democracy. Lübbe's strategy of transforming Nazi supporters or followers into democrats by having them conform to democratic institutions and public rhetoric, with no regard for or change in their "internal condition," will not work. The interior state of being must be specifically addressed and changed; Nazi supporters or followers will not become democrats on their own simply by imitating official democratic guidelines.

But democratic participation does offer a chance for transformation. Previous supporters of dictatorship need not *remain* mendacious and hypocritical (as Hannah Arendt found the Germans to be), not if the creation of new institutions goes hand in hand with inner transformations, or at least if the latter follow the new constitution from an impulse all their own. The psychic structure of human beings is not closed, and it is simultaneously of central importance in determining which values people will adopt and which they will not. As such, it is also essential to the creation and preservation of a basic normative consensus in democracy. And this psychic structure is influenced—and thus influenceable—by the public that surrounds it, and especially by the intimate atmosphere in which it lives, not so much by social status as by personal life experiences and encounters.[75]

If self-esteem has such a central and positive effect on the psychic and normative equipment of a democratic citizenry, if vague and silenced guilt has such a central and negative effect, and if silenced guilt has such strategic importance in destroying or damaging our capacity to democracy, the question inevitably arises: How can we overcome the silence?

7

Overcoming Silence Together

THE RESULTS OF OUR FINDINGS

We have arrived at the following conclusion: the way in which individuals determine guilt and deal with it on a practical level expresses their fundamental self-understanding as well as their relationship to their fellow human beings and, where appropriate, to a transcendental authority, God.

For the sake of a peacefully ordered life together, human beings have drawn a distinction between good and evil since time immemorial. Although the content of this distinction has been expanded and relativized over the course of history, a core of traditional morality exists to this day. We find it, first, in the experience and formal definition of guilt as a rupture of relationship to God, to fellow human beings, and to oneself; second, in the concrete commandments to show mutual respect for our physical and psychic integrity, to stand up for the weak and the needy, to care for one's "neighbors," and to love them as one does oneself.

Since ancient times people have experienced transgressions against this core content, that is, guilt, as a heavy burden. This burden threatens to destroy the sense of self-esteem, and people therefore seek to rid themselves of it. Methods of relief such as the rejection of responsibility or various forms of blindness toward one's own acts appear to be easier than a clear-sighted engagement with guilt; they are therefore more readily resorted to and frequently practiced. Yet they bring no real liberation from guilt, for instead of "clarifying" it they cover it in silence.

Using the experiences with National Socialism as a test case allowed us to analyze the empirical manifestation of silenced guilt and define it more precisely. We discovered that silenced guilt describes the silencing of the clash between actions and norms, not only at the time the acts occurred, but also subsequently. It describes the refusal to acknowledge one's guilt and take responsibility for it. Part of silenced guilt is the silencing of the reasons why this clash of actions and norms occurred. It also includes the refusal to subject oneself to an honest self-examination, to bring to mind one's standards of values and one's freedom, to acknowledge one's responsibility and fundamental capacity for guilt not simply in general terms, rhetorically and half-heartedly, but consciously, clearly, and in reference to concrete cases. Silenced guilt is at the same time and above all the guilt of silence, the abandonment of conscience and personal identity. One can recognize this in a number of specific forms of behavior by those who maintain this silence.

Central importance in all of this attaches to the splitting off of emotion: it is a primary reason why a person becomes guilty, a condition for the elimination of conscience during the act, and finally the precondition and result of the subsequent silence. Silenced guilt has a destructive effect in a variety of ways. It damages a person's sense of self-esteem and self-confidence, sometimes to the point of destroying them. It "amputates" important parts of the personalities of the perpetrators and creates a cold, distanced, and mistrustful atmosphere in their personal relationships, especially their families. It impairs or blocks the ability of subsequent generations to develop whole and integrated personalities, capable of taking on responsibility on their own, and capable of working and loving and forming stable personal relationships. It is no coincidence that the Germans—compared to other European nations and the United States—are a nation with a striking lack of warmth and trust toward themselves and others.

These effects have consequences for democracy, for its quality and in the long run undoubtedly also for its stability. For in the German case one can discern, even against the backdrop of an essentially positive state of democratic stability, considerable deficiencies in the liberal sense of community and responsible solidarity. We can attribute these deficiencies with a high degree of plausibility to silenced guilt.

In the future, liberal democracy will depend increasingly on the capacity to establish communities in the face of a rising potential for conflict and on hardworking cooperative politics in the face of the increasing uncertainties of international entanglements. Silenced guilt undermines—in an almost strategic way—all that is required: the civic ethos, the foundations of a basic democratic consensus, and everyday common sense. It destroys the citizens' self-esteem (which is necessary for democracy) and their capacity for empathy and mutual trust. It corrodes our personal and social relationships and promotes a broad internal dissolution of our liberal polity on the national and international level.

The effect of silenced guilt thus confirms age-old human experiences as expressed in ancient myths and religious traditions.

Guilt thus divides a person and society. Silencing guilt continues the division in a destructive and especially dangerous way because the ravages occur "below the surface": "Nothing is visible from the outside, everything is whole and in order."[1] But if a person is not immediately aware of the destruction and is unable to grasp clearly its causes or consequences, he will not do anything to counter it. This book is intended as an attempt to do something about it. What do we mean by overcoming guilt together, and how is it supposed to happen?

To begin with, we must define the goal of this endeavor. For the opposite of silence is not merely talk and aimless chatter. What we need to overcome is *guilt* and the destructive *split* it causes. We are thus talking about a restoration of the unity of self and of personal identity and about a new social unity, the (re)creation of a social communality. To put it more narrowly in terms of politics or political science: we must find a new *vibrant* basic consensus, build democratic "common sense," and restore (or perhaps create in the first place) our psychic abilities as individuals, which allow us to form sustainable personal relationships and live out a democratic ethos.

NORMS FOR LIVING TOGETHER
IN PEACE AND FREEDOM

Once we recognize the behaviors that promoted or caused the unspeakable crimes of the Nazi period (as well as the central failures in the East German system: lies, betrayal, breach of trust, the arbitrary and unjust destruction of psychic and physical integrity), and once we understand how the silencing of the guilt inherent in them carries on its destructive effects, we can perhaps formulate jointly what should be part of our new basic moral consensus. The murder of millions (in the Nazi era) and the destruction of personal integrity (in East Germany) was generally not done by perpetrators who consciously and single-mindedly wanted to do evil, who acted out of a lust for murder, who deliberately wanted to harm their neighbors, and who were ideologically sealed off and permanently blind to moral reality. Instead, the predominant traits were the abandonment of conscience and personal responsibility to blind obedience, the desire to participate (being part of the crowd), emotional coldness, looking the other way, thoughtlessness, and limiting one's concern to the most narrow personal welfare.

Evil arose not because people wanted evil; it arose out of indifference and a lack of empathy. Its opposite is therefore not indifference (which actually promoted evil) or the simple refusal to harm others; rather, it is a positive concern, care, altruism, and the willingness to acknowledge one's share of responsibility within the larger context. Having witnessed the experiences of National Socialism and the destructive aftereffects of guilt, we can say that this positive element of the traditional moral core is not simply something "additional," a "surplus" one could just as well leave aside without harming moral integrity. It is in fact *essential*, an indispensable part of a shared morality if we wish to prevent anything resembling the Nazi murders or the East German lies in the future.

And so Cain's answer to God's question—"Cain, where is your brother?"—offers an important clue. For Cain did not answer, "Do I have to know where my brother is?" but, "Am I my brother's keeper?" Logically, this response comes as a surprise but not ethically and psychologically, and that is the point. Cain expresses in his words that the opposite to his murder of Abel would not have been his indifference, his ignorance of Abel's situation, but brotherly care. Brotherliness, not indifference, would have prevented Cain from feeling envious of his brother Abel and killing him.

Looking back at National Socialism and recalling the murder of a young woman in New York before the eyes of her neighbors who did nothing, Telford Taylor, who succeeded Robert Jackson as chief prosecutor in the Nuremberg trial, was entirely consistent in raising this question: To what extent must we be "our brother's keeper?" In all likelihood we cannot formulate this guilt in legal terms; we can only articulate it and demand it in moral terms. This is one more reason why we should come to an explicit agreement on our basic moral consensus beyond what is legally enforceable.[2]

The conclusions we have drawn from the experiences of the past coincide not only with the biblical story of Cain and Abel, but also with the findings of contemporary democratic theory we outlined earlier: a truncated liberalism, which concentrates on protecting and demarcating an undisturbed private sphere and on preventing harm to others, is no longer sufficient if we want to survive together in peace and freedom. We also need an active desire for communality and the wish to reach out to others. Invoking the profit interests of the capitalist economy, for example, is no longer sufficient or morally tenable. It amounts to a theoretical-analytical relapse into a time before the social market economy, and it destroys our democracies. If leaders in commerce and industry "look away" when it comes to these issues they take guilt upon themselves.

How Far Does the Demand Placed on Individual Responsibility Reach?

The experience with the consequences of silenced guilt teaches us that the concrete commandment to reach out to others and expand one's concern beyond the narrow sphere of private interests is essential if we wish to survive together in freedom. From this flow a host of highly controversial and perhaps inconvenient consequences when it comes to demarcating our individual sphere of responsibility and mustering the necessary courage to take risks, if necessary, out of loyalty to our moral convictions. What is the reach of our conscience, and how loyal must we remain to it even in the face of danger? It is not wise to avoid these sensitive questions.

Yet there is strong resistance to raising the bar for responsibility and courage too high. One strand of this resistance is opposed to asking too much of people, demanding too high a moral standard from their limited nature—asking them to be heroes. This is unrealistic, the argument goes, and proves counterproductive in the end because it creates defiance and resignation. But the "reality" implied in this critique is not defined or fleshed out in greater detail; instead, it is simply taken for granted. Of course, human beings are not heroes on average, but saying that does not clarify the boundaries of what we can ask of them. Incidentally, drawing those boundaries is not an empirical but a moral decision, even for those who would tend to put the bar rather low.

And we still have not determined which demands of morality and decency prove counterproductive in the end. For example, the self-evident moral decency of the Bulgarians not to abandon their Jews to the murderous demands of the Nazis saved the vast majority of them, and it spared the Bulgarians from having to act as individuals because they were acting together.[3] In the end, it is *our* moral decision where to draw the boundary between acceptable demands on responsibility and non-responsibility. Moreover, rejecting heroism does not mean that we must all regard ourselves as cowards or villains. A broad spectrum lies between these two poles.

A second strand of the argument against excessive moral demands imputes a kind of phariseeism to those who are unwilling to accept the low morality of the "average person." They are accused of raising themselves above their fellow human beings, perhaps because they can live up to their own standards, and taking it upon themselves to apply their yardstick to others. This critique is based on a double misunderstanding. Phariseeism means that I consider myself better than those around me and thank God for it: "I thank thee, O God, that I am not like the rest of men, greedy, dishonest, adulterous; or, for that matter, like this tax-gatherer" (Luke 18:11). But that is not all we are talking about here. The moral demands that are raised arise not from a hubristic sense of self, but from the consequences we must draw from the past experiences of suffering. Negating these demands amounts, conversely, to the conscious acceptance of the fact that such suffering repeats itself. And raising such moral demands does not entail an elevation of self but an inconvenient self-obligation, for, indeed, without embarrassing ourselves we cannot invoke an ethical system from which we simply exempt ourselves. Whether we actually live up to that system is very much an open question. The moral demand contains first of all only the obligation to make the effort—and it contains a great risk. We would rather not take that risk, understandably enough, and so the bar for the normal citizen is placed rather low. Whatever goes beyond that is admired and at times is shifted into the realm of aesthetics as something "beautiful" (although aesthetics, of course, carries its own ethical implications, something we have known even before Kant's *Critique of Judgment*).

To be sure, the objections I have presented do contain a seed of truth. We can put the bar too high and then fall. We can also secretly consider ourselves better with our moral demands, but if we do so we feel our insincerity. Precisely where we should draw the boundary for a minimum standard of responsibility and courage that is valid within a polity is a question of voluntary agreement and habituation. If there were no room for movement on this matter everything would always have to stay the way it is, and our prospects would be grim. Perhaps they are.

This much, at least, we can say: both the fact that we should listen to our conscience at all (the first basic requirement of a moral life) and that conscience includes the basic norms of mutual respect and care for one another follow as a plausible conclusion from the painful experiences of silenced guilt. This conclusion is less trite than one might assume— after all, Hitler was explicitly intent on revolutionizing the centuries-old "Jewish" morality of conscience.[4] And although the call for conscience provides uplifting experiences in public speeches on formal occasions, in everyday discourse it tends to strike people as unpleasantly moralizing.

Conscience is indeed a very old-fashioned thing. How can we overcome the silence to heal the fractures within us and within our society?

ARTICULATING GUILT

The familiar path known to us from tradition (especially of the great religions) embraces the stages of admission, contrition, changing one's ways, repentance (or atonement), and restitution in order to attain reconciliation. Is that path still valid today? If so, what form could it take? How could a renewal of our basic consensus, of our common sense, follow from this path?

In the great religions, the stages of a genuine liberation from guilt are coupled to the belief in God and in God's forgiving and reconciling love. That is why in the ancient Greek understanding there was no escape from guilt understood as a fateful tragedy. The prevailing attitude in the secular world today tends to be that we are at our own disposal, and oftentimes people escape into the "Greek" tragedy of contextualized guilt. Faith in God's forgiving love is much rarer now. Must we therefore simply do without liberation from guilt?

Nicolai Hartmann proudly argued and demanded precisely that: "Being guilty for an evil deed cannot be taken from anyone because it is inseparable from the guilty person." [5] It is indeed an open and very urgent question whether we can still deal with our guilt in a liberating way in this day and age without the perspective of the transcendental and without faith in God. This is the much more far-reaching and quite disquieting dimension of the problematic connection between politics and guilt that I have tried to address in this book. And in the final analysis it is this dimension that concerns me.

Admission as Reconstruction:
Alternatives Did Exist

Hinderk Emrich, laying aside any transcendental and religious preconditions and following Sigmund Freud and Michael Theunissen, has developed a model of "correct" forgetting that is neither repressive nor destructive. This model gives secular form and validity to *admission* as an inner process that clarifies the past to oneself. One must be able to forget in a good way to avoid being depressively submerged by the past's sway over the present and the future and to go on living creatively. This good forgetting presupposes and simultaneously constitutes a mindful remembering. Remembrance knows that the picture we draw of our past always contains value judgments. We are inclined to eliminate those events in which our self-image and our ego ideal diverge too drastically. But doing so causes us to forget badly: we repress, deny, and split things off. What we must seek to do instead is to reconstruct the past, especially in its sensitive points, not only in terms of the way it actually happened but also in terms of the alternatives that would have been possible. If we bring these alternatives to mind, often with great difficulty and sometimes with help from others, we can recognize how much broader the possibilities were and why we made the choice we did (for example, a morally false one). As Michael Theunissen has said, this allows us to break free from well-set ways, to be more creative for the future, and— as Emrich hints at without elaborating-to learn how to do things differently and better in the future. Only then can we "check off" what was wrong and forget in peace. This "actualizing deactualization," a psychological version of the *contritio cordis* (inner contrition), reconciles us to the conflict-laden elements of our selves that disturb our self-image. But those elements that are to be "erased" must first be activated and become known. However, the purely formal process of reconstructing the past (though it demands radical honesty) is not sufficient. In and of itself it does not relieve guilt or take the place of atonement. But by holding out the prospect of relief (in psychoanalytical terms) it "tempts" us to engage in a process of overcoming the split of individual personality, a process that is at least partly in our own hands.[6]

Still, the lump of pain and remorse over choices that were not merely technically but morally wrong and constitute guilt in the true sense remains. We must take the next steps along the path: in the form of grief over one's own failure and over the pain one has inflicted on others. We cannot simply "secularize away" this sorrow. The same is true of the step after that, the—sometimes strenuous—determination of will not to make the wrong choice again, but to truly change one's ways because it is the only way to overcome the pain of remorse.

Here is where we face a problem that has taken on the form of a vicious circle. Many people sense that they should not simply downplay their guilt permanently because that is not good for them. And so they take half a step. They practice "honesty" by openly "admitting" transgressions and failures, sometimes almost too easily and especially in too sweeping a manner. But they avoid the question of why they failed in specific situations, the painful remorse about their failure, and the genuine will to change their ways, which imposes the need for action. In this way, they can retain a remnant of "morality" and regard themselves as moral persons without truly "investing" in the process.

Perhaps behavior like this is adopted out of laziness or superficial convenience. But perhaps it is also adopted because we no longer believe in the possibility of a change of ways, a genuine transformation in ourselves or others, and because we no longer hope for reconciliation or a happy ending. Without this hope, and "disillusioned" by a public opinion that dismisses the expectation of a change of ways as rather naive, it is presumably difficult for us to muster the strength and initiative to go down the road of a genuine liberation from guilt. To be sure, it is almost miraculous to witness a person undergoing a genuine change of heart, especially if she is already older. The hope that it can happen demands perhaps as much strength of faith as the belief in God; or, to put it differently: one can only muster this hope through faith in God. This is the vicious circle in our secularized world.

But it can go the other way round. After 1945, the oldest son of Martin Bormann found the answer he had been searching for in the Christian promise that we always have the possibility of changing our ways if we follow our conscience, the promise that we are not hopelessly lost in our guilt. This answer brought him to faith and opened his life to a new beginning.[7]

There are also encouraging secular experiences of happiness that arise out of the "miracle" of a change of heart. Ralph Giordano has rightly emphasized that it is not enough to persist in a feeling of shame without obligation. Without inner sincerity we shall not arrive at the goal of redemption but will remain stuck in "inner petrifaction." Yet sometimes we have surprising and joyous experiences of genuine remorse and a change of heart:

Redemption sometimes comes unexpectedly. When it does come the dam bursts, and the torment that has been building up for decades erupts, for example, in a surge of talkativeness toward a surviving victim of Nazi persecution, not with the intent of winning absolution but simply because of the coincidence of the moment. I have witnessed this on several occasions. The unfeigned behavior, the release of tension in staggered breaths, the bewildered surprise at oneself and the gratitude for the other person's understanding—all this led to a mutual enrichment. After my liberation, there is little in life that has moved me as deeply or meant as much to me as these unorganized, unplanned confessions made in accidental encounters by people whose basic problem was their feeling of guilt.[8]

It is possible to achieve truthfulness and honesty by admitting one's own moral failure without subsequent attempts to gloss over it or obtain goodwill through false pretenses. Norbert Bobbio gave an exemplary demonstration of this by admitting bluntly to the loyal address he made to Mussolini in 1935. Not only was he able to preserve or regain his self-respect, he also offered encouragement to others and their self-respect.[9]

The Spirit of Forgiveness

Truthfulness and admission need such encouragement, especially if they have to get by without a faith in the transcendent. They show to perpetrators and victims the worldly fruits of truth and demonstrate that one *can* be honest and can *admit* to one's acts. This encouragement comes from individuals.

But all of us, as a social and political community, can contribute to encouragement and confession by creating a climate of leniency and by living in the spirit of forgiveness. Leniency and forgiveness do not mean that we see no differences, that we abolish the distinction between good and evil, lower the standards, and simply wipe guilt away. Leniency and forgiveness declare that we are willing to preserve moral demands and not forget the baseness of the deed, while at the same time making a distinction between the deed and the perpetrator and honoring a change of heart. "The spirit of forgiveness lives in the 'between' of the distinction between person and deed."[10]

This is the "between" of the essential noncongruence of the person that we identified at the beginning of the book as the foundation of conscience. We are always more than our deeds, good or bad. That is why we can become guilty in the first place: we always have the potential for something else inside of us. A good deal of empirical evidence attests that it is not only presumptuous but also unwise to deny a person this noncongruence once and for all, that is, to declare him devoid of conscience. Franz Stangl, Adolf Eichmann, Rudolf Höß—they all had a conscience. Franz Stangl probably would never have admitted his guilt without his conversations with Gitta Sereny: "I never talked to anyone like this," he told her at one point. Toward the very end he declared: "So yes . . . in reality I share the guilt. . . . Because my guilt . . . my guilt . . .

only now in these talks . . . now that I have talked about it all for the first time."[11]

In an exemplary and impressive manner Gitta Sereny conducted these conversations in the spirit of forgiveness. She never lessened her moral demands or allowed the suffering of the victims to be forgotten for even a single moment. But she did not engage her subjects out of the spirit of stigmatization. Instead, she was driven by the joint search for truth. Her interviews are suffused with the palpable intent of making it possible for Stangl to admit his guilt in the quiet confrontation with his "false options," giving room to the "between" between him and his deeds. Eventually, this allowed Stangl to admit openly what he had always "known": that the deliberate restriction of his responsibility to the "administration of valuables" in Treblinka, whose commander he was, was morally untrue and dishonest. The example also shows that a change of heart requires conversation and an open exchange. It rarely succeeds if a person is all by himself; at most, solitude can prepare the way: "It is only in confession that the self begins to acknowledge the deed."[12]

Let us assume, then, that the spirit of forgiveness rests in the "between" and in the fact that conscience cannot be abrogated, that it seeks to overcome the ruptured relationship within the self and between people through leniency. In that case, the "freeing" from the entanglement in past guilt that Bernhard Schlink proposes is wrong: he maintains that in our collective (national) identity we should "disavow" not only the "past" (thus, for instance, the crimes and the motives and attitudes that lead to them) but also the people whose individual past we will not or cannot accept into our present collective identity on moral grounds. We should decide "to reject and exclude those whose individual pasts should not be made part of the collective past." Otherwise, we share in their guilt and remain caught in the context of guilt. Of course, Schlink argues, we also take on guilt by renouncing these individuals because our renunciation does not include all those who are guilty and perhaps some who are not.[13]

I believe this is a false dilemma. For we do not become morally guilty as individual perpetrators (in analogy to legal responsibility, which Schlink invokes as a comparison) if we disavow a deed but keep the perpetrator reliably in our community and offer her, in every possible way, the opportunity to renounce her deeds. On the contrary, by doing so we promote the healing of the broken relationship within herself, that is, the overcoming of guilt. Exclusion and disavowal deepen the rupture instead of healing it; they are merely an attempt to save one's own moral skin.

They reinforce a serious deficit in general human solidarity, which was precisely one of the reasons why the guilt was incurred in the first place. Even perpetrators who show no sign of a consciousness of guilt and of remorse are not identical with their deed. This noncongruence is not created by confession but exists in principle, and we never know when the opportunity for confession will occur and whether we ourselves have done enough to make it happen.

In Bernhard Schlink's novel *The Reader* (1995), the camp guard Hanna let hundreds of captive women die horribly in a burning church. She could have opened the door, could have saved the women, had she not been so fixated on her task of effecting an "orderly" return of the camp inmates that even an elementary feeling of compassion had no power to counter it. But Hanna was not identical with her deed. During a lengthy incarceration she evidently recognized openly the mistakes in her life that had led her down the disastrous path; she had atoned and had chosen a new option. The clues in her cell after the suicide also suggest that she repented and wanted to make amends. No, there was and is no moral reason to disavow Hanna, to disavow people whose deeds we reject.

But there are many reasons for us to develop, out of the interweaving of individual and collective identity, a clear understanding of what is described as "guilt entanglement," often in rather apologetic or tragic-fatalistic terms and fundamentally with a sense of resignation. That we are all called upon to help create a climate of leniency, to live in the spirit of forgiveness and thereby make it easier or even possible for each other to admit guilt, has its deeper meaning precisely in this context of guilt in which we have always lived. The Bible brings this context to life in the metaphor of original sin. As Ricoeur has noted with regret, today we barely understand the meaning of this metaphor. Instead, we trivialize it by insisting that guilt is a thoroughly individual phenomenon and by blocking out our interdependence and reliance upon one another. We belong together in guilt not only from the feeling of humility ("Let him throw the first stone . . . "). Often times we are, unintentionally and unknowingly, the reason why another person falls into temptation and becomes guilty: for example, if we hurt another person's feelings or humiliate him and he takes it out on someone else.

What made the biblical understanding of *sin* special was precisely the connection it made between collective and individual transgression. But it does *not* follow from this connection that I need not worry about my individual share anymore. The apologetic use of the notion of entanglement promotes an attitude that we should "just forget about it" and make a clean break; it favors superficial calls for amnesty and fails to do justice to the twofold perspective of perpetrators and victims. Hence, this use is misleading and inappropriate to guilt and to the suffering that follows from it.

The spirit of forgiveness, which does *not* exclude or disavow the perpetrators for the sake of one's own moral purity, is "Janus-headed" (in Klaus M. Kodalle's vivid term): one head looks at the perpetrator; the other head looks at the victim and the violation of moral norms. This spirit does not fail to appreciate individual guilt, which is why it does not devalue individual responsibility to something exceptional that one supposedly cannot ask of the average person. How much choice, freedom, and responsibility we have or take upon ourselves depends on "how much attention, sensitivity, far-sightedness, and willingness to suffer we expect from a person" or are willing to muster ourselves.[14]

An objective measure of this does not exist. We must ask ourselves whether we have summoned enough of these qualities, and no guilt entanglement exempts us from this self-examination. For the sake of our basic normative consensus we must bring ourselves to answer the question of what we want: once more to take the risk of crimes and the pain of silenced guilt or to hazard a change of heart. The spirit of forgiveness, like Emrich's "correct" forgetting," leaves behind "traces" in the present and for the future. It helps us to learn. Along with the new basic consensus it brings us the gift of a "new normality" in which we cannot simply remain the same. The defiant cry "Leave us the way we are," which can be psychologically attributed to a lack of leniency, cannot be the final word for overcoming the silence and the individual and social fractures, the final word for a new democratic beginning.[15]

Turning Away from Dangerous Mentalities and Psychic Dispositions

In the spirit of forgiveness, it is important to reconstruct, not only individually but also communally, the path we have traveled and the alternatives that were possible because our learning and our "new normality" depend not only on the stock of values we all recognize. As we have seen in chapter 4, traditional attitudes and insidious mentalities that cannot be readily deciphered morally and shape our behavior are also part of it.

The fictive, and yet "authentic," example of Hanna in Bernhard Schlink's novel illustrates how important and difficult it is to reconstruct these mentalities and attitudes and that this reconstruction concerns not only the "perpetrators" but society as a whole. As a camp guard, Hanna accompanied one of the infamous death marches in 1945. As we noted earlier, at one point a catastrophic fire occurs in a church in which the women inmates have been locked up. Hanna could have saved them, but she "neglects" to unlock the burning church, in which the women die a horrible death. In the trial against her and other camp guards the presiding judge asks:

"Why did you not unlock the doors?"

"We were . . . we had . . ." Hanna was groping for the answer. "We didn't have any alternative."

"You had no alternative?" . . .

"We didn't know what to do. It all happened so fast, with the priest's house burning and the church spire, and the men and the cart were there one minute and gone the next, and suddenly we were alone with the women in the church. They left behind some weapons, but we didn't know how to use them, and even if we had, what good would it have done since we were only a handful of women? How could we have guarded all those women? A line like that is very long, even if you keep it as tight together as possible, and to guard such a long column you need far more people than we had." Hanna paused. "Then the screaming began and got worse and worse. If we had opened the doors and they had all come rushing out . . ."

The judge waited a moment. "Were you afraid? Were you afraid that the prisoners would overpower you?"

"That they would . . . no, but how could we have restored order? There would have been chaos, and we had no way to handle that. And if they'd tried to escape . . ."

Once again the judge waited, but Hanna didn't finish the sentence. "Were you afraid that if they escaped, you would be arrested, convicted, shot?"

"We couldn't just let them escape! We were responsible for them. . . . I mean, we had guarded them the whole time, in the camp and on the march, that was the point, that we had to guard them and not let them escape. That's why we didn't know what to do. We also had no idea how many of the women would survive the next few days. So many had died already, and the ones who were still alive were so weak . . ."

Hanna realized that what she was saying wasn't doing her case any good. But she couldn't say anything else. She could only try to say what

she was saying better, to describe it better and explain it. But the more
she said, the worse it looked for her. Because she was at her wits' end, she
turned to the judge again.

"What would you have done?"

But this time she knew she would get no answer. She wasn't expect-
ing one. Nobody was. The judge shook his head silently.[16]

Hanna had put the same question to the judge once before in a different context of the trial. On that occasion as well, the judge had been
entirely at a loss, either because he had been unable (or unwilling) to put
himself in the concrete situation of Hanna's action or because he too was
so shaped by Hanna's ethos of duty and knew so few stirrings of spontaneous compassion that could have led to actions that he simply did not
have an answer. But, in essence, the answer was clear: faced with the
agony in the church, compassion alone could have made Hanna unable
to bear it and open the doors. She did recognize that everything around
her was coming apart. Her fixation on the orderly completion of the
death march demonstrates—together with her emotional shielding—a
blockage that need not have been there. We can never in the end judge
what concretely takes place in an individual and keeps him or her from
acting in a morally correct way. But if we make ourselves aware of other
criteria and accept other forms of behavior and internal dispositions, we
can opt for alternative behaviors that prevent crimes. To do this, we—
society as a whole and that means also the presiding judge—must make
these alternatives clear in our minds; in such a concrete situation of decision making like Hanna faced we must think through and carry out the
change of heart. Some would prefer, and consider it wiser, to leave this
event in the darkness of tragic moral entanglement. Are they giving
enough thought to the victims?[17]

Are There Forms of Atonement, Penance, Restitution, Reconciliation, and Redemption That Are Appropriate for Our Day and Age?

What about the other traditional stages of atonement (penance), restitution, reconciliation, and redemption of guilt? In both the secular and
the religious spheres, atonement is often replaced by punishment or
goes hand in hand with it. In the Judeo-Christian tradition, however, the
meaning of punishment is only fulfilled if it promotes atonement (which
includes a change of heart alongside penance) and has as its aim recon-

ciliation, the restoration of relationship. Excluding the perpetrator or merely taking her into custody to protect society is contrary to this understanding of punishment. Psychological observations suggest that for their part perpetrators have a desire for atonement, that it can be inappropriate to deny it to them in favor of psychiatric treatment (which falsely negates responsibility), and that penance can restore a perpetrator's self-confidence and relieve tension.[18]

This desire for atonement may be driven by an archaic inner wish to make up for harm done with personal sacrifice and to cleanse oneself in the process. It becomes problematic if it *replaces* confession, repentance, and a change of heart. This would be the case in the interpretation contemplated by Tilmann Moser, wherein many Germans believed they could dispense with reconstructing their mistakes under National Socialism because they had already "atoned sufficiently" during the bombings at the end of the war (or earlier through personal losses). One indication for such a false understanding of atonement can be found wherever people reckon the "bombing terror" of the Allies against the Nazi crimes. This kind of reckoning takes place if a person has not truly overcome the inner split but seeks to hide it—also from himself—behind the misdeeds of others, without any lasting success. Atonement and even punishment are by no means outmoded provided the form of punishment and the manner in which it is served do not stand in the way of atonement.

All the steps we have mentioned so far are ones that perpetrators can take on their own (though more easily with support). When it comes to restitution, reconciliation, and redemption, they need someone on the other side: their victims, their God, or both. The last three steps are therefore the most difficult. Restitution and secular reconciliation in the narrower sense are often not possible anymore, either because the damage simply cannot be undone or because the victims are no longer alive or cannot bring themselves to forgive. Nevertheless, it is often a great joy and blessing, not only to the perpetrators but also to the victims, if restitution and reconciliation occur. That is why it is very important for victims to bring themselves to confront the perpetrators. If it is possible, by confronting perpetrators with the suffering they have caused, to arouse empathy in them and thereby trigger a genuine examination of conscience, confession, repentance, and a change of heart, the most important step will have been taken toward overcoming the individual as well as social split. Then, even the "antagonists" of an act can come together again, and one piece is created in the mosaic of a sustainable moral consensus that needs to be rebuilt. In this way, the negative circle of emotional numbness, the "hardness of heart" that promoted the crimes and was further solidified by silenced guilt, can be reversed. This requires from the victims a magnanimity of soul one cannot demand or expect but that one can plead and hope for. This, then, would be genuine reconciliation: overcoming the split within oneself and in society. It could lay the groundwork for a new and vibrant consensus, for a common sense and a civic ethos.

ONCE AGAIN: CHANCES FOR
OVERCOMING THE SILENCE TOGETHER

Basic Consensus, Common Sense, Civic Ethos

Before we take a closer look at the various ways in which one can promote confession, a change of heart, and reconciliation in the public and private spheres, it seems imperative to define more precisely the difference between the notion of a basic normative consensus, commonly used in German political language, and the notion of common sense, borrowed from the Anglo-Saxon world. In her compelling and subtle study of the relationship between political reconciliation and democratic consolidation in Germany, Anne Sa'adeh introduced the concept of a "new common sense" as being the result of successful democratization. She finds the background to this in her historical studies of an analogous problem in postrevolutionary France and in the United States after the Civil War.[19]

The German concept of a basic normative consensus describes a canon of values, one that should be derived with the greatest possible precision and through theoretical-systematic reflection. Common sense, by contrast, refers more to historically evolved everyday behavior, notions of decency, and concrete customary rules about how to deal with one another, what not to do, how to react to something, and how to ignore it. Therein lies a piece of wisdom, which is legitimated not by philosophical derivation but by evolved experience and—this is important—by the experience of successful political coexistence or successful reconciliation (e.g., following the American Civil War). It is no coincidence that one of the American theoreticians of this basis of political life, Richard Rorty, clashed with the German philosophers Habermas and Apel over the question of whether one needs a final, compelling foundation for ethical-political decisions (something Rorty considers potentially totalitarian) or whether one can simply rely on what has historically evolved (something that strikes Habermas and Apel as dangerous, given their German experience). Behind this argument are two entirely different political experiences: successful democracy in the United States, failed democracy in Germany.[20]

It seems to me very useful to include the Anglo-American concept of common sense in our reflections, in spite of, or because of, the fact that it is not philosophically demanding. For the concrete problems of moral failure can be more readily tackled on the level of "self-evident" everyday experiences than on the abstract level of philosophical norms. Common sense, for instance, is part of every decision by a judge, which incorporates necessary assumptions about the interpretation of behavior and about what a person does and refrains from, what can be demanded in a concrete situation, and so on. And it is also found in abundance in written legal norms: for example, in determining negligent conduct (how much thoughtlessness does common sense accept?) or in defining the motives that distinguish murder from manslaughter. Even legal principles such as proportionality and equitableness cannot do without premises grounded in common sense. The problem, at least in the German legal system, is that these premises are frequently not articulated and reflected clearly enough, which creates the impression of a false precision of legal statements.

One of the main tasks for a public overcoming of silence lies in transforming this always-present common sense from an antidemocratic into a democratic one.

What Can Legal Proceedings Achieve?

Within the public sphere, trials or legal proceedings appear at first glance to be suitable means for changing the public consciousness of values and common sense. Perpetrators who do not wish to confess voluntarily can be summoned authoritatively before the bar of justice. Proceedings can render authoritative judgments whose normative implications are binding. But legal proceedings also have their problems. The first stems from the complicated relationship between law and morality. This book has looked at guilt primarily in its moral dimension, a dimension destroyed by silence. But not every legal guilt is a moral guilt (e.g., in private law). Most importantly, not every moral guilt is understood as a legal guilt. In part, this has to do with very compelling reasons involving the personal safeguards in a state based on the rule of law; in part, with reasons that are not compelling on historical-cultural grounds, which means they are subject to change, though not unlimited change, within the legal system.

Because of the possible discrepancy between morality and law, some turn their backs on the law in disappointment, while others think they are very sophisticated and free of illusions by proclaiming the complete separation of law and morality. But common sense—here it is again—tells us that, whatever the specific difficulties there may be in the relationship between law and morality, these two extreme reactions are unacceptable.

Let me indicate a few reasons for the necessary discrepancy between morality and law in order to define more precisely the possibilities, and limitations, for overcoming silence through trials and legal proceedings. To begin with, the legal system must not define and demand specific moral *motivations* from its citizens, as this would run counter to the pluralism and freedom of opinion in a democratic society. I discussed this point briefly at the beginning of the book. In our (inner) moral convictions we must remain free; our (external) conduct the state may regulate—within limits—through its laws.

Second, the primary goal of a state based on the rule of law, a goal that also drove its historical evolution, is to guarantee the safety of the individual. That goal is served by the prescribed procedures of the state based on laws (chiefly, "In case of doubt, the decision goes in favor of the accused"). Although all of these procedures are bound to the truth, in a possible conflict between truth and the absence of doubt they work in favor of the latter so as to protect the accused in every case against unjustified, arbitrary sentencing, even if this violates our sense of justice. The protective legal principles and procedural rules that are especially important for our purposes include also those of equal treatment and the prohibition against retroactivity. They entail a whole series of implications and difficulties that one cannot annul simply to satisfy the (legitimate) desire for justice.

On the other hand, at times these protective hedges collide so strongly with our basic moral understanding that people seek remedies in one form or another. This problem was particularly pronounced at the Nuremberg trials, especially at the first trial. Here the chief prosecutor, Robert H. Jackson, professor of international law and later Supreme Court justice, found himself obliged to "attach" the crime of the murder of the Jews to war crimes already "established" in legal theory, which led to a number of severe inconsistencies and injustices. And since the end of the East German state we are once again faced with the problem that a state based on the rule of law can only condemn an act that was previously forbidden by law.

In general, there are two strategies for overcoming this difficulty: either one cuts the Gordian knot and formulates temporal or substantive exceptions to the prohibition on retroactivity (e.g., for certain "revolutionary" transition periods or for horrendous crimes such as crimes against humanity) and in so doing takes the risk of an expansion of this kind of "arbitrariness," or one adheres to the prohibition and in so doing violates in many concrete cases a fundamental moral understanding. Both paths have their costs. The path of articulating exceptions also has moral implications because it can eat at the substance of a state based on the rule of law—unless a solid common sense draws limits.

At the same time, the importance that everyday self-evident truths play in securely anchoring the positive law in society reveals the limits that legal proceedings face in overcoming silence and renewing the basic moral consensus, common sense, and the civic ethos. Laws and verdicts must link up with common everyday understanding and with people's perceptions of reality. Any gap between written law and judicial verdicts, on the one hand, and people's "reality" and sense of justice, on the other, undermines the acceptance of the law and the state based on the rule of law. This point is especially sensitive in the transition from dictatorships to democracies, as it gets to the heart of the expectations that trials will ensure justice following a regime's injustice and will contribute to a new consciousness of the law. For there is much that is knotted together in this "reality," which also concerns the judicial common sense that flows into the verdicts.

How much were the Nazi trials *permitted* to depart from the "reality" of the German postwar population; how much did they *have* to depart to still deserve to be called "law"? Anne Sa'adeh has worked this out vividly by examining two examples from the Auschwitz trial. State prosecutor Fritz Bauer, who deserves our moral and legal gratitude in connection with the trial, sought to demonstrate with the Auschwitz trial "that a new Germany, a German democracy, is willing to preserve the dignity of every person." Who would have gainsaid the value of preserving every person's dignity in the abstract? But the concrete issue in the trial was the question of whether the fact that someone was a "cog in the entire 'machinery of destruction'" indicated guilt or innocence within the common sense of the Germans at that time.[21] There was a tendency among the Germans at the time, and in part still today, to believe that being a "cog" bespoke innocence. The reason for this view was that the sphere of responsibility was theoretically defined very narrowly and there were undoubtedly many Germans who would have been personally affected if being a "cog" had qualified as "guilt," something they did not want. In this case, because there was a failure to explain sufficiently that the dignity of the individual cannot be safeguarded without individual responsibility, close adherence to German "reality" would thus not have meant overcoming silence but reinforcing it.

As the alternative to the exculpatory "cog in the machinery of destruction" interpretation, which set extremely narrow boundaries to the sphere of responsibility, Fritz Bauer articulated the theory of the "action chain." It pointed to the responsibility of every single person in this machinery, although it did not form the basis of the verdict in the Auschwitz trial (in which jurors were also significantly involved). The theory went like this:

The activities of every member of an extermination camp constitute, from the moment of entry into the camp—which was usually connected with the immediate understanding of its function as a killing machine— to the moment of departure, a natural act, regardless of what a particular person contributed physically to the administration of the camp and thereby to the Final Solution. Every member participated continuously and without interruption. If one looks at the entire activity from a natural point of view, it presents itself as a coherent act connected from one hour to the next. All expressions of will are nonautonomous elements of a whole act; the mere presence is psychic aiding and abetting, which— from a sociological perspective—must not be discounted, especially in mass phenomena. Every person lends support to the next; he makes it easier for him or her to engage in criminal actions. The blood of the victims during his stay in the camp is upon his hands.[22]

And what would common sense look like today with respect to individual responsibility? If it had not changed we would not have learned much. We cannot simply give up the principle that the law must be anchored in reality. But we must also become aware that reality is an important place in which the old common sense is blocking the new, democratic common sense.

This also takes us into the controversial area of the regulations and—above all—the guiding principles for legal interpretations and verdicts that are not dictated by the need to safeguard the state based on the rule of law, but depend strongly on the mentality of the jurists involved and on the state of public opinion and public morality. For example, at the Auschwitz trial, the crime "murder" was restricted so much that de facto only few (provable!) acts were so classified, a move that simultaneously drew very narrow boundaries around the sphere of individual responsibility: "A guilty will [*Täterwillen*] must be inferred only if perpetrators showed special zeal beyond what they were commanded to do, if they participated in the extermination activities with a special lack of restraint, and if they encouraged their subordinates or demonstrated in some other way that they considered the mass killings right and necessary." And the verdict noted "that any person who came to Auschwitz was no longer able to 'react normally' after two weeks."[23] Was no longer *able*? How did the judges and jurors know that? After all, there were examples to the contrary. In reality, this common sense statement is not a descriptive but a normative one: the judges did not expect the accused to still react in a "normal" way after a fortnight. This (negative and exculpatory) norm was thereby established. It was grounded in the common sense of its time.

Thus, it appears that legal proceedings are rather unsuitable for overcoming silence, though the opposite seems the case at first glance. But that is not the entire truth. The public nature of these proceedings sets all sorts of things into motion: discussions about indisputable justiciable facts, which can also stand up to the strain of a legal defense (Peter Steinbach sees a central benefit in this), and about arguments that are put forth to defend camp guards and slowly become enveloped in public doubt—for example, when the accused Hofmann defends himself by saying, "I did my duty. Wherever I was put, I just did my job," or when the attorney Laternser tries to save his client, the camp guard Mulka, with this "argument": "It is true that he did not join the SS voluntarily until he was mature in years, namely, at a point when he had to expect that he would become involved in crimes. However, it is not clear . . . that he ever thought about being misused to commit crimes."[24] This argument de facto reduces the sphere of personal responsibility to zero and proclaims a person's right to be thoughtless. At least the public, legal proclamation of such positions makes it possible to challenge them in an equally public manner, to show their consequences, and to advocate a different, new determination of individual responsibility demanded by society. For instance, in the late 1950s, in a climate that witnessed the— at times—provocative demands for rehabilitation by convicted Nazi perpetrators, the *Einsatzgruppen* trial in Ulm did cause a "shock" that countered a rollback of common sense. One should therefore not underestimate the significance of that trial.[25]

One important (if rather implied) function of verdicts that are carefully argued legally is thus to provide material and impulses for public debates, the real place where common sense is changed. One example is the debate in 1965 over the statue of limitations that was carried on in the German parliament at a high level. In addition, such verdicts can give shape to norms (especially in an international context) that overarch positive law and have a chance of being generally accepted, particularly if they are carefully formulated and circumscribed. A verdict by the German Federal High Court on 13 December 1993, on the question of perversion of justice shows that change is possible in this regard over the course of decades. What emerges from this verdict as the core of injustice transcending positive law is "a clear and gross violation of basic notions of justice and humanity," "excessive or arbitrary acts by judges," that is, cases that violate the law and human rights in such obvious and serious ways that the verdict presents itself as an "arbitrary act." In other words, this core norm is a continuation of the formulation put forth by Radbruch. After 1945, Radbruch revised his original position grounded in positive law to accommodate the following qualifications: "It should be possible to solve the conflict between justice and legal security such that positive law, secured by statute and power, takes precedence even if it is unjust and unsuitable in terms of its content, unless the contradiction between positive law and justice has reached a point that is unbearable and the law, as 'unjust law,' must give way to justice."[26] The specific articulations of the core injustice are by no means precise, and undoubtedly one cannot readily derive legal decisions from them. Because of the prohibition on retroactivity, they are expressed in a "minimalist" form and therefore almost invariably disappoint those who are looking for full material justice. And they require interpretations of common sense (what do we mean by "gross," "obvious," "serious violations of the law and human rights"?) that in turn highlight once more its importance. It is doubtful, as Alexy has claimed, that in the final analysis "arguments can decide" these articulations and that they can be arrived at solely through a rational, discursive examination. But these articulations establish the principle that the norm of human rights sets limits on a state's power to make law, that human rights constitute a foundation that transcends positivism, and that the clear violation of these rights cannot expect to escape punishment.[27]

In international law this principle has also found institutional reinforcement for some years now through the activities of the UN, whose General Assembly voted in 1989 to prepare for the establishment of an International Criminal Court. In the wake of these initiatives, the UN Tribunal for Bosnia was set up in The Hague in 1993 and a similar one for Bosnia in 1994. In spite of the many difficulties the tribunals face in doing their work and enforcing their verdicts, they are a striking public institutionalization of basic norms of human rights and attest to the development of a basic, international moral consensus.

However, on the whole, the positive contribution of legal proceedings to the overcoming of silence lies only to some small degree in the authoritative change of the living basic consensus. This consensus cannot be compelled by institutions. If it is to be truly valid, it can only be created by people together thinking it, struggling for it, living it. Confession and a change of heart, the central elements of the talking that overcomes the fracture, depend on voluntary impulses. But in cases of gross violations of human rights (recognized because of what we have learned after 1945), legal trials can hold perpetrators responsible. They can uncover facts and make them accessible to public debate far more effectively than scholarship is usually able to do. And as long as legal procedures are adhered to, this does not constitute an abuse of the law or an instrumentalization of the accused. Because trials are backed up by the threat of conviction, they provide an occasion for sometimes passionate debates, which are the real element of a new public basic consensus. And as much as we need trials, we also need accompanying professional commentary—not simply to contain the negative consequences of the understandable but at times unavoidable disappointments that verdicts can trigger. We also need it above all to refashion common sense—which is also the informal lining of legal proceedings—in the most transparent way possible, so it can do justice to the suffering caused by silenced guilt.

"Truth Commissions" and Public Debates

What other options are available to us in the public sphere? South Africa, mindful of the unavoidable drawbacks of legal proceedings for punishing past crimes, embarked on the experiment of a Truth and Reconciliation Commission. In Archbishop Desmond Tutu the Commission found a chairman of great and widely accepted authority. This method of clarifying guilt is inspired by the idea of giving restitution and reconciliation precedence over conviction and punishment: "Our emphasis is on resti-

tution and reconciliation—not on repression and revenge," Archbishop
Tutu explained. Anybody who presented himself to the commission
within two years of its establishment would be eligible for amnesty. To be
sure, there is a danger that the process will be manipulated coldblood-
edly by perpetrators who feel no real remorse. But Tutu is putting his
trust in the effect that is produced when a crime is merely articulated:
"We are taking a risk, but we hope that a person who talks about having
killed a human being will realize that this human being is not a cipher."
The suffering of the victims is at the center of the process and is supposed to trigger remorse and atonement. Moreover, limiting the time
frame of the chance for amnesty—so goes the thinking of the founders
of the commission—can create the confidence that scandals will not be
revisited or uncovered at some time in the future, a confidence that legal
proceedings cannot offer. The hope is that remorse and atonement will
come from the cleansing effect of the heart-wrenching and shocking reports and from the confrontation of the perpetrators with the agonies of
their victims. The commission is to create good conditions for forgiveness (which is solely a matter for the victims) and reconciliation as well
as for the betterment of the perpetrators. More than that it cannot do.
The actual change of heart must come from the individual: "In the end
every South African must say to himself: 'For the sake of my country and
for my own sake I can no longer carry the burden of guilt around with
me.' Forgiveness and reconciliation are necessary to get rid of this burden. Without forgiveness there can be no future here. If you and I quarrel and we don't forgive each other, our relationship is ruined. It's that
simple." [28]

The initial experiences with the Truth Commission suggest that, at
least in South Africa, the unspeakable suffering of the victims is in fact
stirring up pity, empathy, and remorse on the part of the perpetrators
and setting in motion a clarifying public debate. As in the large trials in
Germany after the war, the real effect comes from the confrontation with
the facts and the suffering of concrete human beings, against which even
perpetrators seem unable to shut themselves off completely. Conversely,
the trial of the South African general Magnus Malan once again revealed
how limited are the chances for overcoming silenced guilt through a legal process.

Other possibilities for overcoming the silence lie in official public debates
(e.g., in parliament), in speeches by eminent persons, in debates in the
media, in works of art and literature, in the theater, and in films. So far,

there has been little empirical research on the effect and influence these have on individuals, the basic carriers of common sense, and given the methodological problems it is undoubtedly difficult to arrive at a representative determination. Here is one piece of evidence that they *do* have an effect: during his interviews, Philipp Lutz met someone for whom Richard von Weizsäcker's speech on 8 May 1985, was of central importance in his own processing of National Socialism and in the clarification of his self-conception.[29] It is, therefore, possible to reach people, even if it usually happens more readily through experiences in the private sphere—as the American psychologist Sniderman has discovered—than through experiences in the public arena.

At this point, I shall mention explicitly one *disastrous* form of public debate over past guilt: its political instrumentalization, which is diametrically opposed to the spirit of mercy and forgiveness. It poses a particularly big temptation for the political parties, which is why it is practiced all too often. Since the boundary between complete exposure and defamation is not always unequivocal, what is needed once again is a common sense that is focused on truthfulness, a common sense that does not reward the flagrant dishonesty of instrumentalization but punishes it and thereby puts a stop to it. In this arena, we need to call especially upon individual personalities to throw the weight of their authority, of their "reputation for honesty and trustworthiness" (Putnam), into the public scale. And they must be willing to risk sensitive judgments, in the process offering—especially in controversies—a model of fairness in dealing with one another, a model that shames the ruthless instrumentalizers in the long run and makes their propagandists shrink from spreading their poison in the public sphere.

Openness in Private Conversation

The process of defining the content of common sense, precisely because it is "common," must take place fundamentally in public debate. But its personal anchoring, its safeguarding in the civic ethos, depends chiefly on the family as well as on the schools and informal social organizations such as unions, churches, and ideological groups. The freedom of these spheres must be institutionally secured, though that alone is no guarantee that they will in fact contribute their share. In the final analysis, it all depends on the personal initiative of every individual, in the family as well as in the circle of friends and in social organizations; on his and her sense of responsibility, courage, honesty, fairness, nonconformism, empathy;

and on the capacity to trust others and oneself. We have to pull ourselves up by our own bootstraps—there is simply no way around that.

It is difficult to answer the question of whether it is at all possible to
repair the profound damage to personality (such as emotional frigidity
and a lack of trust in oneself and others) that was inflicted in the familial
atmosphere of silenced guilt and undermines the civic ethos. Is it not too
late for the second generation, which is the one we are talking about in
the German case? Is it possible to recover the capacity for commitment,
relationship, and love in "old age"? And if it is not possible, does the third
generation simply outgrow the damage or is it intensified and shifted?

The many broken families, which today are so often "pieced together" again as patchwork families or "postfamilial families," would seem
to indicate that the capacity for relationships has not recovered.[30] To be
sure, this damage should not be attributed only to silenced guilt; as in
most modern societies, it is the result of many factors. But the desire for
reliable and stable relationships continues to exist, especially on the part
of the children. Of course, it is one thing to sadly note the lack of a capacity for relationships (also in oneself) and quite another to respond to
it by making the effort to change one's ways, especially if one does not
know whether this attempt can be successful without help. This much, at
least, can be said: change becomes easier if the growing, vague pain (and
the oppressive burden of pain) is accompanied by a growing insight into
how all the elements are interconnected. Once that happens people are
no longer alone in their psychological and emotional "deformation." And
there are certainly examples of people who made the effort to carefully
reconstruct their own lives and the points at which wrong turns were
taken so they could start over also on an emotional level and be able to
enter into trusting and rich relationships.

However, a person must genuinely desire this, not only for the sake
of giving meaning to his or her own life but also for the sake of the next
generation. For whatever name we will give in the future to the forms of
cohabitation in which the transmission of the generations takes place,
this much seems clear: there is a good deal of evidence that the possibility of identifying with loved and trustworthy persons is a necessary
condition for children and adolescents to become adults themselves,
adults who are able to live as democratic citizens. That is why a family
policy supportive of this process is so important for the future of our
democracy.

Incidentally, the chances that a renewal in openness and honesty will
take place are improved by the next generation's declared primal need

for it. Truthfulness and trust constitute the "primeval stuff" of success-ful cohabitation. It is a marvelous experience to observe how children, before they are "distorted," nearly always speak and desire the truth. Their psychic development all but depends on their desire to receive truth also from their parents, and any person who does not entirely close himself off to parental love will feel challenged by it. This "mechanism" unfolded in the familial conflicts of many members of the generation of '68, and precisely because both sides participated emotionally and the "stakes" were so high it was often deeply hurtful. At the same time, this challenge to the trustworthiness of the parents (nourished by the natu-ral emotional bonds between them and their children) triggered a push for the truth on an individual level and also in society at large. And in later years, the generations were at times successful in arriving at a more un-derstanding and conciliatory attitude on both sides. In any case, the pri-mal desire of children and adolescents for the truth offers a chance not to remain stuck in the old ways.

In societies where the dictatorial past is still fresh, the understand-ing of the destructive effect of silenced guilt may provide an incentive not to repeat the mistakes of earlier, less fortunate generations of per-petrators and to speak openly with the children. It is important to real-ize that parents and teachers will not lose their authority by doing so, but will gain their authority in the first place. For children, it is an ines-timably valuable and happy experience to see the honesty of their mod-els and their attempt to undo past mistakes.

". . . But the Greatest of Them All Is Love"

Where do we find the strength for a new beginning? We find it where re-ligious experience, art, and poetry have always described it: in love. In his novel *The Misused Love Letters*, Gottfried Keller, for example, offered a moving description of how love provides the strength to change and find the basis for a new life, not only for an individual person but for society as a whole.

And Dostoyevsky's Raskolnikov remained seriously ill in Siberia as long as he was unable to repent of his guilt. Repentance came only with the help of Sonia's love and the miracle that he was able to requite it af-ter hardening himself to it for so long. Prior to that, his "unrepentant conscience" would not allow him to admit his guilt, and this threw him into a "purposeless and aimless unrest." As a result, his life became mean-ingless to him at the time, and as he looked toward the future after his imprisonment, he asked: "What had he to live for? What would his aim in life be? To live in order to exist? . . . And if fate had only sent him repentance—burning repentance that would have rent his heart and deprived him of sleep, the sort of repentance that is accompanied by terrible agony which makes one long for the noose or the river! Oh, how happy he would have been if he could have felt such repentance! Agony and tears—why, that, too, was life! But he did not repent of his crime." The price that Raskolnikov pays for his "quiet," unrepentant conscience is a feeling of inner lifelessness and the aimlessness of his existence. He feels that those around him avoid him, even hate him, all these rough men who, to Raskolnikov's surprise, are fond of Sonia. The transformation occurs when he receives word that Sonia has taken ill. How many times he had contemptuously rebuffed her love, the love that had impelled her to follow him to Siberia. He was *unable to repent, unable to live, unable to love. These things were interconnected.* But now, upon receiving a note from her, "his heart beat fast." Early the following morning, Raskolnikov goes off to work. He looks across the river and can hardly take his eyes off the view spread before him:

His thoughts passed into daydreams, into contemplation; he thought of nothing, but a feeling of great desolation came over him and troubled him. Suddenly Sonia was beside him. She had come up noiselessly and sat down close to him. It was still very early; the morning chill had not yet abated. She wore her old shabby coat and the green shawl. Her face still showed traces of illness: it was very thin and pale. She smiled at him joyfully and tenderly, but, as usual, held out her hand to him timidly. . . . How it happened he did not know, but suddenly something seemed to seize him and throw him at her feet. He embraced her knees and wept. At first she was terribly frightened, and her face was covered by a deathly pallor. She jumped to her feet and, trembling all over, looked at him. But at once and at the same moment she understood everything. Her eyes shone with intense happiness; she understood, and he had no doubts at all about it, that he loved her, loved her infinitely, and that the moment she had waited for so long had come at last.

They wanted to speak, but could not; tears stood in their eyes. They were both pale and thin; but in those sick and pale faces the dawn of a new future, of a full resurrection to a new life, was already shining. It was love that brought them back to life: the heart of one held inexhaustible sources of life for the heart of the other.

Raskolnikov felt how his relationship to his fellow convicts was also changing and that his self, impoverished in mere thinking and theorizing, was opening up to feeling. And so this was "the beginning of a new story, the story of a gradual rebirth of a man, the story of his gradual regeneration, of his gradual passing from one world to another, of his acquaintance with a new and hitherto unknown reality. That might be the subject of a new story—our present story is ended."[31]

Notes

INTRODUCTION

1. Quoted in *Der Tagesspiegel*, 6 June 1995.
2. McNamara 1995, xvf.
3. Niethammer 1991.

1. GUILT—A BASIC HUMAN CONDITION

1. Kolakowski 1967, 90.
2. Bolz 1993, 269, 271, and passim.
3. Colpe 1993, 21.
4. Colpe 1993, 49. Cold, dryness . . . : 28. Trimborn 1925, 220;
5. Aztecs: Höltker 1936, 222, 225.
6. Latte 1920/21, 256–63.
7. Latte 1920/21, 276–80.
8. Dodds 1951, 36–37; the preceding discussion, 1–18.
9. Ricoeur 1969, 9, 26–29.
10. Ricoeur 1969, 64; purity and separation: 37f. and 32.
11. Ricoeur 1969, 104; sin objectified: 81f.
12. Buruma 1994, 10, 115ff., 127f.; Ricoeur 1969, 18; Africa: Sembebwa 1983, 123f.
13. An interesting piece of evidence for the persistence of mythical notions of guilt is Erika Fischer-Lichte's observation that times of crisis witness an increase in the archaic and graphic depiction of ritual acts of sacrifice on the theater stage. In Europe it happened before the World War I as well as in the 1960s. Evidently, the kind of thinking that works with categories of guilty pollution and symbolic cleansing is always present, at least in a latent state. Fischer-Lichte 1997.
14. Ricoeur 1967, 20.
15. Quoted in Kaufmann 1976, 129.
16. Kaufmann 1976, 118.

17. Kaufmann 1990, 39 ff.; "substitute conscience": 51; Kaufmann 1976; "lead-up": 189; "minimal ethical standard": 198 ff.
18. Kaufmann 1976, 206–9.
19. Ellscheid and Hassemer 1975, 273–76, emphasis added.
20. Ellscheid and Hassemer 1975, 277 ff.
21. Kaufmann 1976, 179, 171.
22. Ellscheid and Hassemer 1975, 281–88; "natural law": compare Arndt 1955.
23. Günther 1991, 205.
24. Gschwind and Rautenberg 1987, 6 ff.; problems with prognosis: Hassemer 1981, 259 ff.
25. Günther 1989, 149 ff.; compare also Günther 1991, 206 f., 1994, 147; Roxin 1974, 193.
26. Arndt 1955, 24 ff.; Rautenberg 1984, 163 ff.

2. HISTORICAL NOTIONS OF GUILT

1. Compare Bader 1964; Böckle 1987, 49.
2. Syberberg 1994, 124 ff.; Zitelmann 1994, 174 ff.; Buruma 1994, 8 f. and 97 f. The year 1968 was pivotal in the left-inspired student movement in Germany—Trans.
3. Lapide 1983, 44; Ricoeur 1969, 71–74, 52, 88; Rahner 1964, 165.
4. Kreiner 1986, 67; Gründel 1993, 128; Molinski 1986, 80; Altmeyer 1973, 95 ff.; Sievernich 1983, 14 f.
5. Todorov 1996. 67; Ricoeur 1985, 1; Honnefelder 1985, 25, 30.
6. Bujo 1991, 182 ff.
7. Kant 1949, 424 f.
8. Honnefelder 1985, 35, 28, 32.
9. Oeing-Hanhoff 1981, 173.
10. Todorov 1996, 65; Oeing-Hanhoff 1981, 182.
11. Todorov 1996, 69; Arendt 1987, 67.
12. Marquardt et al. 1980.
13. Todorov 1993, 194, 175 ff.; Staub 1989, 28 f., 83; Baumann 1992.
14. Lenz 1991, 75.
15. Krappmann 1993, 82, 79 f.; compare also Tenbruck 1974.
16. Krappmann 1993, 69, 52, 149 ff.
17. On this, see the extensive discussion in Schwan 1990.
18. Jaspers 1947, 11 f., 18.
19. Jaspers 1947, 32 f.
20. Jaspers 1947, 90, 97, 115, 120, 119 ff.

21. Jaspers 1947, 121.
22. See Kittsteiner 1990, 175, 194.
23. Hole 1989, 84 ff.; Gründel 1990, 102 f.
24. Dodds 1968, 31.
25. Breasted 1934, 345, 341.
26. Transition to subjective-individual morality: Kittsteiner 1990, 156.
27. Kant 1949, 425 f.
28. Jaspers 1947, 66; Kerber 1982, 100.

3. TRADITION AND MODERN PSYCHOLOGY

1. Lidsay-Hartz 1984, 695; Morris 1988, 64, 67; Lapide 1983, 50 f.;
    Hoffmann 1982, 298; "core of the self": Hole 1989, 84, 88; "internal
    diminution": Ricoeur 1969, 102; "basic fact": Haeffner 1993, 12;
    "stigmatization": Lipp 1990, 126 f.
2. Ricoeur 1969, 95 f., 144 ff.
3. Höltker 1936, 217; Trimborn 1925, 226; Latte 1920/21, 294; Kreiner
    1986, 67; Sievernich 1983, 10, 13; Khoury 1983, 62; Hummel 1983,
    107, 112; Sempebwa 1983, 132.
4. Hagemann 1986, 54; Gründel 1990, 101; Lapide 1983, 57.
5. Kukutz 1990, 33; Lidsay-Hartz 1984, 693; Buruma 1994, 288 f.;
    Gründel 1993, 135; Lipp 1990, 136; Altmeyer 1986, 107; Sievernich
    1983, 32; Erlinghagen 1983, 85; Sempebwa 1983, 133; Giordano
    1990, 40; "humiliation": Latte 1920/21, 293.
6. Lapide 1983, 51–54; "Common bond of relief": Molinski 1986, 85 f.;
    "self-respect": Köpcke-Duttler 1990, 393.
7. Buruma 1994, 98; "archaic restitution": Gründel 1993, 135; "Ger-
    mans after 1945": Moser 1992, 393.
8. de Boor and Kohlmann 1980, 4, 11; "impossibility of restitution":
    Hoffmann 1982, 298; "self-punishment": Lidsay-Hartz 1984, 693.
9. Ricoeur 1969, 227.

4. SILENCED GUILT

1. Lübbe 1983, 332 ff., 341.
2. Arendt 1963, 134, 47 f., 92.
3. Goldhagen 1996, 76, 32, 15 f., 393, 80 ff., 582.
4. Jäger 1982, 187, 72 f., 183, 179.
5. Kelman 1989, 15; "Nazi perpetrators": Jäger 1982, 59, 272, and Lang-
    bein 1987, 315.
6. Document 1919-PS, 145.

7. Document 1919-PS, 122 f.; "unauthorized actions": Buchheim et al. 1968, 351 ff., 362 f.
8. Document 1919-PS, 150–53.
9. Boberach 1984, vol. 13, 5128–32.
10. Boberach 1984, 5134 f.
11. Buchheim et al. 1968, 317.
12. Frank 1993, 182.
13. Hohenstein 1963; also: Müller-Hohagen 1988; Höß 1959, 115 f.; Sereny 1974, 113; Jäger 1982, 94 ff.
14. Quoted in Jacobsen 1968, 532.
15. "Soldat im Volk" 1995, 2; "officers": Fest 1996, 175 ff.
16. Browning 1994, 22 ff.; Fest 1996, 15 ff.; Jäger 1982, 77.
17. Buchheim et al. 1968, 362 f.
18. Rousseau 1964, 132.
19. "Eichmann": Hull 1964, 38, 40; Höß 1994, 11; Sereny 1974, 21; Browning 1992, 187, 129 f., 174 f., 185. Incidentally, Monika H., a former citizen of East Germany who spied on her friends Katja Havemann and Bärbel Bohley, among others, for the Stasi reports in her "confession" that one of her motives was to do "a good job" in her work for the Stasi and to be a good member of the party: Kukutz 1990, 15, 33.
20. Höß 1959, 30.
21. The "Altreich" refers to Germany exclusive of the Sudeten region and Austria—Trans.
22. Quoted in Aly 1995, 124; "American psychologists": compare Dimsdale 1980, 284.
23. Sereny 1974, 200.
24. Höß 1959, 153 f.
25. Todorov 1996, 129.
26. Sereny 1974, 167. Incidentally, what we have shown here in the case of National Socialism has also been observed in other crime situations: in My Lai, American soldiers invited a Vietnamese girl who just an hour before had escaped their massacre to join them for breakfast (Kelman and Hamilton 1989, 9). Within an hour they changed from murderous frenzy to hospitality.
27. Sereny 1974, 157; Levi 1988, 56, 130 ff.
28. Gilbert 1947, 45 f.
29. Browning 1992, 69.
30. Kelman and Hamilton 1980, 17.
31. Incidentally, herein lies one of Daniel Goldhagen's fundamental sim-

plifications. While he does refer to the relevant American literature (Goldhagen 1996, 377 ff., 384 f.), he does not really engage the arguments presented there; in particular, he does not address the interpretation of "fragmentation."

32. Sereny 1974, 201 ff.
33. See Baumann 1992; Kelman and Hamilton 1989, 16.
34. Sereny 1974, 164.
35. Levi 1988, 27.
36. Lifton 1986, 421, 433, 423.
37. Arendt 1992, 16; Jäger 1982, 257.
38. Browning 1992, 61, 149, 151; Treblinka: Sereny 1974, 26; Lifton 1986, 443; Höß 1959, 146 f.
39. Quoted in Browning 1992, 183, 28, 32, 35.
40. Gilbert 1947, 260; Zeiler 1991, 345.
41. Gauch 1996, 128; Vesper 1995, 329 ff., 344 f., 401; Westernhagen 1988, 73, 85.
42. Arendt 1963, 121 ff. (the Frank quote cited by Arendt is taken from *Die Technik des Staates* [1942]).
43. Kant 1996, 199 f.
44. Kant 1996, 205.
45. Smith 1977.
46. On the moral function of sentiment in Kant, compare Olin 1990, 17 ff.
47. Lifton 1986, 442.
48. Schöpf 1990, 57, 60.
49. Sereny 1995, 697, 719.
50. Dostoyevsky 1951, 430, 554.
51. Hilberg 1985, 993 f.; Jäger 1982, 164, 194, 202; Fest 1996, 175 f.
52. Jäger 1982, 256.
53. Reik 1925, 40 (emphasis added), 115–19, 123.
54. Jaspers 1947, 119.
55. Bar-On 1989b.
56. Schlink 1997, 91.
57. Hilberg 1985, 1013–25; Jäger 1982, 72 f.; Sereny 1974, 113; Levi 1988, 46 f.; Höß 1959, 71 f.
58. Browning 1992, 25, 117 f.; Arendt 1963, 253 f.; Langbein 1987, 465 ff.
59. Gauch 1996, 16; compare also Browning 1992, 69, 94; Langbein 1987, 465; Frank 1993, 67.
60. Adorno et al. 1955, 300 f.; "fixation": Koebner 1987, 303 f.
61. Browning 1992, 158, 147 ff.

62. Bergmann and Erb 1991, 270, 243 f., 240.
63. Ensslin was a member of the RAF, a left-wing German terrorist or-
    ganization active in the 1970s and 1980s—Trans.
64. Vesper 1995, 484 ff.; "apologia": Adorno et al. 1955, 385, 480.
65. Höß 1959, 81; Arendt 1963, 41 f.; Sereny 1974, 39; Reik 1925, 116 f.
66. Arendt 1963, 220 f., 254 f., 89.
67. Hull 1964, 102, 129, 77, 89, 94, 35.
68. Sereny 1974, 364 f.
69. Sereny 1974, 349, 360 f., 344, 253.
70. Jäger 1982, 202.
71. Boberach 1984, vol. 9: 3245–48.
72. Boberach 1984, vol. 8: 3020 ff.
73. See also Kershaw 1983, 224 ff., 373 ff.
74. Langbein 1987, 502 ff.; Ullrich 1991; Goldhagen 1996, 131 ff.
75. Schwarz 1990, 150 ff., 221.
76. Boberach 1984, vol. 10: 3978 f.
77. Schwarz 1990, 40, 133, 201 f.
78. Hoch [1982], 277–81.
79. Noele/Neumann 1967, 48; Bankier 1995, 139; Rürup 1991, 8; *Die
    Zeit* nos. 14 and 18 / 1995.
80. Funke 1996, 10; Schreiber 1996, 55 ff.
81. Hilberg 1985, 994; Aly 1995, 386 ff; Jäger 1982, 51 ff.
82. Hoch [1982], 298.
83. Frei 1996, 399.

5. PSYCHOLOGICAL AND SOCIAL CONSEQUENCES OF SILENCE

1. Noelle-Neumann and Köcher 1987, 15–27.
2. Noelle-Neumann and Köcher 1987, 22 f.
3. Sniderman 1975.
4. Noelle-Neumann and Köcher 1987, 103, 74, 100.
5. Noelle-Neumann and Köcher 1987, 79 ff.; Stierlin 1992, 250 ff.;
    Kohut and Elson 1993, 51, 42 ff.
6. Noelle-Neumann and Köcher 1987, 93, 75 ff.
7. Noelle-Neumann and Köcher 1987, 94–99; compare also Pross
    1982: 74 ff.
8. Noelle-Neumann and Köcher 1987, 91, 301 f.; 193, 290 f., 296.
9. Tenbruck 1972, 290 ff.
10. Tenbruck 1972, 305–10; compare also Bohleber 1990, 79.
11. Noelle-Neumann 1967, 145.

12. Noelle-Neumann and Köcher 1987, 28, 35; 358; 31. (On the centuries-old roots of political cultures, see also Craig 1982, 21 ff.)
13. Noelle-Neumann and Köcher 1987, 34 f.
14. Noelle-Neumann and Köcher 1987, 390.
15. Noelle-Neumann and Köcher 1987, 47, 393, 369 ff.
16. Weißmann 1987, 187.
17. Noelle-Neumann and Köcher 1987, 96.
18. Sereny 1995, 42.
19. Noelle-Neumann and Köcher 1987, 96.
20. Anhalt 1992, 39; Brendler 1991, 235 f.; Hauer 1994, 12; Heimannsberg and Schmidt 1992, 11 f.; Bohleber 1990, 80.
21. Mitscherlich and Mitscherlich 1975, 24.
22. Kittel 1993, 359–63, 378.
23. Segev 1993, 477.
24. Perrez 1979.
25. Condrau 1981, 102.
26. Rottgart 1993, 297; Hardtmann 1992b, 46.
27. Bar-On 1989b, 328; compare also Eckstaedt 1992 174.
28. Schwan 1989 and 1990; Stierlin 1982.
29. Schneider 1987, 113; Hauer 1994, 31; Bohleber 1990, 76 ff.; Koebner 1987, 321.
30. Eckstaedt 1992, 19.
31. Hardtmann 1992b, 44; "double morality": Bohleber 1990, 76.
32. Anhalt 1992, 56, 46, 53.
33. Noelle and Neumann 1967, 197–201, 176.
34. Quoted in Schornstheimer 1995, 130 f., 133.
35. Schornstheimer 1995, 217, 202, 204, 214.
36. Schwan 1990a, 11; Walser 1965.
37. Simenauer 1981, 10.
38. Rottgart 1993, 298.
39. Eckstaedt 1992, 97 f., 122; Moser 1993, 76.
40. Bauriedl 1995, 37; Kohut and Elson 1993, 163 f., 304; Bohleber 1990, 74; Stierlin 1992, 255; Schäfer 1983, 156 ff.
41. Bar-On 1989b, 143; Hardtmann 1992b, 51.
42. Adelson 1971, 1039 f.; Eckstaedt 1992, 165 f., 304; Bohleber 1990, 74; Stierlin 1992, 255; Schäfer 1983, 156 ff.
43. Eckstaedt 1992, 40, 89, 143, 146; Hauer 1994, 12; Coleman 1982, 183 f.; Hardtmann 1995, 243; Hardtmann 1992a, 253; Brendler 1991, 221, 224; Sichrovsky 1987; "survivor's guilt": Segev 1993, 153 ff.; Levi 1988, 72 ff.; Bohleber 1990, 72.

44. Müller-Hohagen 1988, 142; Bohleber 1990, 76; "shame": Wurmser 1981, 46; "guilt": Eickhoff 1989, 323 ff.
45. Bar-On 1989, 263; Bar-On 1993, 300, 291; Hardtmann 1992b, 45 ff.
46. Frank 1993, 52; compare also Bar-On 1989b, 138, 163; Hecker 1992, 245; Bohleber 1990, 78.
47. Anhalt 1992, 54; Bohleber 1990, 77.
48. See also Hardtmann 1992b, 45; "parentalization": Stierlin 1982, 16.
49. Stierlin 1980, 122, 52 f.
50. Tömmel 1992; Treplin 1992; in a different vein, see Moser 1993a.
51. Eckstaedt 1992, 143, 21 ff.
52. Kohlstruck 1995, 287; "deformations": Moser 1993b, 64; "self-definition": Brendler 1991, 229 ff. and passim; Kohlstuck 1995, 277 ff.
53. Eckstaedt 1992, 499.
54. Gampel 1995, 151; Gubrich-Simitis 1995, 361.
55. Bar-On 1989b, 33, 51, 83 f., 92, 125 f., 134, 265 f.; Bar-On 1993, 290, 296 f.; Rosenkötter 1995, 213; Coleman 1982, 192; Anhalt 1992, 39, 42; Salm 1992, 201; Hecker 1992, 242; Bar-On 1992, 290; Rottgart 1993, 303; Schneider 1987, 116 f.; Hardtmann 1992b, 44 ff.; Müller-Hohagen 1988, 138 f., 178; Bohleber 1990, 75 f., 80.
56. Hardtmann 1992b, 44.
57. Brendler 1991, 235 ff.
58. Eckstaedt 1992, 113.
59. Schneider 1987, 126.
60. Bar-On 1993, 297.
61. Eckstaedt 1992, 145, 152 ff.; Rosenkötter 1995, 214; Schneider 1987, 123; Bar-On 1993, 294 f.
62. Bar-On 1993, 294 f.
63. Rosenkötter 1995, 215; Hardtmann 1995, 250; Eckstaedt 1992, 166 f.
64. Stierlin 1985, 251 f.; Eckstaedt 1992, 102 f.; "instrumentalization": Rottgart 1993, 59.
65. Stierlin 1980, 69.
66. Hardtmann 1992, 47.
67. Hardtmann 1992, 52 f.
68. On the "psychopathology" of the German family from the perspective of guilt, see Gaudard 1995, 151 ff.
69. Appy 1987, 35.
70. Vesper 1995, 340 ff.; Härtling 1993, 23.
71. Kohut 1993, 84; Hecker 1992, 245; Stierlin 192, 256 f.
72. Bar-On 1990, 230.
73. von Schlippe 1992, 159 f.; "self-respect": Anhalt 1992, 54; help for a

change of ways: Bauriedl 1995, 41; Leggewie 191, 13 ff.; "loneliness": Rosenthal 1987, 30, 35.

74. Brendler 1991, 239, 251, 231 f.

6. DAMAGE TO DEMOCRACY

1. Almond and Verba 1963, 429, 496.
2. Conradt 1980, 255, 228, 230, 241, 263, 252.
3. Conradt 1980, 265, 251, 221, 264.
4. Kaase 1989, 214, 204 ff., 208, 210, 252.
5. Kaase 1989, 214 f.; Schöbel 1994, 184 f.
6. Berg-Schlosser 1990, 45, 33, 42 ff.
7. Lutz 1992, 285, 277 ff., 282 f.; on the continuity of everyday culture, see also Schäfer 1983, 114 ff.
8. Lutz 1992, 283 f.
9. Stolleis 1996, 14.
10. See the subtle reflections by Bohleber 1994.
11. Beiner 1995, 3 f., 6, 9; Barber 1994, 93 ff.; "potential for conflict": Walzer 1995, 154; Dahl 1992, 49 ff.; Kymlicka and Norman 1994, 352, 355; Stewart 1995, 75 ff.; Beiner 1995, 4, 6, 9.
12. Dahl 1992, 50 f.; Beiner 1995, 4.
13. Offe and Preuss 1991, 165 f.; Buchstein and Schmalz-Bruns 1994, 300 f.; Kymlicka and Norman 1994, 352.
14. Offe and Preuss 1991, 161 f., 166 ff.; compare also Walzer 1995, 155 f.
15. Fraenkel 1964, 64 f.
16. Münkler 1992, 41.
17. Riesenberg 1992.
18. Locke 1955, 5 f.
19. Galston 1988, 1277 ff.
20. Frankenberg 1996, 139 ff.; Münkler 1992, 39 f.
21. Compare also Dahl 1992, 46.
22. Lindner 1990, 91 ff.; Schwan 1995.
23. Maslow 1957, 92 ff.
24. Inkeles 1971, 231; on this compare also Lasswell 1951; Maslow 1957, 100 ff., 128; Lane 1962; Allport 1958.
25. Frankenberg 1996, 133, 193; Barber 1994, 171 f.; Galston 1988, 1285; "dichotomous model": Offe and Preuss 1991, 169.
26. Gilligan 1982, 19 ff.
27. Walzer 1995, 154.
28. Gilligan 1982, 2.

29. Gilligan 1982, 20.
30. Compare also Benjamin 1990.
31. Scheler 1973, 70, 76, 66, 17 ff., 36, 50 ff., 56.
32. Scheler 1973, 143 ff., 24, 78 ff., 147, 137 ff., 107.
33. Hoffmann 1982, 282 ff., 298 ff.; Hoffmann 1984, 284 f., 297; Goleman 1994, 96 ff.
34. Lerner 1958, 49 f.
35. Hoffmann 1984, 289 f.; "sense of responsibility": Weinreich-Haster 1986, 402 ff.; Kant 1952, 152; Arendt 1985.
36. Hoffmann 1982, 295–98, 310 f.
37. See also Goleman 1994, 96 ff.; Dahl 1992, 57; Barber 1994, 190 ff.
38. Frankenberg 1996, 147.
39. Frankenberg 1996, 147 ff.; Barber 1994, 231; Göhler 1996.
40. Erikson 1970.
41. Schwan 1990.
42. Ostrom 1990, 183–88.
43. Putnam 1993, 164, 12 15.
44. Putnam 1993, 168–74.
45. Putnam 1993, 185, 181.
46. Dahl 1992, 54 ff.; Kymlicka and Norman 1994, 359; Walzer 1989, 214; Barber 1994, 147, 181.
47. Walzer 1989, 215 ff.; Kymlicka and Norman 1994, 362; compare also Burtt 1993, 363 ff.; Walzer 1995, 169 ff.
48. Kymlicka and Norman 1994, 363; Galston 1988, 1282.
49. Emrich 1994.
50. Compare Schwan 1992.
51. Freud 1964, 65 f.
52. Freud 1955b, 14; "anxiety": Freud 1964, 78, and Freud 1961a, 49; "masochism": Freud 1961b, 166, and Freud 1955a, 188 f.; "expectant anxiety": Freud 1959, 123; "sadism": Freud 1964, 108 f.
53. Mitscherlich and Mitscherlich 1975, 26 f., xxv, 13, 8.
54. Mitscherlich 1992, 416.
55. Moser 1992, 390–97.
56. Wurmser 1990, xvi. (Quotation taken from the preface to the German edition).
57. Wurmser 1981, 46 f., 17.
58. Moser 1992, 401 f.
59. Wurmser 1981, 76.
60. Vogt 1986, 897; Parin 1990.
61. Parin 1990, 650 f.; "scapegoat": Vogt 1986, 899.

62. Lynd 1961, Witte 1986, 343; Ickes and Layden 1978; Geppert and Hackhausen 1990, 184 (Buss quotation), 187.
63. Geppert and Heckhausen 1990, 184–87. (Quotation "While guilt feelings . . . ," from Buss 1980, 159).
64. Sniderman 1975, 171 ff.
65. Sniderman 1975, 62, 67, 202, 222.
66. Sniderman 1975, 31 ff., 66 f.
67. Sniderman 1975, 66; Buber 1962, 502.
68. Sniderman 1975, 84 f., 73 ff., 70, 102; compare also Kuhl 1986, 33.
69. Sniderman 1975, 90 f., 37.
70. Schöbel 1994, 183.
71. Sniderman 1975, ix, 93–99.
72. Sniderman 1975, 318
73. Sniderman 1975, 125 ff., 178.
74. Sniderman 1975, 311, 321; compare also Schöbel 1994, 184.
75. Sniderman 1975, 107.

7. OVERCOMING SILENCE TOGETHER

1. Noelle-Neumann and Köcher 1987, 358.
2. Taylor 1970, 8.
3. Arendt 1963, 163 ff.
4. Heinsohn 1996, 23.
5. Hartmann 1926, 818.
6. Emrich 1996, 75, 56–63, 44 ff.
7. Bormann 1996, 80 f.
8. Giordano 1990, 40; "petrefaction": Giordano 1990, 281.
9. Kodalle 1994, 52.
10. Kodalle 1994, 53 33.
11. Sereny 1974, 364, 349.
12. Reick 1925, 115; "differently": Böckenförde 1992, 172.
13. Schlink 1988, 68 f.; 1995a, 355.
14. Kodalle 1994, 41, 51–54.
15. Schlink 1995a, 355; Kodalle 1994, 57.
16. Schlink 1997, 127–28.
17. The example of Hanna and the judge's reaction in the 1960s in the Federal Republic, although it is literary fiction and cannot strictly speaking be held up against historical reality, does show how shaky the assumption is that apart from a deadly rage of anti-Semitism,

there could have been no other reason, no other motive, for the continuation of the death marches (Goldhagen 1996, 417ff.).

18. Bleuler 1964, 103f., 113f.; "exclusion": Hirschmann 1962, 141ff., 146; Rich 1964, 53.
19. Sa'adeh 1990; 1992; 1998, 28, 57.
20. Rorty 1988; Apel 1988.
21. Bauer et al. 1979, 595a-68, 448; "dignity": quoted from Werle and Wandres 1995, 43.
22. Quoted in Giordano 1990, 135.
23. Bauer et al. 1979, 595a-74, 454; 595a-68, 448.
24. Bauer et al. 1979, 595a-74, 455; "public nature of legal proceedings": Steinbach 1984, 70; "Hofmann": Langbein 1995, 226.
25. Frei 1996, 399.
26. Radbruch 1946, quoted in Kaufmann 1990, 89; compare Alexy 1993, 3f.; "debate on the statute of limitations": Steinbach 1984, 77; "violation": Rautenberg 1993b, 72; "arbitrary act": quoted in Roggemann 1994, 776.
27. Limbach 1993, 71; Alexy 1993, 24f., 29f.
28. Archbishop Tutu in *Der Tagesspiegel*, 1.29.1996.
29. Lutz 1992, 280.
30. Leggewie 1995, 200ff.
31. Dostoyevsky 1951, 551–59.

Bibliography

Adelson, Joseph. 1971. "The Political Imagination of the Young Adolescent." *Daedalus. Journal of the American Academy of Arts and Sciences* 100, no. 4.

Adorno, Theodor W. 1973. *Studien zum autoritären Charakter.* Frankfurt am Main.

Adorno, Theodor W., and Walter Dirks. 1955. "Gruppenexperiment. Ein Studienbericht, bearb. von Friedrich Pollock u. einem Geleitwort von Franz Böhm." In *Frankfurter Beiträge zur Soziologie, im Auftrag des Instituts für Sozialforschung,* Bd. 2. Frankfurt am Main.

Alexy, Robert. 1993. *Mauerschütze. Zum Verhältnis von Recht, Moral, und Strafbarkeit.* Hamburg.

Allport, Gordon W. 1958. *Werden der Persönlichkeit.* Stuttgart.

———. 1970. *Gestalt und Wachstum in der Persönlichkeit.* Meisenheim am Glan.

———. 1971. *The Nature of Prejudice.* Cambridge MA.

Almond, Gabriel A., and Sidney Verba. 1963. *The Civic Culture.* Princeton.

———. 1980. *The Civic Culture Revisited. An Analytical Study.* Boston.

Altmeyer, Hermann. 1986. "Schuld, Umkehr und Versöhnung im Christentum." In Bernhard Mansen SVD, ed., *Schuld und Versöhnung in verschiedenen Religionen.* Sankt Augustin.

Aly, Götz. 1999. *"Final Solution." Nazi Population Policy and the Murder of the European Jews.* Trans. Belinda Cooper and Allison Brown. London.

Améry, Jean. 1980. *At the Mind's Limits: Contemplations by a Survivor on Auschwitz and Its Realities.* Trans. Sidney Rosenfeld and Stella P. Rosenfeld. Bloomington IN.

Anhalt, Irene. 1992. "Abschied von meinem Vater." In Barbara Heimannsberg and Christoph J. Schmidt, eds., *Das kollektive Schweigen. Nationalsozialistische Vergangenheit und gebrochene Identität in der Psychoanalyse.* Cologne.

Apel, Karl Otto. 1988. "Zuruck zur Normalität? Oder könnten wir aus der nationalsozialistischen Katastrophe etwas Besonderes gelernt haben? Das Problem des weltgeschichtlichen Übergangs zur post-konventionellen Moral und spezifisch deutschen Sicht." In *Zerstö-rung des moralischen Selbstbewußtseins: Chance oder Gefährdung? Praktische Philosophie: Deutschland nach dem Nationalsozialismus.* Published by Forum der Philosophie, Bad Homburg. Frankfurt am Main.

Appy, Gottfried. 1987. "Einige Gedanken zur Sprachlosigkeit." *DVP-Infor-mationen*, Nr. 2, October, 35–39.

Arendt, Hannah. 1946. "Organisierte Schuld." *Die Wandlung*, Jg. 1, Heft 4, April, 333–44.

———. 1963. *Eichmann in Jerusalem. A Report on the Banality of Evil.* New York.

———. 1982. *Lectures on Kant's Political Philosophy.* Ed. with an inter-pretive essay by Ronald Beiner. Chicago.

———. 1987. *Wahrheit und Lüge in der Politik. 2 Essays.* Munich.

———. 1992. *Eichmann in Jerusalem. Ein Bericht von der Banalität des Bösen*, with an essay by Hans Mommsen. Munich.

Arndt, Adolf. 1955. "Rechtsdenken in unserer Zeit. Positivismus und Na-turrecht. Ein Vortrag." In Adolf Arndt, *Recht und Staat in Geschichte und Gegenwart.* Tübingen.

Arnim, Gabriele von. 1991. *Das große Schweigen. Von der Schwierigkeit, mit den Schatten der Vergangenheit zu leben.* Munich.

Bader, Karl S. 1964. "Schuld—Verantwortung—Sühne als rechtshisto-risches Problem." In Erwin Frey, ed., *Schuld, Verantwortung, Strafe im Lichte der Theologie, Jurisprudenz, Soziologie, Medizin und Philoso-phie.* Zurich.

Bankier, David. 1992. *The Germans and the Final Solution: Public Opin-ion under Nazism.* Oxford.

Bar-On, Dan. 1989a. "Holocaust Perpetrators and Their Children: A Paradoxical Morality." *Journal of Humanistic Psychology* 29, no. 4, 424–43.

———. 1989b. *Legacy of Silence: Encounters with Children of the Third Reich.* Cambridge MA.

———. 1990. "Die Kinder der Holocaust-Täter und ihre Suche nach moralischer Identität." *Integrative Therapie*, Heft 3, 222–45.

———. 1992. "A Testimony on the Moment before the (Possible) Oc-currence of a Massacre: On a Possible Contradiction between the

Ability to Adjust Which Means Mental Health and the Maintaining of Human Moral Values." *Journal of Traumatic Stress* 5, no. 2, 289–301.

―――. 1993. *Die Last des Schweigens. Gespräche mit Kindern von Nazi Tätern.* Frankfurt am Main.

Barber, Benjamin. 1994. *Strong Democracy: Participatory Politics for a New Age.* Berkeley.

Bauer, Fritz, et al. 1979. *Justiz und ns-Verbrechen. Sammlung deutscher Strafurteile wegen nationalsozialistischer Tötungsverbrechen 1945–1966.* Amsterdam.

Baumann, Wolfgang. 1992. *Das Schuldanerkenntnis.* Berlin.

Baumann, Zygmunt. 1989. *Modernity and the Holocaust.* Ithaca.

Bauriedl, Thea. 1994. *Auch ohne Couch. Psychoanalyse als Beziehungstheorie und ihre Anwendungen.* Freiburg.

―――. 1995. *Wege aus der Gewalt. Analyse von Beziehungen.* Freiburg.

Beiner, Ronald, ed. 1995. *Theorizing Citizenship.* New York.

Benedict, Ruth. 1977. *The Chrysanthemum and the Sword.* London.

Benjamin, Jessica. 1988. *The Bonds of Love: Psychoanalysis, Feminism, and the Power of Domination.* New York.

Bergmann, Martin S., Milton E. Jucovy, and Judith Kestenberg, eds. 1982. *Generations of the Holocaust.* New York.

Bergmann, Werner, and Rainer Erb. Antisemitismus in der Bundesrepublik Deutschland: Ergebnisse der empirischen Forschung von 1946–1989. 1991.

Berg-Schlosser, Dirk. 1990. "Entwicklung der politischen Kultur in der Bundesrepublik Deutschland." *Aus Politik und Zeitgeschichte* B7/90, 30–46.

Binion, Rudolph. 1976. *Hitler among the Germans.* New York.

Bleuler, Manfred. 1964. "Sühne und ärztliche Behandlung in ihrer heilenden Bedeutung." In Erwin Frey, ed., *Schuld, Verantwortung, Strafe im Lichte der Theologie, Jurisprudenz, Soziologie, Medizin und Philosophie.* Zurich.

Boberach, Heinz, ed. 1984. *Meldungen aus dem Reich. Die geheimen Lagerberichte des Sicherheitsdienstes der SS 1938–1945.* Herrsching. (Index. 1985)

Böckenförde, Ernst-Wolfgang. 1992. "Der Beitrag politischen Handelns zur Verwirklichung von Gerechtigkeit." In W. Ernst, ed., *Gerechtigkeit in Gesellschaft, Wirtschaft und Politik.* Studien zur theologischen Ethik, 34. Freiburg im Breisgau.

Böckle, Franz. 1987. "Was bedeutet 'Natur' in der Moraltheologie?" In

Franz Böckle, ed., *Der umstrittene Naturbegriff. Person—Natur—
Sexualität in der kirchlichen Morallehre.* Düsseldorf.

Bohleber, Werner. 1990. "Das Fortwirken des Nationalsozialismus in der
zweiten und dritten Generation nach Auschwitz." *Babylon. Beiträge
zur jüdischen Gegenwart,* Heft 7, September, 70–83.

———. 1994. "Autorität und Freiheit heute: Sind die 68er schuld am
Rechtsextremismus?" *Psychosozial,* 17 Jg., Heft 2, Nr. 56, 73–85.

Bolz, Norbert. 1993. "Das Böse jenseits von Gut und Böse." In Carsten
Colpe and Wilhelm Schmidt-Biggemann, eds., *Das Böse. Eine historische Phänomenologie des Unerklärlichen.* Frankfurt am Main.

Boor, W. de, G. Kohlmann. 1980. *Obzessionsdelikte. Tiefenmotive bei
Eigentumsdelinquenz.* Basel.

Bormann, Martin. 1996. *Leben gegen Schatten. Gelebte Zeit—
geschenkte Zeit. Begegnungen—Erfahrungen—Folgerungen.*
Paderborn.

Breasted, James Henry. 1934. *The Dawn of Conscience.* New York.

Brendler, Konrad. 1991. "Die Unumgänglichkeit des Themas Holocaust
für die Enkelgeneration." In Konrad Brendler and Günter Rexilius,
eds., *Beiträge zum internationalen Forschungskolloquium Lernen und
Pseudo-Lernen in der Aufarbeitung des Holocaust.* Wuppertaler
Sozialwissenschaftliche Studien, Bd. 4. Wuppertal.

Browning, Christopher. 1992. *Ordinary Men: Reserve Police Battalion
101 and the Final Solution in Poland.* New York.

Buber, Martin. 1962. "Schuld und Schuldgefühle." In Martin Buber,
Werke, Bd. 1, Schriften zur Philosophie. Munich.

Buchheim, Hans et al. 1968. *Anatomy of the SS State.* Trans. Richard
Barry, Marian Jackson, and Dorothy Lang. New York.

Buchstein, Hubertus, and Rainer Schmalz-Bruns. 1994. "Nachwort. Re-
publikanische Demokratie." In Benjamin Barber, *Starke Demokratie.
Über die Teilhabe am Politischen.* Trans. from the English by Chri-
stiane Goldmann and Christel Erbacher-von Grümbkow, with a fore-
word by the author of the German edition and an afterword by
Hubertus Buchstein. Hamburg.

Bude, Heinz. 1992. *Bilanz der Nachfolge.* Frankfurt am Main.

Bujo, Bénézet. 1991. "Gibt es eine spezifische afrikanische Ethik? Ein An-
frage an westliches Denken." In Walter Kerber, ed., *Das Absolute in
der Ethik.* Munich.

Burns, Angelika. 1978. "Persönlichkeit und Demokratie bei Gordon Allport. Anthropologische und sozialpsychologische Betrachtungen zur
Genese eines Demokraten." Diss., Basel.

Burtt, Shelley. 1993. "The Politics of Virtue Today: A Critique and a Proposal." *American Political Science Review* 87, no. 2, June, 360–68.

Buruma, Ian. 1994. *The Wages of Guilt: Memories of War in Germany and Japan.* New York.

Buss, A. H. 1980. *Self-Consciousness and Social Anxiety.* San Francisco.

Coleman, M. Donald, and Anonymous. 1982. "Children of the Victims." In Martin S. Bergmann and Milton E. Jucovy, eds., *Generations of the Holocaust.* New York.

Colpe, Carsten. 1993. "Religion und Mythos im Altertum." In Carsten Colpe and Wilhelm Schmidt-Biggemann, eds., *Das Böse, Eine historische Phänomenologie des Unerklärlichen.* Frankfurt am Main.

Condrau, Cion, and Franz Böckle. 1981. "Schuld und Sünde." In Franz Böckle et al., eds., *Christlicher Glaub in moderner Gesellschaft.* Teilband 2. Freiburg.

Conover, Pamela Johnston. 1995. "Citizen Identities and Conceptions of the Self." *Journal of Political Philosophy* 3, No. 2, 133–65.

Conradt, David P. 1980. "Changing German Political Culture." In Gabriel Almond and Sidney Verba, *The Civic Culture Revisited. An Analytical Study.* Boston.

Craig, Gordon. 1982. *The Germans.* New York.

Dahl, Robert A. 1992. "The Problem of Civic Competence." *Journal of Democracy* 3, No. 4, 45–59.

Die Zeit. 1995. Nr. 10, March 3, "Forum," 14–20.

Dimsdale, Joel E. 1980. *Survivors, Victims and Perpetrators. Essays on the Nazi Holocaust.* Washington.

Dodds, E. R. 1951. *The Greeks and the Irrational.* Berkeley.

Dokument 1919-PS: 145, Himmler's Speech at the SS Gruppenführer Meeting in Posen on October 4. 1943. In *Der Prozeß gegen die Hauptkriegsverbrecher vor dem Internationalen Militärgerichtshof Nürnberg 14. Nov. 1945—I. Okt. 1946.* Published in Nuremberg. 1948. Bd. 29.

Dostoyevsky, Fyodor. 1966. *Crime and Punishment.* Trans. with a introduction by Davis Magarshack. New York.

Eckstaedt, Anita. 1992. *Nationalsozialismus in der 'Zweiten Generation.' Psychoanalyse von Hörigkeitsverhältnissen.* Frankfurt am Main.

Eickhoff, F. W. 1989. "On the "Borrowed Unconscious Sense of Guilt" and the Palimpsestic Structure of a Symptom—Afterthoughts on the Hamburg Congress of the IPA." *International Review of Psycho-Analysis* 16, 323–29.

Ellscheid, Günter, and Winfried Hassemer. 1975. "Strafe ohne Schuld.

Bemerkungen zum Grund strafrechtlicher Haftung." In Klaus Lüders-
sen and Fritz Sack, eds., *Seminar: Abweichendes Verhalten II. Die
gesellschaftliche Reaktion of Kriminalität*. Bd. 1: *Strafgesetzgebung
und Strafrechtsdogmatik*. Frankfurt am Main.

Emrich, Hinderk M. 1994. "Identität und Versprechen." In Helmut Girndt
and Wolfgang H. Schrader, eds., *Realität und Gewißheit*. Fichtestu-
dien, Bd. 6.

————. 1996. "Über die Notwendigkeit des Vergessens." In Hinderk M.
Emrich and Gary Smith, eds., *Vom Nutzen des Vergessens*. Berlin.

Enzensberger, Hans Magnus, ed. 1990. *Europa in Trümmern. Augenzeu-
genberichte aus den Jahren 1944–1948*. Frankfurt am Main.

Erikson, Erik H. 1970. *Jugend und Krise. Die Psychodynamik im sozialen
Wandel*. Stuttgart.

Erlinghagen, Helmut S. G. 1983. "Im geistigen Zustand bewußter Ober-
flüchlichkeit. Schuld und Umkehr im Verständnis des Buddhismus." In
Michael Sievernich and Klaus Philipp Seif, eds., *Schuld und Umkehr
in den Weltreligionen*. Mainz.

Faimberg, Haydée. 1985. "Die Ineinanderrückung (Téléscoping) der
Generationen. Zur Genealogie gewisser Identifizierungen." *Jahrbuch
der Psychoanalyse*, Bd. 20, 114–42.

Fest, Joachim. 1996. *Plotting Hitler's Death. The German Resistance to
Hitler. 1933–1945*. London.

Fischer-Lichte, Erika. 1997. "Das theatralische Opfer. Zum Funktions-
wandel von Theater im 20. Jahrhundert." Manuscript of the Inaugural
Address at the Freie Universität Berlin.

Fraenkel, Ernst. 1964. *Deutschland und die westlichen Demokratien*.
Stuttgart.

Frank, Niklas. 1993. *Der Vater—Eine Abrechnung*. Munich.

Frankenberg, Günter. 1996. *Die Verfassung der Republik. Autorität und
Solidarität in der Zivilgesellschaft*. Baden-Baden.

Frei, Norbert. 1996. *Vergangenheitspolitik. Die Anfänge der Bundesrepublik und die NS-Vergangenheit*. Munich.

Freud, Sigmund. 1955a. "A Child Is Being Beaten: Contribution to the
Study of the Origins of Sexual Perversions." *The Standard Edition of
the Complete Psychoanalytical Works of Sigmund Freud*. Translated
from the German under the General Editorship of James Strachey.
London. Vol. 17: 175–204.

————. 1955b. "Beyond the Pleasure Principle." *Standard Edition*.
Vol. 18: 3–64.

————. 1959. "Obsessive Actions and Religious Practices." *Standard Edition.* Vol. 9: 115–28.

————. 1961a. "The Ego and the Id." *Standard Edition.* Vol. 19: 3–66.

————. 1961b. "The Economic Problem of Masochism." *Standard Edition.* Vol. 19: 155–72.

————. 1964. "New Introductory Lectures on Psychoanalysis." *Standard Edition.* Vol. 22.

Frey, Erwin, ed. 1964 *Schuld, Verantwortung, Strafe im Lichte der Theorie, Jurisprudenz, Soziologie, Medizin und Philosophie.* Zurich.

Funke, Manfred. 1996. "Der letzte Sieg der Wehrmacht. Deutsche Kriegsverbrechen und Besatzungspolitik in Italien." Review of Gerhard Schreiber (1996). *Frankfurter Allgemeine Zeitung,* October 21, Nr. 245, 10.

Futterknecht, Franz. 1976. *Das Dritte Reich im deutschen Roman der Nachkriegszeit. Untersuchungen zur Faschismustheorie und Faschismusbewältigung.* Bonn.

Galston, William A. 1988. "Liberal Virtues." *American Political Science Review* 82, no. 4, December. 1277–89.

Gampel, Yolanda. 1982. "A Daughter of Silence." In Martin S. Bergmann and Milton E. Jucovy, eds., *Generations of the Holocaust.* New York.

Gauch, Sigfrid. 1996. *Vaterspuren. Erzählungen.* Frankfurt am Main.

Gaudard, Pierre-Yves. 1995. "Mémoire et culpabilité en Allemagne. Contribution à l'étude du processus de deuil collectif allemand après le national-socialisme. Thèse doctorat en sociologie sous la direction de Nicole Elzner." Paris x Nanterre.

Geppert, Ulrich, and Heinz Heckhausen. 1990. "Ontogenese der Emotionen." In Klaus R. Scherer, ed., *Enzyklopädie der Psychologie,* Bd. 3, *Psychologie der Emotionen.* Göttingen.

Gilbert, Gustave M. 1947. *Nuremberg Diary.* New York.

Gilligan, Carol. 1982. *In a Different Voice: Psychological Theory and Women's Development.* Cambridge MA.

Giordano, Ralph. 1990. *Die zweite Schuld oder Von der Last, Deutscher zu sein.* Munich.

Göhler, Gerhard. 1997. *Institutionen—Macht—Repräsentation: Wofür politische Institutionen stehen und wie sie wirken.* Baden-Baden.

Goldhagen, Daniel Jonah. 1996. *Hitler's Willing Executioners: Ordinary Germans and the Holocaust.* New York.

Goleman, Daniel. 1995. *Emotional Intelligence.* New York.

Grosser, Alfred. 1990. *Die Ermordung der Menschheit. Der Genozid im Gedächtnis der Völker.* Munich.

————. 1996. *Les identités difficiles*. Paris.

Gründel, Johannes. 1990. "Schuld—Strafe—Versöhnung aus theologischer Sicht." In Arnold Köpcke-Duttler, ed., *Schuld—Strafe—Versöhnung. Ein interdisziplinäres Gespräch*. Mainz.

————. 1993. "Schuld und Vergebung im christlichen Verständnis." In Gerd Haeffner, ed., *Schuld und Schuldbewältigung. Keine Zukunft ohne Auseinandersetzung mit der Vergangenheit*. Düsseldorf.

————. n.d. "Moralpsychologische und theologische Aspekte zum Umgang mit der Schuld." In Günter Eifler and Otto Saame, eds., *Die Frage nach der Schuld*. Mainz.

Gschwind, Martin, and Erardo C. Rautenberg. 1987. *Kriminalpsychopathologie*. Berlin.

Gubrich-Simitis, Ilse. 1995. "Vom Konkretismus zur Metaphorik." In Martin S. Bergmann, Milton E. Jucovy, and Judith Kestenberg, eds., *Kinder der Opfer. Kinder der Täter. Psychoanalyse und Holocaust*. Frankfurt am Main.

Günther, Klaus. 1989. "Natürlich sind wir für die Abschaffung des Strafrechts! Sind wir es wirklich? Über einige moralische Aporien gegenwärtiger Kriminalpolitik." In Gerhard Gamm and Gerd Kimmerle, eds., *Vorschrift und Autonomie: Zur Zivilisationsgeschichte der Moral*. Tübingen.

————. 1991. "Möglichkeiten einer diskursethischen Begründung des Strafrechts." In Heike Jung, Heinz Müller-Dietz, and Ulfried Neumann, eds., *Recht und Moral. Beiträge zu einer Standortbestimmung*. Baden-Baden.

————. 1994. "Kampf gegen das Böse? Zehn Thesen wider die ethische Aufrüstung der Kriminalpolitik." *Kritische Justiz*, Jg. 27, Heft 2, 135–57.

Haeffner, Gerd. 1993. *Schuld und Schuldbewältigung. Keine Zukunft ohne Auseinandersetzung mit der Vergangenheit*. Düsseldorf.

Hagemann, Ludwig. 1986. "Schuld und Versöhnung im Islam." In Bernhard Mensen svd, ed., *Schuld und Versöhnung in verschiedenen Religionen*. Sankt Augustin.

Hardtmann, Gertrud. 1982. "The Shadows of the Past." In Martin S. Bergmann and Milton E. Jucovy, eds., *Generations of the Holocaust*. New York.

————. 1988. "Von unerträglicher Schuld zu erträglichem Schuldgefühl?" In Dan Bar-On, F. Beiner, and M. Brusten, eds., *Der Holocaust. Familiale und gesellschaftliche Folgen. Aufarbeitung in Wissenschaft und Erziehung? Ergebnisse eines internationalen Forschungskolloquiums an der Bergischen Universität—Gesamthochschule Wuppertal.*

―――. 1992a. "Ein Volk ohne Schatten." In Gertrud Hardtmann, ed., *Spuren der Verfolgung. Seelische Auswirkungen des Holocaust auf die Opfer und ihre Kinder.* Gerlingen.

―――. 1992b. "Begegnung mit dem Tod. Die Kinder der Täter." *Psychosozial,* Jg. 15, Heft 3, Nr. 51, 42–53.

Härtling, Peter. 1993. *Nachgetragene Liebe.* Munich.

Hartmann, Nicolai. 1932. *Ethics.* 3 vols. New York.

Hassemer, Winfried. 1981. *Einführung in die Grundlagen des Strafrechts.* Munich.

Hauer, Nadine. 1994. *Die Mitläufer. Oder: Die Unfähigkeit zu fragen. Auswirkungen des Nationalsozialismus auf die Demokratie von heute.* Opladen.

Hecker, Margarete. 1992. "Familienrekonstruktion in Deutschland. Ein Versuch, sich der Vergangenheit zu stellen." In Barbara Heimannsberg and Christoph J. Schmidt, eds., *Das kollektive Schweigen. Nationalsozialistische Vergangenheit und gebrochene Identität in der Psychotherapie.* Cologne.

Heimannsberg, Barbara, and Christoph J. Schmidt, eds. 1992. *Das kollektive Schweigen. Nationalsozialistische Vergangenheit und gebrochene Identität in der Psychotherapie.* Cologne.

Heinsohn, Gunnar. 1996. "Auschwitz ohne Hitler? Die Tafeln von Sinai und die Lehre von den drei Weltzeitaltern." *Lettre International,* summer, 21–27.

Henkys. 1964. *Die nationalsozialistischen Gewaltverbrechen. Geschichte und Gericht,* ed. Dietrich Goldschmidt. With an introduction by Kurt Scharf and a contribution by Jürgen Baumann. Stuttgart.

Hilberg, Raul. 1967. *The Destruction of the European Jews.* New York.

Hoch, Gerhard. 1982. *Zwölf wiedergefundene Jahre. Kaltenkirchen unter dem Hakenkreuz.* Bad Bramstedt.

Hoffmann, Martin L. 1982. "Development of Prosocial Motivation: Empathy and Guilt." In Nancy Eisenberg, ed., *The Development of Prosocial Behavior.* New York.

―――. 1984. "Empathy. Its Limitations and Its Role in a Comprehensive Moral Theory." In William M. Kurtines and Jacob L. Gewirtz, eds., *Morality, Moral Behavior, and Moral Development.* New York.

Hohenstein, Alexander. 1963. *Wartheländisches Tagebuch 1941/42.* Munich.

Hole, Gunter. 1989. "Schuld und Schuldgefühle." In Walter Poeldinger and Wolfgang Wagner, eds., *Aggression, Selbstaggression, Familie und Gesellschaft.* Das Mayerling-Symposium. New York.

Höltker, Georg. 1936. "Das Sündenbewußtsein bei den Azteken im alten Mexiko." *Anthropos. Revue Internationale d'Ethnologie et de Linguistique,* Heft 1, 2, 213–33.

Honnefelder, Ludger 1985. "Gewissen und Identität." In *Gewissensbildung heute—zwischen Standfestigkeit und Anpassung. Referate und Berichte der Jahrestagung der Vereinigung Deutschen Ordensschulen und -internate (Sektion Schule) vom 28.–30. Oktober 1985 in Freising.* Materialien 7. Published by the Arbeitskreis katholischer Schulen in freier Trägerschaft.

Höß, Rudolf. 1958. *Commandant of Auschwitz.* London.

Hull, William L. 1964. *Kampf um eine Seele. Gespräche mit Eichmann in der Todeszelle.* Wuppertal.

Hummel, Reinhard. 1983. "'Im Räderwerk des Karma.' Schuld und Umkehr im Hinduismus." In Michael Sievernich and Klaus Philipp Seif, eds., *Schuld und Umkehr in den Weltreligionen.* Mainz.

Ickes, William, and Mary A. Layden. 1978. "Attribution of Styles." In John H. Harvey et al., eds. *New Directions in Attribution Research.* Vol. 2. Hirrsdale NJ.

Ignatieff, Michael. 1995. "The Myth of Citizenship." In Ronald Beiner, ed., *Theorizing Citizenship.* New York.

Inkeles, Alex. 1972. "National Character and Modern Political Systems." In Francis C. K. Hsu, ed., *Psychological Anthropology.* Cambridge MA.

Jacobson, Hans-Adolf. 1968. "The *Kommissarbefehl* and Mass Executions of Soviet Russian Prisoners of War." In Hans Buchheim et al., eds., *Anatomy of the SS State.* Trans. Richard Barry, Marian Jackson, Dorothy Long. New York.

Jäger, Herbert. 1982. *Verbrechen unter totalitärer Herrschaft. Studien zur nationalsozialistischen Gewaltkriminalität.* With an afterword for the reprint by Adalbert Rückerl. Frankfurt am Main.

Jaspers, Karl. 1947. *The Question of German Guilt.* Trans. E. B. Ashton. New York.

Kaase, Max. 1989. "Bewußtseinslagen und Leitbilder in der Bundesrepublik Deutschland." In Werner Weidenfeld and Hartmut Zimmermann, eds., *Deutschland-Handbuch. Eine doppelte Bilanz 1949–1989.* Bonn.

Kant, Immanuel. 1949. *Religion within the Limits of Reason Alone*. New York.

―――. 1952. *The Critique of Judgment*. Trans. James Creed Meredith. Oxford.

―――. 1996. "Critique of Practical Reasoning." Trans. Mary J. Gregor. In Paul Guyer and Allen W. Wood, eds., *Immanuel Kant: Practical Philosophy*. Cambridge.

Kaufmann, Arthur. 1976. *Das Schuldprinzip. Eine strafrechtlich-rechtsphilosophische Untersuchung*. Heidelberg.

―――. 1990. "Das Problem der Schuld aus strafrechtlich-rechtsphilosophischer Sicht." In Arnold Köpcke-Duttler, ed., *Schuld, Strafe, Versöhnung. Ein interdisziplinäres Gespräch*. Mainz.

Keller, Gottfried. 1993. *The Misused Love Letters*. Trans. Michael Bullock. New York.

Kelman, Herbert C., and V. Lee Hamilton. 1989. *Crimes of Obedience. Toward a Social Psychology of Authority and Responsibility*. New Haven.

Kerber, Walter. 1982. "Geschichtlichkeit konkreter sittlicher Normen aus der Sicht der Philosophie und der Humanwissenschaften." In Walter Kerber et al., eds., *Sittliche Normen. Zum Problem ihrer allgemeinen und umwandelbaren Geltung*. Düsseldorf.

Kershaw, Ian. 1983. *Popular Opinion and Political Dissent in the Third Reich: Bavaria 1933–1945*. Oxford.

Kestenberg, Judith S. 1982. "A Metapsychological Assessment Based on an Analysis of a Survivor's Child." In Martin S. Bergmann and Milton E. Jucovy, eds., *Generations of the Holocaust*. New York.

―――. 1993. "What a Psychoanalyst Learned from the Holocaust and Genocide." *International Journal of Psycho-Analysis* 74, 1117–29.

Khoury, Theodor A. 1983. "Die Seele verlangt gebieterisch nach dem Bösen. Schuld und Umkehr im Islam." In Michael Sievernich and Klaus Philipp Seif, eds., *Schuld und Umkehr in den Weltreligionen*. Mainz.

Kittel, Manfred. 1993. *Die Legende von der 'Zweiten Schuld.' Vergangenheitsbewältigung in der Ära Adenauer*. Berlin.

Kittsteiner, H. D. 1990. *Gewissen und Geschichte. Studien zur Entwicklung des moralischen Bewußtseins*. Heidelberg.

Klee, Ernst, Willi Dreßen, and Volker Rieß. 1991. *Those Were the Days: The Holocaust as Seen by Its Perpetrators and Bystanders*. Trans. Deborah Burnstone. London.

Kodalle, Klaus-M. 1994. "Verzeihung nach Wendezeiten? Über Unnach-

sichtigkeit und mißlingende Selbstentschuldigung." Inaugural
Address at the Friedrich-Schiller-Universität Jena, June 2. 1994.
Erlangen.

Koebner, Thomas. 1987. "Die Schuldfrage. Vergangenheitsverweigerung
und Lebenslügen in der Diskussion 1945–1949." In Thomas Koebner,
Gert Sautermeister, and Sigrid Schneider, eds., *Deutschland nach
Hitler.* Opladen.

Kohlstruck, Michael. 1995. "Die Enkel der Mitläufer. Die Thematisierung
des Nationalsozialismus bei jungen Männern." Diss., Berlin.

Kohut, Heinz, and Miriam Elson. 1993. *Auf der Suche nach dem Selbst.
Kohuts Seminare zur Selbstpsychologie und Psychotherapie mit jün-
geren Erwachsenen.* Ed. Miriam Elson. Munich.

Kolakowski, Leszek. 1967. "Ethik ohne Kodex." In Leszek Kolakowski,
Traktat über die Sterblichkeit der Vernunft. Philosophische Essays.
Munich.

Köpcke-Duttler, Arnold. 1990. *Schuld—Strafe—Versöhnung. Ein interdisziplinäres Gespräch.* Mainz.

Koppert, Claudia. 1991. "Schuld und Schuldgefühle im westlichen Nach-
kriegsdeutschland: Zur Wirksamkeit des Vergangenen im Gegen-
wärtigen." *Beiträge zur feministischen theorie und praxia,* 30–31,
217–29.

Krappmann, Lothar. 1993. *Soziologische Dimensionen der Identität.
Strukturelle Bedingungen für die Teilnahme an Interaktionsprozes-
sen.* Stuttgart.

Kreiner, Josef. 1986. "Schuld und Versöhunung im Shintoismus." In Bernhard Mensen svd, ed., *Schuld und Versöhnung in verschiedenen Religionen.* Sankt Augustin.

Kuhl, Ulrich. 1986. *Selbstsicherheit und prosoziales Handeln. Zivil-
courage im Alltag.* Munich.

Kukutz, Irene, and Katja Havemann. 1990. *Geschützte Quelle: Gespräche mit Monika H. alias Karin Lenz.* Berlin.

Kymlicka, Will, and Wayne Norman. 1994. "Return of the Citizen: A Survey of Recent Work on Citizenship Theory." *Ethics* 104, January,
352–81.

Lane, Robert E. 1962. *Political Ideology. Why the American Common
Man Believes What He Does.* New York.

Langbein, Hermann. 1987. *Menschen in Auschwitz.* Vienna.

Lapide, Pinchas. 1983. "'Ist meine Schuld zu groß zum Vergeben?'
Schuld und Umkehr im Judentum." In Michael Sievernich and Klaus
Philipp Seif, eds., *Schuld und Umkehr in den Weltreligionen.* Mainz.

Lasswell, Harold D. 1951. "Democratic Character." In *The Political Writings of Harold D. Lasswell.* Illinois.

Latte, Kurt. 1920–21. "Schuld und Sühne in den griechischen Religionen." *Archiv für Religionswissenschaften,* Bd. 20 (reprint 1965), 465–525.

Leggewie, Claus. 1991. *Nachgetragenes Mitleid.* Göttingen.

———. 1995. *Die 89er. Portrait einer Generation.* Hamburg.

Lenz, Siegfried. 1991. "Zeit der Schuldlosen." In Siegfried Lenz, *Zeit der Schuldlosen und andere Stücke.* Munich.

Lepsius, Juliane. 1991. *Es taucht in Träumen wieder auf. Schicksale seit 1933.* Düsseldorf.

Lerner, Daniel. 1958. *The Passing of Traditional Society: Modernizing the Middle East.* London.

Levi, Primo. 1961. *Survival in Auschwitz.* Trans. Stuart Woolf. New York.

———. 1988. *The Drowned and the Saved.* Trans. Raymond Rosenthal. New York.

Lidsay-Hartz, Janice. 1984. "Contrasting Experiences of Shame and Guilt." *American Behavioral Scientist* 27, no. 6, July-August, 689–704.

Lifton, Robert Jay. 1986. *The Nazi Doctors: Medical Killing and the Psychology of Genocide.* New York.

Limbach, Jutta. 1993. "Vergangenheitsbewältigung durch die Justiz." *DtZ,* Heft 3, 66–71.

Lindner, Clausjohann. 1990. *Kritik der Theorie der partizipatorischen Demokratie.* Opladen.

Lipp, Wolfgang. 1990. "Schuld und gesellschaftliche Mechanismen der sozialen Zuschreibung, Bewältigung und Wandlung von Schuld." In Arnold Köpcke-Duttler, ed., *Schuld—Strafe—Versöhnung. Ein interdisziplinäres Gespräch.* Mainz.

Locke, John. 1955 [1689]. *Of Civil Government.* Indiana.

Lübbe, Hermann. 1983. "Der Nationalsozialismus im politischen Bewußtsein der Gegenwart." In *Deutschlands Weg in die Diktatur. Internationale Konferenz zur nationalsozialistischen Machtübernahme im Reichstagsgebäude zu Berlin. Referate und Diskussionen. Ein Protokoll.* Berlin.

Lutz, Felix Philipp. 1992. "Geschichtsbewußtsein und individuelle Wertesysteme." In Helmut Klages, Hans-Jürgen Hipper, and Willi Herbert, eds., *Werte und Wandel. Ergebnisse und Methoden einer Forschungstradition.* Frankfurt.

Lynd, H. M. 1961. *On Shame and the Search for Identity.* New York.

Marquard, Odo, et al. 1980. "Malum." In *Historisches Wörterbuch der Philosophie.* Bd. 5. Darmstadt.

Maslow, A. G. 1957. "Power Relationships and Patterns of Personal Development." In Arthur Kornhauser, ed., *Problems of Power in American Democracy.* Detroit.

Massing, Almuth, and Ulrich Benshausen. 1986. "'Bis ins dritte und vierte Glied.' Auswirkungen des Nationalsozialismus in den Familien." *psychosozial,* Jg. 9, Nr. 28, 27– 42.

McNamara, Robert. 1995. *In Retrospect: The Tragedy and Lessons of Vietnam.* With Brian Van de Mark. New York.

Mitscherlich, Alexander and Margarete. 1975. *The Inability to Mourn. Principles of Collective Behavior.* Preface by Robert Jay Lifton. Trans. Beverly R. Placzek. New York.

Mitscherlich-Nielsen, Margarete. 1992. "Die Unfähigkeit zu trauern in Ost- und Westdeutschland. Was Trauerarbeit heißen könnte." *Psyche,* Jg. 5/46, 406 –18.

Molinski, Hans. 1986. "Schuld und Versöhnung in der säkularisierten Gesellschaft der Bundesrepublik." In Bernhard Mensen, ed., *Schuld und Versöhnung in verschiedenen Religionen.* Sankt Augustin.

Morris, Herbert. 1988. "The Decline of Guilt." *Ethics* 99, October.

Moser, Tilmann. 1992. "Die Unfähigkeit zu trauern: Hält die Diagnose einer Überprüfung statt? Zur psychischen Verarbeitung des Holocaust in der Bundesrepublik." *Psyche,* Jg. 5/46, 389– 405.

———. 1993a. "Nationalsozialismus im seelischen Untergrund von heute. Über die Nachwirkungen von Holocaust, Krieg und NS-Diktatur. Zur Rezeption von Anita Eckstaedts Buch 'Nationalsozialismus in der 'zweiten Generation.'" In Tilmann Moser, *Politik und seelischer Untergrund,* Frankfurt am Main.

———. 1993b. "Der braune Untergrund der Charaktere. Die deutsche Seele vor und nach der Einheit aus westlicher Sicht." In Tilmann Moser, *Politik und seelischer Untergrund.* Frankfurt am Main.

Müller-Hohagen, Jürgen. 1988. *Verleugnet, verdrängt, verschwiegen. Die seelischen Auswirkungen der Nazizeit.* Munich.

Münkler, Herfried. 1992. "Politische Tugend. Bedarf die Demokratie einer sozio-moralischen Grundlegung?" In Herfried Münkler, ed., *Die Chancen der Freiheit. Grundprobleme der Demokratie.* Munich.

Nielsen, Henrik Kaare. 1987. "Zur Sozialpsychologie des Generationenkonflikts der Nachkriegszeit in Dänemark." In Klaus Schulte and Wolf Wucherpfenning, eds., *Die Gegenwart der Vergangenheit.*

Geschichte und nationale Identität in Deutschland und Dänemark. Roskilde.

Niethammer, Lutz. 1991. *Die volkseigene Erfahrung. Eine Archäologie des Lebens in der Industrieprovinz der DDR.* Berlin.

Noelle, Elisabeth, and Erich Peter Neumann, eds. 1967. *The Germans: Public Opinion Polls 1947–1966.* Westport CT.

Noelle-Neumann, Elisabeth, and Renate Köcher. 1987. *Die verletzte Nation. Über den Versuch der Deutschen, ihren Charakter zu ändern.* Stuttgart.

Oeing-Hanhoff, Ludger, and Walter Kasper. 1981. "Negativität und Böses." In Franz Böckle et al., eds. *Christlicher Glaube in moderner Gesellschaft.* Teilbd. 9. Freiburg, Basel, Vienna.

Offe, Claus, and Ulrich K. Preuss. 1991. "Democratic Institutions and Moral Resources." In David Held, ed., *Political Theory Today.* Stanford.

Olin, Susan Möller. 1990. "Reason and Thinking about Justice." In Cass R. Sunstein, ed., *Feminism and Political Theory.* Chicago.

Ostrom, Elinor. 1990. *Governing the Commons: The Evolution of Institutions for Collective Action.* Cambridge.

Parin, Paul. 1990. "Der nationalen Schande begegnen. Eine ethnopsychoanalytischer Vergleich der deutschen und italienischen Kultur." *Psyche,* Nr. 7, Jg. 44, 643–59.

Perrez, Meinrad. 1979. *Ist die Psychoanalyse eine Wissenschaft?* Bern.

Pocock, J. G. A. 1995. "The Idea of Citizenship since Classical Times." In Ronald Beiner, ed., *Theorizing Citizenship.* New York.

Pollock, Friedrich. 1955. *Gruppenexperiment. Ein Studienbericht.* Bearbeitet von Friedrich Pollock. Mit einem Geleitwort von Franz Böhm. Frankfurter Beiträge zur Soziologie. Im Auftrag des Instituts für Sozialforschung. Ed. Theodor W. Adorno and Walter Dirks. Bd. 2. Frankfurt am Main.

Pross, Helge. 1982. *Was ist heute deutsch? Werteorientierungen in der Bundesrepublik.* Reinbek b. Hamburg.

Putnam, Robert D. 1993. *Making Democracy Work: Civic Traditions in Modern Italy.* With Robert Leonardi and Raffaella Y. Nanetti. Princeton.

Rahner, Karl. 1964. "Schuld—Verantwortung—Strafe in der Sicht der katholischen Theologie." In Erwin Frey, ed., *Schuld, Verantwortung, Strafe im Lichte der Theologie, Jurisprudenz, Soziologie, Medizin und Philosophie.* Zurich.

Rautenberg, Erarado C. 1993a. *Verminderte Schuldfähigkeit. Ein beson-
    derer fakultativer Strafmilderungsgrund?* Heidelberg.

————. 1993b. "Anfangsverdacht wegen Rechtsbeugung gegen Staats-
    anwälte und Richter der früheren DDR—ein Beitrag zum Meinungs-
    stand in der Praxis." *DtZ*, Heft 3, 71–75.

Reik, Theodor. 1925. *Geständniszwang und Strafbedürfnis.* Leipzig.

Rich, Arthur. 1964. "Verantwortung—Schuld—Strafe in der Sicht der
    protestantischen Theologen." In Erwin Frey, ed., *Schuld, Verantwor-
    tung, Strafe im Lichte der Theologie, Jurisprudenz, Soziologie, Medi-
    zin und Philosophie.* Zurich.

Ricoeur, Paul. 1969. *The Symbolism of Evil.* Trans. Emerson Buchanan.
    Boston.

————. 1986. *Fallible Man.* Rev. trans. Charles A. Kelbley. Introduction
    by Walter J. Lowe. New York.

Riesenberg, Peter. 1992. *Citizenship in the Western Tradition: From
    Plato to Rousseau.* Chapel Hill.

Roggemann, Herwig. 1994. "Richterstrafbarkeit und Wechsel der
    Rechtsordnung. Das BGH-Urteil zur Rechtsbeugung durch DDR-
    Richer." *J.Z.*, 15/16, 769–78.

Rorty, Richard. 1988. "Der Vorrang der Demokratie vor der Philoso-
    phie." In *Zerstörung des moralischen Selbstbewußtseins: Chance
    oder Gefährdung? Praktische Philosophie: Deutschland nach dem
    Nationalsozialismus.* Published by Forum der Philosophie, Bad Hom-
    burg. Frankfurt am Main.

Rosenkötter, Lutz. 1982. "The Formation of Ideals in the Succession
    of Generations." In Martin S. Bergmann and Milton E. Jucovy, eds.,
    Generations of the Holocaust. New York.

Rosenthal, Gabriele. 1987. *". . . Wenn alles in Scherben fällt . . ." Von
    Leben und Sinnwelt der Kriegsgeneration.* Opladen.

Rottgart, Elke. 1993. *Elternhörigkeit. Nationalsozialismus in der Genera-
    tion danach. Eltern-Kind-Verhältnisse vor dem Hintergrund der na-
    tionalsozialistischen Vergangenheit.* Hamburg.

Rousseau, Jean-Jacques. 1964. "Discourse on the Origin and Founda-
    tions of Inequality (Second Discourse)." In Roger D. Masters, ed.
    The First and Second Discourses. New York.

Roxin, Claus. 1974. "'Schuld' und 'Verantwortlichkeit' als strafrechtliche
    Systemkategorien." In Claus Roxin, ed., *Grundfragen der gesamten
    Staatsrechtswissenschaften. Festschrift für Heinrich Henkel zum 70.
    Geburtstag am 12. Sept. 1973.* Berlin.

Rürup, Reinhard, ed. 1991. *Der Krieg gegen die Sowjetunion 1941–1945. Eine Dokumentation*. Berlin.

Sa'adeh, Anne. 1990. *The Shaping of Liberal Politics in Revolutionary France: A Comparative Perspective*. Princeton.

———. 1992. "Forgiving without Forgetting: Political Reconciliation and Democratic Citizenship." *French Politics and Society* 10, no. 3, 94–113.

———. 1998. *Germany's Second Chance: Trust, Justice, and Democratization*. Cambridge MA.

Salm, Heidi. 1992. "'Auch ich war dabei.' Konfrontationen mit der eigenen Geschichte in der Familientherapie." In Barbara Heimannsberg and Christoph J. Schmidt, eds., *Das kollektive Schweigen. Nationalsozialistische Vergangenheit und gebrochene Identität in der Psychotherapie*. Cologne.

Schäfer, Hans Dieter. 1983. *Das gespaltene Bewußtsein. Über deutsche Kultur und Lebenswirklichkeit 1933–1945*. Munich.

Scheler, Max. 1968. *Vom Ewigen im Menschen*. Bd. 5, *Gesammelte Werke*. Bonn.

———. 1973. *Wesen und Formen der Sympathie*. 6th, rev. ed. of *Phänomenologie und Theorie der Sympathiefähigkeit*. Bern.

Schlink, Bernhard. 1988. "Recht, Schuld, Zukunft." In *Loccumer Protokolle, 66. Dokumentation einer Tagung der Evangelischen Akademie Loccum vom 4.-6. 12. 1987*, 57–78.

———. 1994. "Rechtsstaat und revolutionäre Gerechtigkeit." *Neue Justiz. Zeitschrift für Rechtsetzung und Rechtsanwendung*, Jg. 48, Nr. 10, 433–37.

———. 1995. "Vergangenheit als Zumutung? Zum Kündigungsgrund der Unzumutbarkeit weiterer Beschäftigung nach früherer Tätigkeit für das Ministerium für Staatssicherheit nach Kapitel XIX, Sachgebiet A Abschnitt II Nr. 1 Abs. 5 zur Alternative der Anlage I zum Einigungsvertrag." In Rolf Grawert et al., eds., *Offene Staatlichkeit. Festschrift für Ernst-Wolfgang Böckenförde zum 65. Geburtstag*, 341–55. Berlin.

———. 1997. *The Reader*. Trans. from the German by Carol Brown Janeway. New York.

Schlippe, Gunnar von. 1992. "'Schuldig!' Gedanken zum Umgang mit der eigenen Vergangenheit. Briefe an meinen Sohn." In Barbara Heimannsberg and Christoph J. Schmidt, eds., *Das kollektive Schweigen. Nationalsozialistische Vergangenheit und gebrochene Identität. in der Psychotherapie*. Cologne.

Schneider, Christian. 1993. "Jenseits der Schuld? Die Unfähigkeit zu trauern in der zweiten Generation." *Psyche*, Jg. 47, Nr. 8, 754–74.

Schneider, Michael. 1987. "Väter und Söhne, posthum. Über das beschädigte Verhältnis zweier Generationen." In Klaus Schulte and Wolf Wucherpfennig, eds., *Die Gegenwart der Vergangenheit. Geschichte und nationale Identität in Deutschland und Dänemark*, 111–38. Roskilde.

Schöbel, Carolin. 1994. "Persönlichkeit und politisches System. Eine Analyse ihrer Beziehung im Kontext der deutschen Vereinigung." Diss., Berlin.

Schöpf, Alfred. 1990. "Emotion und Ethik." In Arnold Köpcke-Duttler, *Schuld, Strafe, Versöhnung. Ein interdisziplinäres Gespräch*. Mainz.

Schornstheimer, Michael. 1995. *Die leuchtenden Augen der Frontsoldaten. Nationalsozialismus und Krieg in den Illustriertenromanen der fünfziger Jahre*. Berlin.

Schreiber, Gerhard. 1996. *Deutsche Kriegsverbrechen in Italien. Täter, Opfer, Strafverfolgung*. Munich.

Schwan, Alexander. 1992. *Ethos der Demokratie*. Ed. Gesine Schwan. Bd. 66, Rechts und Sozialwissenschaftliche Veröffentlichungen der Görresgesellschaft. Paderborn.

Schwan, Gesine. 1990. "Politik ohne Vertrauen? Ideengeschichtliche und systematische Überlegungen zum Verhältnis von Politik und Vertrauen." In Peter Haungs, ed., *Politik ohne Vertrauen?*, 9–30. Baden-Baden.

———. 1995. "Die 'demokratische Persönlichkeit.' Ein brauchbarer demokratietheoretischer Maßstab? Problem eines politisch-psychologischen Persönlichkeitskonzepts unter demokratietheoretischem Aspekt." In Heiner Timmermann, ed., *Die Kontinentwerdung Europas. Festschrift für Helmut Wagner zum 65. Geburtstag*, 231–43. Berlin.

Schwan, Werner. 1990. *"Ich bin doch kein Unmensch." Kriegs- und Nachkriegszeit im deutschen Roman*. Freiburg.

Schwarz, Gudrun. 1990. *Die Nationalsozialistischen Lager*. Frankfurt am Main.

Schwilk, Heimo, and Ulrich Schacht, eds. 1994. *Die selbstbewußte Nation. "Anschwellender Bocksgesang" und weitere Beiträge zu einer deutschen Debatte*. Frankfurt am Main.

Segev, Tom. 1987. *Soldiers of Evil: The Commandants of the Nazi Concentration Camps*. Trans. Haim Watzman. New York.

————. 1993. *The Seventh Million: The Israelis and the Holocaust.*
Trans. Haim Watzman. New York.

Sempebwa. 1983. "'Ich werde zu meinem Vater zurückgehen.' Schuld
und Umkehr in den afrikanischen Naturreligionen." In Michael Sievernich and Klaus Philipp Seif, eds., *Schuld und Umkehr in den Weltreligionen*. Mainz.

Senger, Valentin. 1995. *Die Heimkehrer. Eine Verwunderung über die
Nachkriegszeit.* Munich.

Sereny, Gitta. 1974. *Into that Darkness: From Mercy Killing to Mass
Murder.* London.

————. 1995. *Albert Speer: His Battle with Truth.* New York.

Sichrovsky, Peter. 1988. *Born Guilty: Children of Nazi Families.* Trans.
Jean Steinberg.

Sievernich, Michael, and Klaus Philipp Seif, eds. 1983. *Schuld und Umkehr in den Weltreligionen.* Mainz.

Simenauer, Erich. 1981. "Die zweite Generation—danach. Die Wieder-
kehr der Verfolger-Mentalität in Psychoanalysen." *Jahrbuch der Psychoanalyse*, Bd. 12, 8–12.

Smith, Adam. 1982. *The Theory of Moral Sentiments.* Ed. D. D. Raphael
and A. L. Macfie. Indianapolis.

Sniderman, Paul M. 1975. *Personality and Democratic Politics.* Berkeley.

"*Soldat im Volk*". 1995. Organ des Verbandes deutscher Soldaten, e. V.
Jg. 44, Nr. 7–8.

Staub, Ervin. 1989. *The Roots of Evil: The Origins of Genocide and
Other Group Violence.* New York, Melbourne, Sydney.

Steinbach, Peter. 1984. "Zur Auseinandersetzung mit nationalsozialistischen Gewaltverbrechen in der Bundesrepublik Deutschland. Ein
Beitrag zur deutschen Kultur nach 1945." *GWU*, Nr. 2, 65–85.

Steinbach, Peter, and Jürgen Weber, eds. 1984. *Vergangenheitsbewältigung durch Strafverfahren? NS-Prozesse in der Bundesrepublik
Deutschland.* Munich.

Stelzenmüller, Constanze. 1996. "Der General war überall. Vor dem
Haager Kriegsverbrechertribunal zeichnen Opfer und Täter das Bild
der Hauptverantwortlichen: Mladíc und Karadzíc." *Die Zeit* 29/96, 3.

Stewart, Angus. 1995. "Two Conceptions of Citizenship." *British Journal
of Sociology* 46, no. 1, 63–78.

Stierlin, Helm. 1976. *Adolf Hitler: A Family Perspective.* New York.

————. 1982. *Delegation und Familie. Beiträge zum Heidelberger fami-
liendynamischen Konzept.* Frankfurt am Main.

————. 1992. "Der Dialog zwischen den Generationen über die Nazi-

zeit." In Barbara Heimannsberg and Christoph J. Schmidt, eds., *Das
kollektive Schweigen. Nationalsozialistische Vergangenheit und gebrochene Identität in der Psychotherapie.* Cologne.

Stolleis, Michael. 1996. "Eine immer gefährdete Errungenschaft. In der
Alltäglichkeit des Rechtsstaats darf das Wissen um seine Kostbarkeit
nicht verloren gehen." *Frankfurter Allgemeine Zeitung,* Nr. 212, September 11, 14.

Syberberg, Hans Jürgen. 1994. "Eigenes und Fremdes. Über den Verlust
des Tragischen." In Heimo Schwilk and Ulrich Schacht, eds., *Die
selbstbewußte Nation. 'Anschwellender Bocksgesang' und weitere
Beiträge zur deutschen Debatte,* 124–33. Frankfurt am Main.

Taylor, Telford. 1970. *Guilt, Responsibility, and the Third Reich.* Cambridge.

Tenbruck, Friedrich H. 1974. "Alltagsnormen und Lebensgefühle in der
Bundesrepublik Deutschland." In Richard Löwenthal and Hans-Peter
Schwarz, eds., *25 Jahre Bundesrepublik Deutschland—eine Bilanz,*
289–310. Stuttgart.

Todorov, Tzvetan. 1996. *Facing the Extreme: Moral Life in the Concentration Camps.* Trans. Arthur Denner and Abigail Pollak. New York.

Tömmel, Sieglinde E. 1992. "Anita Eckstaedt: Nationalsozialismus in der
'zweiten Generation.' Psychoanalyse von Hörigkeitsverhältnissen."
Luzifer—Amor. Zeitschrift zur Geschichte der Psychoanalyse, Jg. 5,
Heft 9, 156–64.

Treplin, Vera. 1992. "Eine Auseinandersetzung mit dem Buch von A. Eckstaedt: Nationalsozialismus in der 'zweiten Generation.' Psychoanalyse von Hörigkeitsverhältnissen." *Luzifer—Amor. Zeitschrift zur
Geschichte der Psychoanalyse,* Jg. 5, Heft 9, 165–87.

Trimborn, Hermann. 1925. "Straftat und Sühne in Alt-Peru." *Zeitschrift
für Ethnologie. Organ der Berliner Gesellschaft für Anthropologie,
Ethnologie und Urgeschichte,* Jg. 57, 194–240.

Ullrich, Volker. 1991. "'Wir haben nichts gewußt'—Ein deutsches
Trauma." *1999: Zeitschrift für Sozialgeschichte des 20. und 21. Jahr-
hunderts,* Jg. 6, Heft 4, October, 11–46.

Vesper, Bernward. 1995. *Die Reise. Romanessay.* Reinbek bei Hamburg.

Vogt, Rolf. 1986. "Warum sprechen die Deutschen nicht?" *Psyche,* Jg.
40, Nr. 10, 896–902.

Walser, Martin. 1965. "Der schwarze Schwan." *Spectaculum VIII. Mo-
derne Theaterstücke.* Frankfurt am Main.

Walzer, Michael. 1989. "Citizenship." In Terence Ball et al., eds., *Political
Innovation and Conceptual Change: Ideas in Context.* Cambridge.

————. 1995. "The Civil Society Argument." In Ronald Beiner, ed., *Theorizing Citizenship*. New York.

Warren, Mark E. 1995. "The Self in Discursive Democracy." In Stephen K. White, ed., *The Cambridge Companion to Habermas*. Cambridge.

Weinreich-Haste, Helen. 1986. "Moralisches Engagement. Die Funktion der Gefühle im Urteilen und Handeln." In Wolfgang Edelstein and Gertrud Nunner-Winkler, eds., *Zur Bestimmung der Moral. Philosophische und sozialwissenschaftliche Beiträge zur Moralforschung*, 377–406. Frankfurt am Main.

Weißmann, Karlheinz. 1987. "Krise der Werte—Demoskopisch." *Criticon* Nr. 102, 182.

West, Rebecca. 1995 [1946]. *Gewächshaus mit Alpenveilchen. Im Herzen des Weltfeindes*. Nuremberg.

Westernhagen, Dörte von. 1988. *Die Kinder der Täter. Das Dritte Reich und die Generation danach*. Munich.

Witte, Erich H. 1986. *Sozialpsychologie. Ein Lehrbuch*. Munich.

Wurmser, Leon. 1981. *The Mask of Shame*. Baltimore.

Zeiler, Joachim. 1991. "Psychogramm des Kommandanten von Auschwitz: Erkenntnis und Begegnung durch Zertstörung. Zur Autobiographie des Rudolf Höß." *Psyche*, Nr. 45, Heft 4, 335–62.

Zitelmann, Rainer. 1994. "Position und Begriff. Über eine neue demokratische Rechte." In Heimo Schwilk and Ulrich Schacht, eds., *Die selbstbewußte Nation. 'Anschwellender Bocksgesang' und weitere Beiträge zur deutschen Debatte*, 163–81. Frankfurt am Main.

Index

In the European Horizons series

The Consecration of the Writer, 1750–1830
By Paul Bénichou
Translated and with an introduction by Mark Jensen
With a preface by Tzvetan Todorov

A Modern Maistre: The Social and Political Thought of Joseph de Maistre
By Owen Bradley

Dispatches from the Balkan War and Other Writings
By Alain Finkielkraut
Translated by Peter S. Rogers and Richard Golsan
With an introduction by Richard Golsan

A Primer of Italian Facism
Edited and with an introduction by Jeffrey Schnapp
Translated by Jeffrey T. Schnapp, Olivia E. Sears, and Maria G. Stampino

Politics and Guilt: The Destructive Power of Silence
By Gesine Schwan
Translated by Thomas Dunlap

Life in Common: An Essay in General Anthropology
By Tzvetan Todorov
Translated by Katherine Golsan and Lucy Golsan
With a new afterword by the author